PELLET B

Study Guide

2025-2026

Detailed Content Review, Proven Strategies, And Full-Length Practice Tests

Zara T. Williamson

Disclaimer

This book is intended for educational and informational purposes only. The content provided is based on the author's research and understanding of the subject matter. While every effort has been made to ensure accuracy, the author and publisher assume no responsibility for errors, omissions, or discrepancies. The strategies, tips, and advice contained in this book are suggestions, and the reader is encouraged to use their own discretion and judgment when applying the information.

The Board was not involved in the development or production of this product, has no affiliation with **''Mintwrite Review'',** and does not sponsor or endorse it.

This book is not intended as a substitute for professional advice. The author and publisher shall not be held liable for any damages or consequences arising from the use or misuse of information in this book. Readers should seek appropriate legal, academic, or professional guidance as necessary.

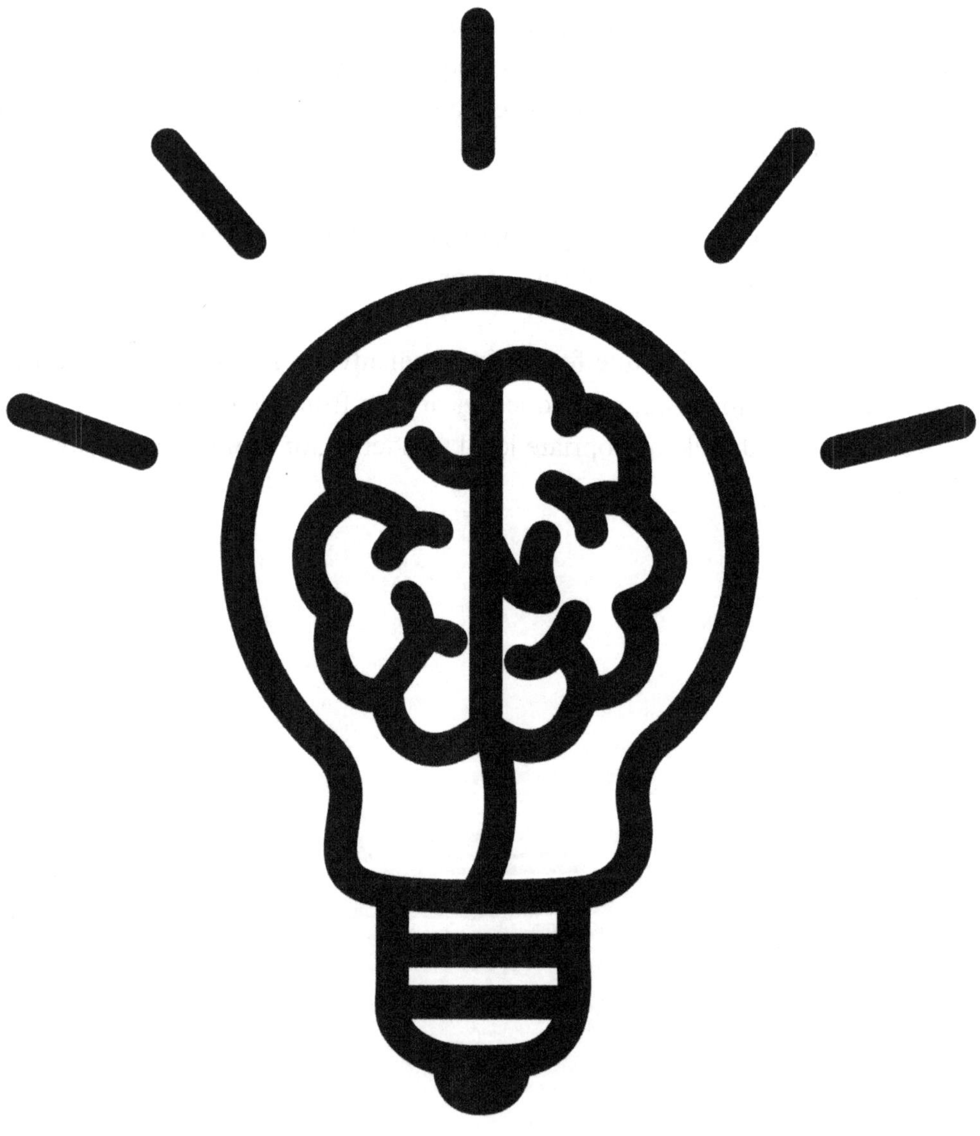

Contents

Introduction 6
    Jake's Journey to Success: The Power of the Right Guide 6
    A Letter From ''Mintwrite Review'' To Our Amazing Readers 7

Chapter 1 8
Introduction to the PELLET B Exam 8
    Overview of the PELLET B Exam 8
    Purpose of the PELLET B Exam 9
    Key Sections of the PELLET B Exam and How They Relate to Law Enforcement Training 10
    Why The Removal of the CLOZE Reading Comprehension Subtest 11
    What to Expect During the Test 12
    Understanding Your Test Results 12

Chapter 2 14
Spelling in the PELLET B Exam 14
    Overview of Spelling in the PELLET B Exam 14
    Key Spelling Rules: Common Spelling Patterns and Exceptions 19
    Strategies for Correctly Identifying Misspelled Words 22
    Practice Questions and Solutions: Spelling 27
    Typical Spelling Mistakes to Avoid on Test Day 32

Chapter 3 36
Vocabulary in the PELLET B Exam 36
    The Significance of Vocabulary in Law Enforcement and Communication 36
    How to Approach Vocabulary Questions on the PELLET B Exam 41
    Understanding the Meaning of Words Based on the Context They're Used In 45
    Tips for Determining the Best Possible Meaning from Options 47
    Building a Law Enforcement Vocabulary: Commonly Tested Words 49
    Practice Questions and Solutions: Vocabulary 54

Chapter 4 60
Clarity in the PELLET B Exam 60
    What Clarity Questions Assess: Sentence Structure and Communication 60
    Identifying the Most Clearly Written Sentence 65
    How to Improve Sentence Clarity for the PELLET B Exam 69
    Tips for Enhancing Sentence Clarity 70
    Practice Questions and Solutions: Example Clarity Questions 75
    Common Pitfalls in Clarity Questions 78

Chapter 5... 84
Reading Comprehension in the PELLET B Exam... 84
- Overview of Reading Comprehension in the PELLET B Exam............................... 84
- Strategies for Efficient Reading.. 90
- Understanding Fact-Based vs. Inference-Based Questions..................................... 94
- Understanding the Importance of Speed and Retention.. 98
- Practice Passages And Questions: Reading Comprehension................................ 103
- Common Challenges in Reading Comprehension... 108

Chapter 6... 114
Strategies for Success.. 114
- Effective Study Techniques for Maximum Retention.. 114
- Test-Taking Strategies for the PELT B Exam... 119
- Common Mistakes to Avoid in All Sections... 122
- Final Review Tips for All Sections... 127

Chapter 7... 132
Full-Length Practice Tests and Detailed Answer Explanations......................... 132
Full-Scale Practice Test 1.. 134
- Practice Test 1: Answer Key.. 158
- Practice Test 1: Answer And Explanation... 162
Full-Scale Practice Test 2.. 174
- Practice Test 2: Answer Key.. 199
- Practice Test 2: Answer And Explanation... 203
Full-Scale Practice Test 3.. 217
- Practice Test 3: Answer Key.. 243
- Practice Test 3: Answer And Explanation... 247
How to Analyze Your Practice Test Results.. 260

Chapter 8... 266
Preparing for Test Day... 266
- What to Expect on Test Day.. 266
- Last-Minute Tips for Reviewing Key Concepts.. 269
- How to Stay Mentally and Physically Prepared in the Week Leading Up to the Test....................... 271
- Relaxation Techniques for a Calm Test Day... 273

Chapter 9... 274
Post-Test Analysis and Next Steps... 274
- Interpreting Your Test Results: Understanding Your T-Score and Its Significance............................ 274
- How to Use Your Test Results for Future Applications... 276
- Next Steps After the Test: How to Move Forward in Your Law Enforcement Career........................ 278
- Tips for Applying to Different Law Enforcement Agencies.................................. 281

Conclusion.. 284
Bonus Section... 285

Introduction

Jake's Journey to Success: The Power of the Right Guide.

Jake had consistently aspired to become a law enforcement officer. Following months of preparation, the significant day arrived. He seated himself to undertake the PELLET B examination, sensing the pressure intensifying with each passing second. However, Jake faced a significant issue—he lacked a comprehensive study guide. Instead, he was burdened with an antiquated guide that inadequately addressed the portions. The spelling inquiries were challenging, the vocabulary appeared daunting, and the reading comprehension passages resembled a foreign language. Each question appeared more challenging than the preceding one. Upon concluding the examination, Jake realized he had not succeeded. His heart plummeted as he contemplated the extent of his desire for this.

While returning home in frustration, Jake encountered a new PELT B Study Guide in a bookstore. The headline caught his eye: The Complete Guide to Passing the PELLET B Exam with Confidence. Curious, he flipped through the pages. The style was sleek, the content was up-to-date, and it even contained practice questions that felt legitimate. The new guide broke down the test sections clearly and presented easy-to-follow tactics that actually made sense. No more old, convoluted tricks that didn't help.

Jake instantly bought the guide and delved into studying. For the first time, he felt like he was actually preparing. The vocabulary component clicked, and the reading comprehension skills let him break down complex texts with ease. The guide gave him confidence and tools that he had never had before.

Test day came again. Jake strolled into the exam room with a calm mind, armed with the knowledge from his new study guide. This time, he breezed through the questions. The spelling was a snap, the vocabulary questions were familiar, and the reading comprehension seemed like a piece of cake. He finished the exam with time to spare and departed feeling confident.

Weeks later, Jake received his results—a terrific grade! He passed with flying colors, and his dream of becoming a law enforcement officer was finally within grasp.

Jake Couldn't Believe The Difference A Real Guide Made. Don't Make The Same Mistake Jake Did. Follow This Study Guide And Pass Your Pellet B Exam With Ease. Your Future Starts Here!

Welcome To This Book "PELLET B Study Guide 2025-2026"

This book is your ultimate resource for acing the POST Entry-Level Law Enforcement Test Battery (PELLET B). This book is specifically designed to help you tackle every section of the PELLET B exam with confidence and precision. Whether you're new to the exam or trying to improve your previous score, this book will serve as your thorough route to success.

Inside this guide, you'll find:

- Clear and succinct analysis of each exam section, including Spelling, Vocabulary, Clarity, and Reading Comprehension, customized to the 2025-2026 revisions.
- Effective solutions for each question type, from detecting the correct spelling to breaking down dense reading passages.
- Hundreds of practice questions with full explanations to strengthen your learning and improve your test-taking skills.
- Tips and tactics to help you manage your time, reduce test anxiety, and maximize your performance on exam day.
- This book is intended: Aspiring law enforcement officers who are studying for the PELLET B exam and require a good, up-to-date resource.
- Students and applicants who have struggled with prior versions of the test and desire a more current and successful study technique.
- Anyone wants to pass the PELLET B exam with flying colors by focusing on the correct tactics, practice, and insights.

A Letter From "Mintwrite Review" To Our Amazing Readers.

We create this handbook with one objective in mind: to empower you to succeed. With the correct study tools and an organized approach, you may simply go through each area of the test and boost your chances of scoring high. We want you to feel ready, relaxed, and in control on test day. With this guide, you'll not only grasp the content but also master it in a way that fits your learning style.

As you go through this study guide, remember that you're taking the first step towards a fulfilling career in law enforcement. Whether you're aiming for a position in the police force, highway patrol, or other public safety departments, this book is your key to opening the door to your future.

Let's Get Started—Your Journey To Passing The Pellet B Exam Begins Now!

Chapter 1

Introduction to the PELLET B Exam

The route to a career in law enforcement is riddled with challenges and barriers, but one of the first stages for aspiring officers is passing the PELT B Exam. If you're reading this, you presumably already know how vital it is to pass the POST Entry-Level Law Enforcement Test Battery (PELLET B) and understand how it fits into your career aspirations. But do you really appreciate the significance of this exam and how it helps shape the future of law enforcement professionals? Let's dive into all you need to know about the PELT B Exam—from its purpose to the important portions it assesses, as well as some major modifications that you need to be aware of. By the end of this chapter, you'll feel empowered and prepared to begin your road toward acing this vital exam.

Overview of the PELLET B Exam

The PELT B Exam is the important first step for anyone wishing to enter law enforcement in California. It is a multiple-choice and fill-in-the-blank exam meant to evaluate reading, writing, and thinking ability. The test is part of the POST (Peace Officer Standards and Training) procedure and is used by law enforcement organizations across California to screen potential recruits.

The exam itself is meant to measure critical cognitive and language skills that are required for a career in law enforcement. While physical fitness and skills training are key components of becoming a law enforcement officer, the PELT B Exam guarantees that applicants possess the intellectual ability necessary to do the job efficiently. This includes the capacity to read, absorb, and evaluate information, solve issues rationally, and communicate clearly—skills that are critical for officers who need to handle enormous volumes of information rapidly and precisely during high-pressure circumstances.

What makes the PELLET B Exam so important is that it works as a filter for law enforcement authorities. A good score on this test can set you apart from other candidates and demonstrate your readiness for training and real-world application of your abilities. For many law enforcement agencies, the PELLET B Exam is not just a formality—it's a key indicator of whether a candidate possesses the intellectual and cognitive aptitude essential to excel in the academy and in the field.

Purpose of the PELLET B Exam

The major goal of the PELLET B Exam is to assess the basic cognitive skills required to conduct law enforcement responsibilities successfully. Law enforcement professionals are expected to make quick choices, analyze legal documents, create reports, and communicate coherently with colleagues, supervisors, and the public. These duties demand more than simply physical strength—they require mental acuity, attention to detail, and effective communication.

By examining these important skills, the PELLET B Exam guarantees that law enforcement agencies are hiring individuals who have the intellectual capacity to handle the demands of the profession. The exam evaluates:

- **Reading comprehension**: Officers need to read and comprehend reports, laws, regulations, and communications from other officers or the public.
- **Spelling and vocabulary**: Officers are expected to write clear and accurate reports and communicate effectively.
- **Clarity and sentence structure**: Writing clearly is a fundamental skill for officers who need to write reports, document evidence, and communicate with the public.
- **Critical thinking and problem-solving**: Law enforcement officers are frequently required to make decisions based on their assessment of a situation, so problem-solving and reasoning are crucial skills.

Passing the PELLET B Exam is the gateway to next stages in the law enforcement recruitment process. It's the first filter that helps agencies decide whether candidates are psychologically equipped for the tough training and demanding responsibilities that will follow.

Why the PELLET B Exam Matters

In the world of law enforcement, the ability to speak clearly and efficiently can make all the difference. Officers must be able to create accurate reports, read legal papers, and communicate well with both their colleagues and the public. The PELT B Exam ensures that only individuals who are capable of these responsibilities are selected. It's more than simply an exam—it's a vital step in ensuring that law enforcement officers are not just physically capable but mentally suited to serve their communities.

The test isn't just a measure of your ability to pass a test—it's a reflection of the abilities you'll use every day in your profession. Whether it's understanding a traffic rule, analyzing a crime scene report, or drafting a clear statement after an arrest, the cognitive skills examined by the PELLET B Exam will be put to use in the field. Your ability to handle these activities can directly impact the outcome of an investigation, the effectiveness of your interactions with the public, and, most importantly, the safety of your community.

Key Sections of the PELLET B Exam and How They Relate to Law Enforcement Training

The PELLET B Exam is broken into several important sections, each meant to measure a distinct aspect of your cognitive ability. Understanding these areas is vital for effective preparation. Below are the key sections and their direct significance to the law enforcement profession.

1. Spelling: Spelling may seem like a basic skill, but in law enforcement, precision is everything. Officers are expected to write reports, documents, and correspondence that may be used as legal evidence. A misspelled word could create confusion or undermine the credibility of a report. This section of the exam tests your ability to correctly identify the spelling of commonly used words in law enforcement contexts, such as "arrest," "suspect," and "evidence."

In law enforcement training, spelling is foundational for effective written communication. Clear and accurate writing is vital for drafting incident reports, issuing citations, or communicating with other officers. The spelling section of the exam helps ensure that recruits have a solid understanding of the vocabulary they'll need in the field.

2. Vocabulary: Vocabulary is another vital component for law enforcement professionals. Officers are required to comprehend and communicate complicated concepts pertaining to the law, processes, and regulations. The vocabulary component of the PELLET B Exam assesses your ability to grasp and use words in context, particularly those that are regularly encountered in the law enforcement profession.

A strong vocabulary enables officers to produce concise, precise reports and connect more successfully with the public. Whether it's reading a criminal code or understanding a victim's statement, a robust vocabulary is vital for absorbing and effectively interpreting material.

3. Clarity: The capacity to articulate oneself clearly is possibly one of the most crucial talents for law enforcement officers. Officers must be able to explain their actions and observations clearly and coherently in their reports and testimonies. The clarity component assesses your ability to determine which of two sentences is clearer, making it a vital skill for effective written communication.

In training, candidates focus on how to create clear, succinct, and professional reports that can hold up in court. The clarity component of the PELLET B Exam guarantees that recruits have the skill set necessary for this critical aspect of law enforcement operations.

4. Reading Comprehension: Reading comprehension is one of the most critical abilities for law enforcement agents. Officers must often read and interpret a range of papers, including case files, witness testimony, and legal documents. The reading comprehension component of the PELLET B Exam examines your ability to interpret written content, extract crucial details, and make inferences based on the information supplied.

This talent is directly applicable to law enforcement training and practice. Whether analyzing a search warrant, interpreting evidence in a case, or reading a crime report, reading comprehension ensures that recruits are capable of acquiring and digesting crucial information effectively and efficiently.

Why The Removal of the CLOZE Reading Comprehension Subtest

Effective January 2025, one of the most important changes to the PELLET B Exam is the removal of the CLOZE reading comprehension subtest. In past editions of the exam, the CLOZE test asked applicants to fill in the blanks inside a paragraph, demonstrating their ability to interpret and finish words based on context. This type of test, albeit effective in certain educational settings, was deemed unneeded for law enforcement recruits, and it has now been superseded.

Why Was the CLOZE Test Removed?

The decision to delete the CLOZE reading comprehension sub-test came following a review of its relevance to the abilities needed by law enforcement professionals. While the ability to complete sentences is crucial, it became evident that the comprehension of real-world documents, such as legal texts, police reports, and public communications, was a stronger indication of an officer's capacity to manage written information.

Instead than focusing on filling in missing words, the exam now places more attention on the capacity to grasp, evaluate, and interpret real-world texts—skills that are directly applicable to law enforcement employment. This adjustment helps streamline the exam and guarantee that it more correctly measures the cognitive talents needed in the profession.

What Does This Change Mean for You?

If you're studying for the PELLET B Exam, this upgrade means you'll have a more easy and meaningful reading comprehension component. The absence of the CLOZE test allows you to focus more on comprehending the essential elements that law enforcement personnel will deal with every day. This makes the exam more aligned with the skills that matter most on the job.

What to Expect During the Test

Taking the PELLET B Exam can feel like a high-stakes challenge, but being prepared and understanding what to expect can help you approach the test with confidence. Below, we'll break down the essential parts of the exam so that you may approach test day properly prepared.

Test Duration and Format

The PELLET B Exam is a multiple-choice and fill-in-the-blank exam designed to measure your reading comprehension, spelling, vocabulary, and clarity of writing. The test is scheduled to be finished within 2 hours and 15 minutes, which includes time for instructions, answering questions, and the actual testing session.

During the test, you will encounter a variety of questions designed to assess your language competence and cognitive abilities. It's vital to manage your time properly, since you'll need to stay focused and complete all portions within the allocated time. Some applicants may feel rushed throughout the test, but with adequate preparation, you'll be able to pace yourself and answer each question successfully.

The exam consists of four essential sections: Spelling, Vocabulary, Clarity, and Reading Comprehension. Each of these parts is designed to assess a specific ability that is vital for law enforcement professionals. Below, we'll take a closer look at each of these categories and what they involve.

Understanding Your Test Results

Once you've taken the PELLET B Exam, the next step is to learn how your performance is judged. In most circumstances, you will obtain a T-score, which is a standardized score used to analyze your performance in relation to other test-takers.

T-Scores: What They Mean and How They Are Calculated

A T-score is a statistical measure that compares your raw score (the number of accurate answers you provided) to the performance of others who have taken the exam. T-scores are utilized to provide you an overview of how well you fared on the test compared to the average test-taker.

The T-score is standardized to have a mean (average) of 50 and a standard deviation of 10. This means that:

- A T-score of 50 represents an average score compared to all test-takers.

- A T-score of 40 or below indicates a **below average** performance, while a score of 60 or above is considered **above average**.
- Higher T-scores indicate stronger performance, with recruits scoring above 60 showing greater proficiency in the tested skills.

T-scores are a significant tool for law enforcement agencies to identify whether a candidate has the intellectual ability required to succeed in the academy and the field. In many agencies, a T-score of 42 or more is considered the benchmark for acceptable performance, and those scoring above this barrier are perceived as more likely to succeed in training and the real-world components of the work.

Interpreting Your Score and Understanding Its Impact on Your Career

Understanding your T-score is vital not just for passing the test, but for making educated decisions regarding your future. Here's how your score can affect your law enforcement career:

- **T-Scores and Test Results:** If you earn a T-score of 60 or greater, this implies that you performed considerably above the average test-taker. Law enforcement agencies often search for people who exhibit high reading, writing, and thinking skills. A higher T-score may set you apart from other applicants and offer you an edge throughout the recruitment process.
- **Score Validity and Retakes:** Many departments recognize the T-score as a valid measure of your ability to handle the demands of law enforcement training. However, some agencies may need you to retake the exam or consider other considerations, such as prior experience or educational background. If your T-score is below average, don't be disheartened. You can retake the exam after 30 days and focus on improving specific areas of weakness.
- **Career Readiness:** The PELLET B Exam is meant to predict how well candidates will succeed in law enforcement training. A higher grade generally suggests that you're better equipped for the academic and intellectual requirements of the training procedure. Your score can also serve as a measure of your general preparation for the duties you'll face as a law enforcement officer.

The PELT B Exam is not just a test—it's a representation of the talents you'll need in your law enforcement profession. From reading comprehension to spelling and vocabulary, each portion of the exam serves a key role in preparing candidates for the obstacles they will experience in the field. By learning what to expect during the exam, how the results are computed, and how to interpret your score, you'll be in a strong position to succeed. With good study and a firm understanding of the exam methodology, you can approach the PELLET B Exam with confidence and take the first step toward a fulfilling career in law enforcement.

Chapter 2

Spelling in the PELLET B Exam

Spelling might seem like a basic skill to many, but in law enforcement, it is a crucial aspect of effective communication. As an officer, you'll need to make concise, accurate reports, fill out legal papers, and interact with your team and the public. Even little errors might generate misunderstanding, diminish your professionalism, or weaken the integrity of your work. Whether you're documenting an incident report or drafting a citation, spelling counts.

In this chapter, we will go deep into the spelling area of the PELLET B Exam. We will cover why perfect spelling is so vital in law enforcement, the types of words you'll likely face on the test, and the tactics you may use to enhance your spelling skills. By the end of this chapter, you'll have the knowledge and tools needed to excel in the spelling section of the exam and apply those abilities to your law enforcement career.

Overview of Spelling in the PELLET B Exam

The PELT B Exam is meant to assess candidates' abilities to read, understand, and write effectively—skills that are vital for anybody joining the law enforcement industry. One of the main elements of the exam is the spelling section, which evaluates your ability to accurately recognize the correct spelling of words used in law enforcement situations.

Why is spelling crucial in law enforcement?

As a law enforcement officer, your job involves much more than merely patrolling the streets and responding to calls. You'll be responsible for documents that could become part of the public record or be utilized in judicial actions. Accurate spelling is crucial in this situation because:

- **Court documents:** When officers are testifying in court, written evidence like police reports and case files must be clear and correct. A misspelled term in a report or affidavit could impair your credibility, or worse, could be used to invalidate your testimony.
- **Clarity:** Clear, clear writing is vital for law enforcement agents. Whether you're filling out a report, writing a citation, or emailing with colleagues, misspellings can mislead the reader and delay operations.

- **Attention to detail:** Correct spelling reveals that you pay attention to detail—a talent that's vital when documenting evidence, recording interviews, or conducting investigations.

The spelling component of the PELLET B Exam specifically focuses on testing your ability to identify correctly spelled words from a list of similar-sounding possibilities. This means that it's not just about knowing how to spell a word but also being able to recognize when a word is misspelled. You'll be asked to choose the correctly spelled word from a list of possibilities, and the issue is typically discerning between words that sound the same but are spelled differently or spotting tiny spelling mistakes.

The Importance of Accurate Spelling in Law Enforcement

In law enforcement, accurate written communication is as crucial as vocal communication. The ability to deliver information clearly and correctly can make or break a case. Law enforcement officials are regularly called upon to create written reports, which may become evidence in criminal prosecutions. Any spelling mistakes, no matter how little, could be disputed in court and may raise issues about the reliability of the document or evidence.

1. Courtroom Impact In the courtroom, precision and attention to detail are paramount. Lawyers, prosecutors, and defense attorneys may review any document filed as evidence. Even a small misspelling could be used to attack the legitimacy of your report or weaken your credibility as a witness. For example, if you mistakenly misspell a suspect's name or the location of a crime scene, it could throw doubt on your ability to recollect precise facts. This could result in substantial consequences, including the loss of a case or the dismissal of evidence.

2. Professionalism The professionalism you demonstrate on paper matters just as much as your conduct in the field. In law enforcement, attention to detail is a core principle, and it's something that's represented in your writing. If you submit a report full of spelling errors, it creates the appearance that you don't take your job seriously, or that you're careless. In contrast, a well-written, error-free report portrays an officer who is diligent, accurate, and reliable—a virtue that is highly regarded in the profession.

3. Clear Communication Misunderstandings can be costly in law enforcement. Accurate spelling guarantees that all communication, whether it's a report, an arrest warrant, or a conversation with fellow officers, is clear and devoid of errors. A miscommunication due to a misspelled term might lead to confusion and possibly mistakes. For example, a misspelled name or address on a search warrant could invalidate the warrant, or a mistake in a witness statement could lead to the wrong result.

4. Documenting Evidence In many circumstances, law enforcement officers will be obliged to document evidence and observations in reports. When producing these documents, it's crucial to ensure that every aspect is appropriately conveyed. A misspelled word could change the meaning of a statement, which could result in vital evidence being rejected or misunderstood. Accuracy is crucial, especially when the outcomes of investigations depend on the integrity of written documents.

Types of Words Commonly Tested in the Spelling Section

The spelling component of the PELLET B Exam is meant to evaluate your knowledge of common law enforcement words as well as general spelling skills. While the terms you'll encounter may vary from exam to test, there are some types of words that regularly occur owing to their significance to the law enforcement profession. These include:

1. Law Enforcement Terminology

Many of the words tested in this section will relate directly to law enforcement tasks. These terms are used often in reports, legal papers, and everyday contacts with the public and colleagues. Some examples of law enforcement terms that may occur on the test include:

- **Arrest**
- **Suspect**
- **Warrant**
- **Evidence**
- **Conviction**
- **Defendant**
- **Accusation**
- **Surveillance**
- **Interrogation**
- **Probation**
- **Subpoena**

These are terms you'll face on a regular basis as a law enforcement officer, and they need to be written correctly in your reports and documents. Misstating any of these terms might create misunderstanding and damage the clarity of your written communication.

2. Commonly Misspelled Words

While law enforcement terminology is crucial, the test will also incorporate commonly misspelled words that test your broad mastery of English spelling conventions. Many of these words can be tricky because they follow unusual patterns or are readily confused with other terms. Common examples include:

- **Occurrence** vs. **Occurance**
- **Necessary** vs. **Necessery**
- **Occurred** vs. **Ocurred**
- **Receive** vs. **Recieve**
- **Separate** vs. **Seperate**
- **Maintenance** vs. **Maintanance**

Understanding the appropriate spelling of such words is vital not just for passing the exam but also for speaking successfully in your law enforcement profession. Officers must prepare reports, statements, and other papers that are clear, succinct, and free from errors.

3. Similar Sounding Words (Homophones)

Homophones are words that sound the same but have various meanings and spellings. These words can be especially challenging, as their wrong use might change the meaning of a statement entirely. Some instances of commonly tested homophones include:

- **Principle** vs. **Principal**
- **Accept** vs. **Except**
- **Complement** vs. **Compliment**
- **Capital** vs. **Capitol**
- **Stationary** vs. **Stationery**

Because homophones are often confused, they appear frequently in the spelling component of the PELLET B Exam. Correctly determining the right spelling for each homophone can assist ensure that your written communication is accurate and professional.

4. Legal and Administrative Terms

As a law enforcement officer, you will regularly deal with legal documents, forms, and processes. The spelling component of the PELLET B Exam may test your knowledge of legal and administrative vocabulary. Some examples of legal terminology you may encounter include:

- **Defendant**
- **Indictment**
- **Testimony**
- **Affidavit**
- **Subpoena**
- **Injunction**

Mastering these terms and ensuring they are spelled correctly is vital for your work, as any error could lead to confusion or delay in legal proceedings. Accuracy is paramount in the legal world.

Strategies to Improve Your Spelling Skills

Mastering the spelling component of the PELLET B Exam demands constant practice and attention to detail. Here are a few ideas to help you improve your spelling skills and guarantee you're prepared for the test:

1. Create a List of Common Law Enforcement Terms

As you study for the PELLET B Exam, establish a list of law enforcement-specific phrases that you may encounter. Review these words periodically and practice spelling them out loud. Using flashcards with the word on one side and the proper spelling on the other might also be helpful for reinforcing these phrases.

2. Focus on Homophones

Homophones are one of the trickiest components of spelling, but they're also vital for law enforcement communication. To strengthen your understanding, construct pairs of homophones and test yourself. You can also utilize context clues to assist you recall which homophone to employ in a certain situation.

3. Pay Attention to Syllable Patterns

Many spelling errors occur because people don't break words down into syllables. Practice identifying the syllables in long or intricate words. Breaking a word into sections will help you recognize the correct spelling.

4. Use Online Tools and Resources

There are many online spelling materials and quizzes available to help you prepare for the exam. Websites and applications that provide daily spelling tests can be a fantastic method to practice spelling in context. This will help you become familiar with the types of words that are assessed on the PELLET B Exam.

5. Proofread Your Work

Before submitting any written project or report, make sure to proofread your work. This is a practice that will not only aid you during the exam but will also improve your written communication as a law enforcement officer. Proofreading lets you spot any spelling problems and polish your content before it's finalized.

Spelling is a key skill in law enforcement, and the PELLET B Exam examines your ability to recognize and use correct spelling in a number of circumstances. Accurate spelling ensures that your written communication is clear, professional, and reliable, which is crucial in the legal and law enforcement areas.

Key Spelling Rules: Common Spelling Patterns and Exceptions

In order to thrive in the spelling area of the PELLET B Exam, it's vital to learn some basic spelling rules and common patterns. These rules assist you approach tough words, especially when you face unexpected terminology during the test. Additionally, being aware of exceptions to these principles can offer you an edge when it comes to selecting the proper spelling in a multiple-choice format.

1. The 'I Before E' Rule (With Exceptions)

One of the most well-known spelling rules is the "**I before E**" rule. It states that in most cases, the letter **'i'** comes before **'e'** in a word, except after **'c'**, or when the word sounds like "ay" (e.g., "neighbor" or "weigh").

- **Example words** that follow the rule:
    - **Believe, Receive, Field, Achieve**

However, there are important **exceptions** to this rule:

- When the **'c'** comes before **'ei'**, such as in the word **"ceiling"**.
- Words where the combination sounds like "ay" (as mentioned earlier), like **"neighbor"** or **"weigh"**.
- Other irregular exceptions include **"science"**, **"seize"**, and **"weird"**.

2. Plurals and Suffixes: Adding 'S' or 'ES'

Adding **'s'** or **'es'** to a word to make it plural is another area where many spelling challenges arise. The basic rule is simple: just add **'s'** to the end of most words. However, when the word ends in **s, x, z, ch, or sh**, you'll need to add **'es'** instead.

- **Examples of plural words with 's'**:
    - **Cats, Dogs, Books**
- **Examples of plural words with 'es'**:
    - **Boxes, Washes, Buzzes**

Also, consider the tricky cases where you need to change a letter before adding the plural suffix:

- For words ending in **'y'** after a consonant, change the **'y'** to **'i'** and add **'es'**:
    - **City → Cities**
    - **Lady → Ladies**

3. Dropping the 'e' Before Adding a Suffix

Many English words end with an **'e'**, and when adding a suffix (such as **'ing'** or **'ly'**), the **'e'** is often dropped.

- **Examples where the 'e' is dropped**:
    - **Make → Making**
    - **Dance → Dancing**
    - **Large → Largely**

However, this rule has **exceptions**:

- Don't drop the 'e' when the suffix begins with a **vowel** that would change the word's pronunciation:
    - **Adorable → Adorably** (the 'e' is kept)

4. Double Consonants

When adding suffixes to words that end with a **single vowel** followed by a **single consonant**, you should **double the consonant** before adding the suffix if the word has a short vowel sound. This ensures that the consonant is pronounced as part of the original syllable rather than a separate one.

- **Examples of doubling consonants**:
    - **Stop → Stopping**
    - **Run → Running**
    - **Hop → Hopping**

Exceptions: If the vowel sound is long, do not double the consonant:

- **Hate → Hating**
- **Race → Racing**

5. Silent Letters and Commonly Misspelled Words

English is full of **silent letters**, which make certain words particularly difficult to spell. It is important to know these silent letters and understand how they affect the word's pronunciation and spelling.

- **Silent letters in common law enforcement terms:**
  - **Knife** (silent 'k')
  - **Doubt** (silent 'b')
  - **Receipt** (silent 'p')
  - **Psychology** (silent 'p')
  - **Subpoena** (silent 'u')

A good strategy for handling these tricky words is to memorize them and recognize the patterns where silent letters typically appear. Additionally, many silent letter words are rooted in foreign languages, so familiarizing yourself with these linguistic roots can be helpful.

How to Identify and Remember Commonly Misspelled Words

No matter how well you know spelling standards, there will always be words that are regularly misspelled, both in the PELLET B Exam and in ordinary writing. The key to excelling in the spelling segment of the exam is to memorize these words and develop ways for recognizing them. Here are a few strategies to help you:

1. Create a Personal Spelling List

One of the most effective strategies to improve your spelling is to keep track of the words that you often misspell. Whether they are popular law enforcement phrases or basic English words, putting them down in a dedicated list and checking them periodically will help encourage correct spelling.

- **Create flashcards** with the word on one side and the correct spelling on the other. You can even write a sentence using the word to provide context.
- **Practice writing the words** several times to reinforce their correct spelling.

2. Pay Attention to Word Patterns

English has a number of recurring patterns that can help you figure out the correct spelling of unfamiliar words. For example, many words with the **'ie'** or **'ei'** pattern follow the **"i before e"** rule, but as mentioned earlier, you should be mindful of the exceptions.

Breaking down unfamiliar words into their component syllables or finding the root of the word can also help you spell it correctly:

- **Experience** → Break it into **ex-per-i-ence**
- **Government** → Break it into **gov-ern-ment**

21

3. Use Mnemonics

Using **mnemonics** (memory aids) can be an excellent way to remember how to spell difficult words. For example, to remember how to spell **"necessary"**, you could use the mnemonic: **"One collar and two sleeves"** (to remind you that it has one 'c' and two 's').

Another effective mnemonic is for the word **"accommodate"**, which is often misspelled. The mnemonic here could be: **"Two c's and two m's make the room for two"**.

4. Visualize the Word

Many people find that **visualizing** the correct spelling of a word helps them remember it. For example, if you are struggling with a word like **"maintenance"**, try to visualize it in your mind's eye and break it down into its syllables. Seeing the word in your mind will often help solidify the correct spelling.

5. Use Spelling Apps and Online Tools

There are several apps and internet programs meant to improve spelling. Many of these tools feature spelling quizzes, flashcards, and writing prompts to help you practice. Regular practice with these materials will not only help you with spelling, but will also help you detect and learn from your mistakes.

6. Recognize the Importance of Context

Context plays a critical role in spelling. Sometimes, a word may be **misspelled because it is used in the wrong context** or because it is confused with a similar word. For example, the words **"affect"** and **"effect"** are often confused because they sound alike, but they have different meanings and spellings. By paying attention to the context in which a word is used, you can often deduce the correct spelling.

Understanding and applying **key spelling rules** will not only help you pass the test but will also prepare you for the precision and professionalism required in your future career.

Strategies for Correctly Identifying Misspelled Words

The PELLET B Exam's spelling part sometimes includes terms that are tough to spell, and misspelled words can have major ramifications, especially in law enforcement. Understanding the procedures for successfully spotting misspelled words will help you tackle this subject with confidence. Here are numerous tactics and recommendations to help you recognize frequent errors and improve your spelling accuracy.

1. Spotting Homophones (Words That Sound the Same but Are Spelled Differently)

Homophones are words that sound the same but have various meanings and spellings. In law enforcement, abusing homophones could lead to major miscommunications, especially when recording legal or procedural phrases. The key to accurately detecting homophones on the PELLET B Exam is understanding their meanings and knowing their right usage. Here are some common examples:

- **Accept vs. Except**
    - **Accept** means to receive something, whereas **except** means to exclude something.
    - **Correct Usage**: "I **accept** the report," and "Everyone was invited **except** John."
- **Principal vs. Principle**
    - **Principal** refers to a person in charge (such as a police chief), while **principle** refers to a fundamental belief or rule.
    - **Correct Usage**: "The **principal** of the police academy spoke at the graduation," and "He violated the basic **principle** of fairness."
- **Stationary vs. Stationery**
    - **Stationary** means something that is not moving, whereas **stationery** refers to writing materials.
    - **Correct Usage**: "The vehicle was **stationary** during the traffic stop," and "I need to buy some new **stationery** for writing reports."
- **Complement vs. Compliment**
    - **Complement** refers to something that completes or enhances something else, while **compliment** refers to praise or admiration.
    - **Correct Usage**: "The badge and uniform are a perfect **complement** to each other," and "The officer gave me a **compliment** on my work."

Tip for identifying homophones: When you encounter a homophone in the PELLET B Exam, pause for a moment to think about the context. Is the word referring to something that completes (complement) or something that's received (accept)? By examining the context, you can often determine which spelling is correct.

2. Recognizing Double Letters in Words

Many law enforcement terminology, as well as regular English words, have double letters, however these can be challenging. Sometimes, people accidentally delete one of the letters or add an extra one while spelling words. On the PELLET B Exam, you may come across terms that require attention to detail when it comes to double consonants.

Here are a few examples of commonly misspelled words with double letters:

- **Occurred** (not **Occured**)

- **Successful** (not **Sucessful**)
- **Aggressive** (not **Agressive**)
- **Embarrassment** (not **Embarassment**)
- **Possessive** (not **Possesive**)

Tip for correctly identifying double letters: When you encounter a word with double letters, pronounce it slowly in your head, and focus on the **sound** of the repeated consonant. Most double-letter words will follow specific patterns, such as doubling the **'s'** in "successful" or the **'r'** in "occurred."

3. Understanding Commonly Misspelled Words in Law Enforcement

As a law enforcement officer, you will frequently encounter terms that are specific to your profession. Some of these words may be unfamiliar, or their spelling may differ from what you'd expect based on their pronunciation. Common law enforcement-related words include:

- **Subpoena** (not **Subpeona**)
- **Warrant** (not **Warant**)
- **Surveillance** (not **Survelance**)
- **Defendant** (not **Defendent**)
- **Interrogation** (not **Interogation**)

These are words you may use on a daily basis, so it's important to **memorize their correct spelling**. Misunderstanding or miswriting these terms can result in incorrect documentation or confusion during legal proceedings.

Tip for identifying misspelled law enforcement terms: Create a list of commonly used terms in your field and review them regularly. Visualize each word and focus on its **pronunciation** and structure. Knowing these terms inside and out will help you identify them more easily on the exam.

4. Applying the 'Rule of E' for Adding Suffixes

A common spelling challenge involves words that end in **'e'**, particularly when adding a suffix. The general rule is to **drop the 'e'** before adding certain suffixes, like **-ing**, **-ly**, or **-ed**. However, **don't drop the 'e'** if the suffix starts with a **vowel** (like **-able** or **-ous**).

For example:

- **Make → Making**
- **Dance → Dancing**
- **Large → Largely**
- **Love → Loving**

Exceptions to this rule include words like:

- **Changeable** (not **Changeable**)
- **Noticeable** (not **Noticable**)

5. Watch Out for Silent Letters

Silent letters can make some words especially challenging to spell. These letters are not pronounced but must be included in the spelling. On the PELLET B Exam, you'll need to recognize when a letter is silent to choose the correct spelling.

Some common examples:

- **Knife** (silent 'k')
- **Subpoena** (silent 'u')
- **Psychology** (silent 'p')
- **Debt** (silent 'b')
- **Receipt** (silent 'p')

Tip for identifying silent letters: Make a mental note of common silent letter patterns. Many silent letters appear in words with roots from other languages (Latin, French), so recognizing these patterns can help you choose the correct spelling on the exam.

Effective Memorization Techniques for Law Enforcement-Related Terms

Memorizing the right spelling of law enforcement-related phrases involves constant practice and deliberate learning. Since many of these terminology are peculiar to the profession, studying them in context will make them easier to recall. Below are numerous efficient memorizing techniques to assist you memorize the correct spelling of law enforcement terminology.

1. Create Flashcards

Flashcards are one of the most effective techniques to memorize information fast. You can design a deck of flashcards with the law enforcement terms on one side and the proper spelling on the other. Additionally, write a brief statement or phrase using the word on the back to reinforce both its meaning and its spelling.

- Example flashcard:
    - Front: **Subpoena**
    - Back: **A legal document that requires a person to appear in court.**

Using an app like **Quizlet** or physical index cards, review the flashcards daily. This constant repetition helps reinforce the correct spelling in your memory.

2. Write the Words Repeatedly

Writing a word multiple times helps **reinforce muscle memory**. It's a simple but effective way to internalize the correct spelling. By writing law enforcement terms repeatedly, you will not only improve your ability to spell the word but also become more familiar with its structure.

- Example: Write **"Subpoena"** 10 times while saying it out loud, focusing on each letter as you write it.

3. Visualize the Words

Visualization is a powerful tool for memorization. To **visualize a word**, try imagining it on paper in your mind's eye. Focus on the shape of the letters and the overall structure of the word. Try to picture the word as it would appear in an official document, such as a police report or legal brief.

- For example, visualize the word **"Warrant"** as it might appear in the context of **"Search Warrant"** or **"Arrest Warrant,"** and mentally see it in a formal legal document.

4. Use Mnemonics

Mnemonics (memory aids) are great for remembering tricky words. A mnemonic uses a phrase, rhyme, or acronym to help recall information. For example, the word **"necessary"** can be remembered using the mnemonic: "**One collar and two sleeves**" (reminding you that it has one 'c' and two 's').

- Example mnemonic for **"accommodate"**: "**Two c's, two m's, and two rooms for two.**"

5. Teach the Words to Someone Else

Teaching someone else how to spell a word is an efficient approach to reinforce your own understanding. If you have a study buddy, practice spelling words together, explaining the rules and exceptions to each other. Teaching helps enhance your comprehension and makes it easier to remember the correct spelling.

6. Group Similar Words Together

Another remembering strategy is grouping related words together. For instance, arrange words with double letters together or construct a list of frequent law enforcement terms that are often misspelled. By grouping terms in comparable categories, you can make them easier to recall.

- Example group: **Necessary, Embarrassment, Successful** (all have double letters).

7. Review Regularly

Consistent review is the key to retaining what you've learnt. Spend a few minutes each day examining your list of law enforcement-related phrases, focusing on any words you find problematic. Reviewing the terms in several formats—flashcards, writing them down, or speaking them aloud—will help reinforce the knowledge in multiple ways.

Mastering the spelling component of the PELT B Exam is about more than just memorizing individual words. It entails understanding the laws and patterns of spelling, spotting typical errors like homophones and double letters, and employing efficient memorizing strategies. With constant preparation and the tactics taught in this chapter, you can confidently approach the exam and ace the spelling section.

Practice Questions and Solutions: Spelling.

Before going into the practice problems, let's take a quick review of how the spelling portion is arranged in the PELT B Exam.

The spelling component consists of multiple-choice questions where you are provided with a word and asked to choose the proper spelling from a list of possibilities. In each example, there will be one correct answer plus a few distractors—incorrect response alternatives that are aimed to test your comprehension of common spelling principles and word patterns. The words you'll be tested on include not simply broad vocabulary but also terminology widely used in law enforcement scenarios.

By practicing the problems in this chapter and examining the breakdown of each answer choice, you'll learn how to confidently recognize the proper spelling for any word on the exam.

Practice Question 1:

Which of the following is the correct spelling?

A) **Defendent**
B) **Defendant**
C) **Defandant**
D) **Defandent**

Answer Breakdown:

- **A) Defendent**
  This option is a common misspelling of the word. The correct spelling is **"defendant,"** with an **'a'** instead of an **'e'**. It's a frequent mistake, but it's important to remember the proper form to avoid losing points on the exam.
- **B) Defendant**
  This is the correct spelling. The word **"defendant"** refers to a person who is being accused or sued in a court of law. The spelling follows standard English conventions and is used consistently in legal documents.
- **C) Defandant**
  This option is incorrect because of the extra **'n'** and the misplacement of the **'a'**. While it may seem like a plausible mistake, the word should only contain one **'n'**.
- **D) Defandent**
  Similar to option **C**, this is also incorrect due to the extra **'e'** and the rearranged letters. This misspelling is not common in standard English, making it easy to identify as a distractor.

Correct Answer: B) Defendant

Explanation: The word "defendant" comes from the Latin term **"defendere,"** which means to defend or to protect. It's important to remember the standard **'a'** in the middle of the word and avoid adding unnecessary letters.

Practice Question 2:

Which of the following is the correct spelling?

A) **Occured**
B) **Occurred**
C) **Ocurred**
D) **Ocurrred**

Answer Breakdown:

- **A) Occured**
  This option is incorrect because it omits one of the **'r's** in the word. The correct spelling contains **two 'r's** after the **'c'**.
- **B) Occurred**
  This is the correct spelling. The word **"occurred"** follows the standard pattern of double

consonants after a short vowel in a word. The 'r' is doubled because the word has a short 'o' sound. This is a standard spelling convention for many words with a similar structure.

- **C) Ocurred**
  This is incorrect because it uses an incorrect vowel combination. The correct form uses 'cc' after the vowel rather than 'c' and 'u'.
- **D) Ocurrred**
  This option is incorrect because it contains an extra 'r'. The word should have only two 'r's, not three.

Correct Answer: B) Occurred

Explanation: The word "occurred" is a verb that means something that took place. The doubling of the consonant 'r' after the short vowel 'o' follows a common English spelling rule, and it's crucial to remember the correct number of letters to avoid errors in your writing.

Practice Question 3:

Which of the following is the correct spelling?

A) **Indictment**
B) **Inditement**
C) **Indictement**
D) **Inditment**

Answer Breakdown:

- **A) Indictment**
  This is the correct spelling. The word **"indictment"** refers to a formal charge or accusation of a serious crime, typically in legal contexts. The spelling has a 'c' and 't' after 'i', following the standard legal term convention.
- **B) Inditement**
  This is incorrect because it uses the incorrect 'i' after the 'd', which is a common mistake. The 'c' should be present in the correct spelling.
- **C) Indictement**
  This is incorrect because it has an extra 'e' in the middle of the word. This misspelling is not common and doesn't follow the usual structure of the word.
- **D) Inditment**
  This is also incorrect because it omits the 'c' and places an unnecessary 'i' in the word. The word should have a 'c' after 'd' to be correctly spelled.

Correct Answer: A) Indictment

Explanation: The word **"indictment"** comes from the Latin **"indictare,"** which means to announce or proclaim. In English, the word is traditionally spelled with a **'c'** after **'d'**, though it is often mispronounced as if it had a **'t'** sound. The key is to remember the proper legal spelling.

Practice Question 4:

Which of the following is the correct spelling?

A) **Accommodate**
B) **Acommodate**
C) **Accomodate**
D) **Acomodate**

Answer Breakdown:

- **A) Accommodate**
  This is the correct spelling. The word **"accommodate"** means to provide room or space for something or someone, and it contains **two c's** and **two m's**. It is a word often encountered in both formal and legal contexts, especially in documents related to housing, transportation, or official arrangements.
- **B) Acommodate**
  This is incorrect because it uses only **one 'c'**, whereas the correct spelling uses **two c's**. This is a common misspelling of the word, and it's important to remember the double consonants.
- **C) Accomodate**
  This is also incorrect because it incorrectly uses **one 'm'** instead of **two m's**. This is another common mistake that many people make, especially when they are unsure about double letters in the word.
- **D) Acomodate**
  This is incorrect due to the missing **'c'** and the **'o'** in place of the correct **'m'**. The word should have **two c's** and **two m's**, and this error is easily avoided with regular practice.

Correct Answer: A) Accommodate

Explanation: The word **"accommodate"** is often difficult for many people due to the double consonants. However, by breaking the word into parts (ac-com-mo-date), you can remember the correct spelling. The key is to always remember **two c's** and **two m's**, which is a common rule for many English words with similar structure.

Practice Question 5:

Which of the following is the correct spelling?

A) **Embarrassment**
B) **Embarassment**
C) **Embaressment**
D) **Embarrasment**

Answer Breakdown:

- **A) Embarrassment**
  This is the correct spelling. The word **"embarrassment"** refers to a state of being embarrassed, and it contains **two r's** and **two s's**. This is a tricky word because it can be easily misspelled due to its double letters.
- **B) Embarassment**
  This is incorrect because it omits the second **'r'**, which is required to correctly spell **"embarrassment."**
- **C) Embaressment**
  This is incorrect because it misses both the **'r'** and the double **'s'**. It is a common mistake, but it does not follow the correct structure of the word.
- **D) Embarrasment**
  This is incorrect because it has only **one 's'** instead of **two**. This is a frequent error, and the correct spelling has a double **'s'**.

Correct Answer: A) Embarrassment

Explanation: The word **"embarrassment"** follows the pattern of doubling consonants for emphasis, which is common in many English words. The key to spelling this word correctly is to remember the double **'r'** and **'s'**. When in doubt, break the word into parts—**em-barr-ass-ment**—to visualize the correct spelling.

The spelling component of the PELT B Exam may appear basic, but it's crucial to practice often and recognize the common mistakes that individuals make. By following the tactics discussed in this chapter—such as recognizing homophones, spotting double letters, and memorizing commonly misspelled law enforcement terms—you'll be well-prepared to handle this portion confidently.

Typical Spelling Mistakes to Avoid on Test Day

Now that we understand the relevance of spelling in law enforcement, let's dive into some typical spelling mistakes that test-takers often make. Being aware of these typical hazards will allow you to spot them more easily and avoid them on test day.

1. Mixing Up Homophones (Words That Sound the Same)

One of the most common spelling mistakes comes with homophones—words that sound the same but are spelled differently and have distinct meanings. These terms can easily trip you up on the PELLET B Exam if you're not careful. Many individuals misunderstand homophones because they sound identical, but understanding the difference between them is important to success.

- **Examples of Common Homophones:**
  - **Accept** vs. **Except**
    - **Accept** means to receive something.
    - **Except** means to exclude something.
    - **Example**: "I **accept** the invitation **except** for the time change."
  - **Compliment** vs. **Complement**
    - **Compliment** refers to praise or admiration.
    - **Complement** means something that completes or enhances something else.
    - **Example**: "Her dress was a perfect **complement** to her shoes, and I gave her a **compliment** on her outfit."
  - **Stationary** vs. **Stationery**
    - **Stationary** means not moving.
    - **Stationery** refers to paper, pens, or office supplies.
    - **Example**: "The car was **stationary** at the light, and I needed to buy more **stationery** for writing my reports."

Tip for Recognizing Homophones: Always take a moment to evaluate the **context** of the sentence. If the word refers to something that's received, it's likely **accepted**. If the sentence is excluding something, it's **an exception**. This careful evaluation helps ensure the correct choice.

2. Misspelling Common Law Enforcement Terms

As you prepare for the **PELT B Exam**, it's important to familiarize yourself with **common law enforcement terms** and their correct spellings. Many of these terms are frequently used in reports, legal documents, and day-to-day police work, making it crucial to get them right.

Here are some examples of commonly misspelled law enforcement terms:

- **Defendant** (not **Defendent**)
- **Warrant** (not **Warant**)
- **Surveillance** (not **Survelance**)
- **Subpoena** (not **Subpeona**)
- **Arrest** (not **Arest**)

These terms are frequently tested on the **PELT B Exam** because they are so important in the legal and law enforcement world. Learning these terms, and practicing them regularly, will help you avoid mistakes.

Tip for Mastering Law Enforcement Terms: Create a list of law enforcement-related words and review them regularly. Flashcards can be an excellent tool to reinforce their correct spelling. The more familiar you are with these terms, the easier it will be to identify them on the exam.

3. Dropping or Adding Letters (Double Consonants)

Another common mistake test-takers make is failing to correctly identify when to **double consonants** or when to leave them as a single letter. Many words require a doubled consonant, especially after a short vowel sound.

- **Examples** of double consonants:
  - **Occurred** (not **Occured**)
  - **Successful** (not **Sucessful**)
  - **Aggressive** (not **Agressive**)
  - **Embarrassment** (not **Embarassment**)

Tip for Avoiding Double Consonant Mistakes: The rule is simple: if a word ends with a single vowel followed by a single consonant, and the vowel sound is short, double the consonant before adding a suffix. This rule applies to many common English words.

4. Silent Letters

English contains many words with **silent letters**—letters that are not pronounced but must be included when spelling the word. These silent letters can easily trip you up if you're not familiar with them.

- **Common examples of silent letters**:
  - **Knife** (silent 'k')
  - **Psychology** (silent 'p')
  - **Subpoena** (silent 'u')
  - **Receipt** (silent 'p')

Tip for Recognizing Silent Letters: If you're unsure about a word, take a moment to think about its pronunciation. Silent letters are often found in words with roots from other languages, such as Latin or French. Knowing the most common silent letter patterns can help you spot them easily.

5. Confusing Words with Similar Spellings

Many words in the English language are **similar in spelling** but differ in meaning. These words are often mixed up on exams, especially when test-takers are in a rush. Here are some common examples:

- **Principal** vs. **Principle**
    - **Principal** refers to a person in charge, such as the principal of a school or a police chief.
    - **Principle** refers to a fundamental law or belief.
    - **Example**: "The **principal** of the academy addressed the cadets," and "The **principle** of fairness was important in the decision."
- **Stationary** vs. **Stationery**
    - **Stationary** means not moving.
    - **Stationery** refers to writing materials.
    - **Example**: "The vehicle was **stationary** during the traffic stop," and "I need to buy new **stationery** for report writing."

Tip for Avoiding Confused Words: Pay attention to the context of the sentence to determine which word is correct. Always take the time to read through the options carefully to avoid mixing up words with similar spellings.

Recognizing These Pitfalls on Test Day

Now that we've discussed some of the most common spelling mistakes, let's explore how you can **recognize and avoid these pitfalls** on test day. The PELLET B Exam is a timed, multiple-choice exam, so it's crucial to be strategic when working through the spelling section.

1. Practice Contextual Reading

When presented with a multiple-choice question, always read the sentence or passage surrounding the word in question. By focusing on the **context**, you can more easily distinguish between similar words and select the correct spelling.

For example, if the test presents the word **"principle"** in a sentence about a **law**, it's likely the correct word is **"principle"** (fundamental belief), not **"principal"** (person in charge).

2. Eliminate Obvious Incorrect Options

The PELLET B Exam includes **distractors**—incorrect answer choices meant to test your knowledge of common misspellings and word patterns. If you come across an option that clearly contains a spelling error (e.g., **"sucessful"** instead of **"successful"**), immediately eliminate that option. This will improve your chances of selecting the correct answer.

3. Take Your Time to Review

Although the exam is timed, it's important to **pace yourself**. After reading through each question, give yourself a few seconds to review the word choices. Don't rush through, as this could lead to careless mistakes. If you're unsure about a word, trust your knowledge of common spelling rules to guide you.

Spelling may seem like an easy ability, but in the context of the PELLET B Exam, it's a critical aspect of displaying your attention to detail and expertise. By avoiding typical errors, such as mixing up homophones, mistaking words with similar spellings, and misplacing double consonants or silent letters, you will boost your chances of earning a good mark on the exam.

Regular practice, comprehending typical spelling problems, and implementing the solutions given in this chapter will guarantee you can successfully handle the spelling area of the PELLET B Exam. With these ideas in mind, you are now more ready to recognize and solve frequent mistakes, providing you a larger advantage as you prepare for this key step in your law enforcement career.

Chapter 3

Vocabulary in the PELLET B Exam

Vocabulary is an essential component of the PELT B Exam, since it directly influences your comprehension and communication efficacy within the law enforcement domain. Possessing a robust vocabulary is essential for effectively and professionally executing your responsibilities, whether engaging with coworkers, composing reports, testifying in court, or reviewing case files. This chapter will examine the significance of vocabulary in law enforcement, its effect on communication, and the many vocabulary questions seen on the PELLET B Exam. Upon concluding this chapter, you will comprehend the significance of vocabulary in law enforcement and how to excel in this segment of the examination.

The Significance of Vocabulary in Law Enforcement and Communication

In law enforcement, language holds significance. The capacity to select the appropriate word at the opportune moment can significantly influence the result of an inquiry, a legal proceeding, or a public conversation. As an officer, you will be obligated to compose reports, conduct witness interviews, make observations, and provide testimony in court. A robust and comprehensive vocabulary enables clear, precise, and professional articulation of thoughts.

Vocabulary is vital not just for good communication but also for comprehension. As a law enforcement officer, you will regularly analyze and evaluate legal documents, reports, and various written materials. A rich vocabulary allows you to rapidly and accurately receive and grasp crucial information. Whether it's comprehending legal language in a statute or grasping the details of a witness's statement, your vocabulary will help you perform your work efficiently.

Why Vocabulary Matters in Law Enforcement

In law enforcement, clear communication is vital for preserving order and solving problems. Officers must communicate with numerous groups, including colleagues, suspects, witnesses, the public, and attorneys. If an officer lacks the ability to deliver information effectively, misconceptions may ensue, leading to errors, delays, or even legal ramifications. The stakes are high—especially when public safety is concerned.

Here are some significant areas where terminology has a crucial role:

- **Report Writing:** Officers are often obliged to produce extensive reports, which can be utilized in criminal investigations or legal procedures. Clear, precise wording helps guarantee that your reports are easily understood by others. An ambiguous or imprecise word choice could create uncertainty and weaken the accuracy of the report.
- **Interviews and Interrogations:** As an officer, you may conduct interviews or interrogations with suspects, witnesses, or victims. Having a decent vocabulary helps you frame inquiries effectively, evaluate replies accurately, and locate crucial information. Misunderstanding a remark owing to poor vocabulary could result in losing essential information or reaching the wrong inferences.
- **Legal Documentation:** Legal documents may involve sophisticated terms and specialist language. A good vocabulary helps you understand these documents and apply the proper wording when creating warrants, subpoenas, affidavits, or other legal material.
- **Court Testimony:** Officers are often forced to testify in court. In these instances, it's crucial to be able to explain your findings and experiences accurately. The use of exact language helps avoid misinterpretations and improves your credibility as a witness.
- **Public Communication:** Officers contact the public regularly. Whether describing a legal process, giving critical information, or de-escalating a tense situation, the ability to utilize clear and accessible language can help you develop trust and minimize misconceptions.

The better your vocabulary, the more successfully you can operate in each of these domains. It's not just about having a large vocabulary; it's about being able to utilize the appropriate words in the proper circumstances.

Types of Vocabulary Questions You Will Face on the PELLET B Exam

The vocabulary component of the PELLET B Exam measures your ability to understand and use words in context. This portion evaluates not just your knowledge of definitions but also your ability to identify which word best fits a specific context, demonstrating how well you comprehend the meanings of words and their suitable usage. Below, we will look at the types of vocabulary questions you might expect on the PELLET B Exam, and how to approach them effectively.

1. Multiple-Choice Definitions

One of the most popular types of vocabulary questions on the PELLET B Exam is the multiple-choice definition question. In these questions, you will be provided with a term and asked to choose the proper definition from a choice of options. These questions are designed to test your knowledge of terminology often used in law enforcement and general vocabulary.

For example:

What does the word "subpoena" mean?

A) A written order requiring someone to appear in court
B) A formal complaint filed in a civil case
C) The process of questioning a witness under oath
D) A report detailing the findings of an investigation

In this case, the correct answer is **A) A written order requiring someone to appear in court**. Understanding the meaning of legal terms like **"subpoena"** is essential for law enforcement officers, as these terms are frequently encountered in daily duties.

Tip for success: When answering multiple-choice definition questions, try to eliminate any options that you know are incorrect. If you're unsure, focus on the most contextually appropriate definition, as many of the words in law enforcement have specific meanings.

2. Word Usage in Context

Another typical sort of vocabulary question is the word usage in context inquiry. In these questions, you will be asked to choose the word that most appropriately matches a statement depending on its meaning. These questions assess your ability to recognize the meaning of a term and apply it correctly in context.

For example:

Choose the word that best completes the sentence:

"The officer had to _____ the situation before the crowd became more agitated."

A) Diffuse
B) Confuse
C) Refuse
D) Suffuse

In this case, the correct answer is **A) Diffuse**, as it means to calm down or make less tense. The word **"diffuse"** fits logically in the context of calming down a potentially dangerous or tense situation. The other options are not appropriate in this context.

Tip for success: For this type of question, focus on the sentence as a whole. Think about the situation and the meaning of each word option. Context clues will guide you toward the best choice.

3. Synonyms and Antonyms

In this type of vocabulary question, you will be asked to select a word that is **synonymous** (has a similar meaning) or **antonyms** (has the opposite meaning) to a given word. These questions test your ability to understand nuances in word meanings.

For example:

Which of the following is a synonym for "arbitrary"?

A) Random
B) Deliberate
C) Precise
D) Systematic

In this case, the correct answer is **A) Random**, because both **"arbitrary"** and **"random"** refer to something decided without a specific reason or plan.

Tip for success: For synonym and antonym questions, try to recall the basic meaning of the word in question. Synonyms will share similar meanings, while antonyms will represent the opposite concept.

4. Recognizing Commonly Confused Words

Some vocabulary questions test your ability to identify **commonly confused words**. These words may look or sound similar but have different meanings. Being able to differentiate between these words is crucial for both the exam and your professional communication.

For example:

Which of the following sentences uses the correct word?

A) The officer made a **capital** mistake when issuing the citation.
B) The officer made a **capitol** mistake when issuing the citation.

The correct answer is **A) capital**, as **"capital"** refers to a serious or major mistake, whereas **"capitol"** refers to a building or location related to government.

Tip for success: Pay attention to words that are often confused. Knowing the difference between similar-sounding words and understanding their correct usage is essential for your success on the exam.

5. Word Parts (Prefixes, Suffixes, and Roots)

Some vocabulary questions may ask you to identify a word's meaning based on its **prefix**, **suffix**, or **root**. This type of question tests your understanding of word construction and how parts of a word can influence its meaning.

For example:

Which of the following words is derived from the root word "dict," which means "to speak" or "to say"?

A) Predict
B) Dissect
C) Subscribe
D) Eject

The correct answer is **A) Predict**, as **"dict"** comes from the Latin word **"dicere,"** meaning to speak or say, and **"predict"** means to say or estimate what will happen in the future.

Tip for success: Familiarizing yourself with common word roots, prefixes, and suffixes will help you recognize the meanings of unfamiliar words, particularly in the law enforcement context.

Tips for Improving Your Vocabulary for the PELLET B Exam

Having a good vocabulary is vital not only for the exam but also for your law enforcement job. Here are some strategies for boosting your vocabulary and ensuring that you're well-prepared for the PELLET B Exam:

1. Read Regularly and Widely

One of the finest methods to expand your vocabulary is to read consistently. Exposure to a range of texts—whether they are books, newspapers, periodicals, or legal documents—will introduce you to new terms and reinforce their meanings in context. Law enforcement personnel routinely read reports, statutes, and legal briefs, so reading broadly will help you become more acquainted with these types of materials.

2. Use Flashcards

Create flashcards with new words on one side and their definitions on the other. You may also offer example phrases to help you comprehend the word in context. Review the flashcards regularly to strengthen your language knowledge.

3. Learn Word Roots, Prefixes, and Suffixes

Understanding the fundamental blocks of words will help you comprehend their meanings and recognize them on the exam. Focus on frequent prefixes, suffixes, and roots, especially those employed in legal and law enforcement situations.

4. Practice using Vocabulary Quizzes

There are several online tools and apps that offer vocabulary quizzes and practice assessments. Use these to test your knowledge and find areas where you need improvement. Regular practice can help you retain new terms and enhance your grasp of them.

5. Use New Words in Conversation

The greatest approach to imprint new vocabulary in your head is to utilize it. Make an attempt to incorporate new words into your talks or writing. The more you use the word, the easier it will be to recall when you need it.

A strong vocabulary is vital for success on the PELT B Exam and in your law enforcement job. It impairs your capacity to read complex materials, interact successfully with coworkers and the public, and portray yourself professionally in reports and legal documents.

How to Approach Vocabulary Questions on the PELLET B Exam

The vocabulary component of the PELT B Exam often contains multiple-choice questions, where you are asked to determine the right meaning of a word based on its usage within a phrase. For each question, you will be given a term and asked to choose the proper definition from a set of possible solutions.

Two essential strategies to tackle these questions are **using context clues** and **decoding words with roots, prefixes, and suffixes**. Let's dive into how each of these strategies works.

1. Context Clues: Using the Surrounding Text to Define Unfamiliar Words

One of the most efficient strategies to discover the meaning of an unfamiliar word on the PELT B Exam is by examining context clues. Context clues are the words, phrases, and sentences around the unfamiliar term that can help you figure out its meaning. When you come across a word you don't know, your first reaction should be to glance at the surrounding text to uncover hints about its meaning.

Types of Context Clues

There are several types of context clues you can use to infer the meaning of a word. Let's look at each of these types:

1. **Definition or Restatement Clues**
   Sometimes, the meaning of an unfamiliar word will be directly stated or restated in the sentence or in the following sentences. In such cases, the context clue is very explicit.
   Example:
   "The officer was **adamant** about the importance of following procedure. She would not tolerate any mistakes."
   In this example, the word **"adamant"** is defined by the context as someone who is firm and unwilling to change their stance. The use of the phrase **"would not tolerate any mistakes"** suggests that **"adamant"** means **uncompromising** or **firm**.
2. **Synonym Clues**
   In some cases, the surrounding text may provide a **synonym**—a word with a similar meaning to the unfamiliar word. These clues can make it easy to understand the unfamiliar word.
   Example:
   "The officer's **inflexible** behavior made it difficult to negotiate. She would not budge on her decision."
   Here, the word **"inflexible"** is a synonym for **"adamant"**, and the clue provided by **"would not budge"** tells us that **"inflexible"** means **rigid** or **unwilling to change**.
3. **Antonym Clues**
   Sometimes, the meaning of an unfamiliar word is clarified by its opposite. These are called **antonym clues**.
   Example:
   "The suspect was **cooperative**, unlike the previous witness who had been **uncooperative** during the interrogation."
   In this case, the context clue **"uncooperative"** helps us infer that **"cooperative"** means **willing to work together or assist**.
4. **Example Clues**
   In some sentences, examples are provided that help define the meaning of the unfamiliar

word.

Example:

"The officer needed to search for **contraband**, such as drugs, weapons, or stolen goods." In this case, the examples of **"drugs," "weapons,"** and **"stolen goods"** help us understand that **"contraband"** refers to **illegal items**.

5. **Cause and Effect Clues**

   Sometimes, the context will show the cause or effect of an action, which can help define a word.

   Example:

   "The suspect's **aggressive** behavior led to his immediate arrest. His violent outbursts were unprovoked."

   In this case, the effect of the suspect's behavior helps define **"aggressive"** as **hostile or combative**.

Tip for Using Context Clues:

When you encounter an unfamiliar word, first try to identify the **clue words** that will help you understand the meaning. Look for surrounding sentences or phrases that provide more information. **Context clues** are often the quickest and most effective way to figure out the meaning of a word without needing to know the definition directly.

---

2. Word Roots, Prefixes, and Suffixes: Decoding Unknown Words

Another useful method for solving vocabulary questions on the PELT B Exam is comprehending **word roots, prefixes, and suffixes.**

The structure of many English words can provide useful clues about their meanings, even if you've never encountered the word before. By breaking down the term into its component pieces, you may often deduce its meaning with a high degree of precision.

Word Roots

A **root word** is the base part of a word, the core unit that carries its primary meaning. Many English words come from Latin or Greek roots, and by recognizing these roots, you can often deduce the meanings of unfamiliar words.

- **Example**: The root **"bene"** means **good** or **well** (from Latin).
    - **Benevolent** (showing kindness)
    - **Beneficial** (producing good results)
    - **Benefit** (an advantage or good result)

- **Example**: The root **"mal"** means **bad** or **evil** (from Latin).
    - **Malevolent** (showing evil intentions)
    - **Malfunction** (a failure to work correctly)
    - **Malicious** (intending to do harm)

Prefixes

A **prefix** is a group of letters added to the beginning of a word to alter its meaning. Knowing common prefixes can help you determine the meaning of unfamiliar words.

- **Example**: The prefix **"un-"** means **not** or **opposite of**.
    - **Unhappy** (not happy)
    - **Unwilling** (not willing)
    - **Uncertain** (not certain)
- **Example**: The prefix **"pre-"** means **before**.
    - **Preview** (to view beforehand)
    - **Preliminary** (something that comes before the main event)
    - **Preschool** (before school age)

Suffixes

A **suffix** is a group of letters added to the end of a word to change its meaning. Suffixes often indicate the word's **part of speech** (such as noun, verb, or adjective).

- **Example**: The suffix **"-able"** means **capable of** or **suitable for**.
    - **Readable** (capable of being read)
    - **Reliable** (capable of being relied upon)
    - **Understandable** (able to be understood)
- **Example**: The suffix **"-ment"** turns a verb into a noun, usually indicating a **state or condition**.
    - **Enjoyment** (the state of enjoying)
    - **Development** (the process of developing)
    - **Establishment** (the process of setting something up)

Combining Roots, Prefixes, and Suffixes

Many English words are formed by combining roots, prefixes, and suffixes. By recognizing the individual parts of a word, you can deduce its overall meaning.

- **Example**: **"Un-"** (prefix) + **"happi"** (root) + **"-ness"** (suffix) = **Unhappiness** (the state of being unhappy)
- **Example**: **"Pre-"** (prefix) + **"view"** (root) = **Preview** (to view before)

Tip for Decoding Words:

When you come across an unknown term, break it down into its base, prefix, and suffix. By understanding the meaning of each component, you can typically extrapolate the entire meaning of the word, even if you've never seen it before. The more you acquaint yourself with common prefixes, suffixes, and roots, the more confident you will be in decoding unknown terminology on the PELLET B Exam.

Mastering vocabulary is vital not only for passing the PELT B Exam but also for flourishing in your law enforcement job. Whether you are communicating in writing or speaking with coworkers, suspects, or the public, the ability to use and interpret language effectively is crucial to your success.

Understanding the Meaning of Words Based on the Context They're Used In

When taking the PELT B Exam, the vocabulary questions are designed to evaluate your ability to comprehend words and phrases within the context in which they are used. In real-world law enforcement circumstances, you often need to grasp legal jargon, witness statements, and police reports that may contain sophisticated or foreign terms.

Vocabulary in context means using surrounding information—whether it's the sentence, paragraph, or the general tone of the document—to determine the meaning of an unknown word. This is particularly crucial during the exam, because you may come across vocabulary that is unfamiliar to you or that you've never encountered in this exact context before.

How Context Influences Word Meaning

Words can take on different meanings depending on how they are used in phrases. For example, the word "charge" could refer to a criminal charge, an electric charge, or even a charge in a military sense. Context is what helps you identify which meaning is correct in a given situation. Let's study how context hints can help you understand terminology in sentences.

1. Context Clues: Types and Examples

When you encounter an unfamiliar word in a sentence, look at the **surrounding context** for clues. Context clues can come in several forms:

- **Definition Clues**
  The sentence or surrounding text may define or explain the meaning of the word directly.
  Example: "The **defendant** is a person who is formally accused or charged with a crime."
  In this example, the sentence defines the word **"defendant"**, making it easy to deduce its meaning.

- **Synonym Clues**
  Sometimes, the meaning of the unfamiliar word is provided through a synonym—a word with a similar meaning.
  Example: "The police officer was **ardent** in his efforts to solve the case, always putting in extra hours."
  The word **"ardent"** can be interpreted as **"eager"** or **"enthusiastic"** because of the context of "efforts" and "putting in extra hours."

- **Antonym Clues**
  An antonym, or opposite word, can also provide insight into the meaning of an unfamiliar word.
  Example: "The suspect's **recalcitrant** attitude was in stark contrast to his cooperation during the first round of questioning."
  The word **"recalcitrant"** (meaning resistant to authority) is made clearer by the contrasting word **"cooperation."**

- **Cause and Effect Clues**
  Context can also indicate the effect of a particular action or condition, helping you understand the meaning of the word.
  Example: "The officer's **inflexible** stance on the policy led to tension with other departments."
  From the cause-and-effect relationship, we can infer that **"inflexible"** means **unwilling to change** or **rigid**.

2. Context and Law Enforcement Terms

In law enforcement, **specific terminology** often arises, and context helps determine how these terms should be understood. Words like **"apprehend," "surveillance,"** or **"probable cause"** all have meanings that are deeply tied to their specific use within the law enforcement context. Let's look at some examples:

- **Apprehend**: To arrest or capture someone.
- **Probable Cause**: The reasonable belief that a crime has been committed and that a specific person is linked to it.
- **Surveillance**: Close observation of a person or group, typically used in investigations to gather evidence.

These terms take on their specific legal meanings because of the **context** in which they are used. A law enforcement officer must be able to quickly identify the meaning of these words in a range of settings—from **interviews** and **report writing** to **testimony** in court.

Tips for Determining the Best Possible Meaning from Options

When taking the PELT B Exam, you may likely face multiple-choice questions that assess your vocabulary knowledge. You will be prompted to select the most acceptable definition or word based on the context of a statement. Here are some ways to assist you determine the correct meaning when you have to choose from a set of options:

1. Analyze the Sentence Structure and Clues

Start by reading the entire sentence or surrounding text carefully. Pay attention to the words around the unfamiliar word, as these will often give you essential clues about its meaning. Is the word being used to describe an emotion, an action, or a person? The context will guide your decision.

Example:

"The officer was very tenacious in his investigation, working long hours to track down the suspect."

Options:
A) Persistent
B) Weak
C) Distracted
D) Lazy

The word **tenacious** is used to describe the officer's approach to the investigation. Based on the context of **"working long hours"** and **"track down the suspect,"** the word must mean something like **"persistent"** or **"determined."**

The correct answer is **A) Persistent**.

2. Eliminate Obviously Incorrect Choices

In a multiple-choice format, it's important to eliminate answers that are clearly wrong. If a word doesn't make sense in the context of the sentence, remove it from your list of options.

Example:

"**The suspect was very subtle in his attempt to hide the evidence, hoping the officers wouldn't notice.**"

Options:
A) Obvious
B) Deceptive
C) Easily detected
D) Discreet

Here, **"subtle"** refers to something that is not obvious or easily noticed. The word **"obvious"** clearly doesn't fit in this context because it's the opposite of subtle.

The correct answer is **D) Discreet**.

3. Consider the Connotation of the Word

Many words have both a **denotation** (literal meaning) and a **connotation** (emotional or cultural meaning). When faced with multiple options, consider the connotation of the word. Is the word being used in a **positive**, **neutral**, or **negative** light? This will help you select the best option.

Example:

"**The officer was cordial in his interactions with the witnesses, making them feel at ease.**"

Options:
A) Rude
B) Polite
C) Hostile
D) Indifferent

In this sentence, the officer is interacting with witnesses, and the word **"cordial"** is used to describe a positive interaction. The correct answer, therefore, is **B) Polite**.

4. Look for Root Words, Prefixes, and Suffixes

As mentioned earlier, understanding word roots, prefixes, and suffixes can be extremely helpful in figuring out the meaning of an unfamiliar word. Many words in English are derived from Latin or Greek roots, and recognizing these roots can help you make an educated guess about the word's meaning.

Example:

"The officer's nonchalant attitude toward the situation caused concern among his colleagues."

Options:
A) Carefree
B) Angry
C) Concerned
D) Hostile

The word **"nonchalant"** contains the root **"chalant,"** which is derived from the French word meaning **"calm"**. The prefix **"non-"** indicates the opposite of calm, so **"nonchalant"** refers to someone who is **carefree** or not emotionally involved.

The correct answer is **A) Carefree**.

5. Practice Regularly

One of the best ways to increase your ability to use context clues and choose the correct vocabulary definitions is through regular practice. By practicing multiple-choice questions and being familiar with how vocabulary is examined on the PELLET B Exam, you will refine your skills and feel more confident.

Use internet tools, study guides, and vocabulary books to enhance your ability to spot patterns in words and interpret them depending on their context.

Whether you're understanding legal jargon or comprehending complex sentences, the ability to discern the meaning of unknown terms based on context can help you perform confidently on the exam. By applying the tactics taught in this chapter—paying close attention to context cues, removing wrong answers, weighing connotations, and understanding word structures—you will be well-equipped to tackle vocabulary issues with ease.

Building a Law Enforcement Vocabulary: Commonly Tested Words

Law enforcement workers generally deal with complex situations, legal language, and specialist vocabulary. Whether you're examining case files, attending briefings, or creating reports, comprehending and accurately employing the right terms is vital. The PELT B Exam assesses vocabulary that is particularly relevant to the profession, therefore it's vital to acquaint yourself with the most usually examined words related to law enforcement and daily responsibilities.

1. Legal Terminology

In law enforcement, you'll frequently encounter terms related to the legal system. These terms are essential for writing reports, filing charges, and understanding the criminal justice process. Here are some of the most commonly tested legal terms:

- **Arrest**: To take someone into custody by legal authority, often due to suspicion of committing a crime.
- **Defendant**: A person accused of committing a crime in court.
- **Probable Cause**: The reasonable belief that a crime has been committed and that a specific individual was involved, which justifies actions like searches or arrests.
- **Subpoena**: A legal order requiring someone to appear in court or produce documents.
- **Indictment**: A formal charge or accusation of a crime issued by a grand jury.
- **Affidavit**: A written statement of facts sworn to be true, often used as evidence in court.
- **Warrant**: A document authorizing the police to search, seize property, or make an arrest.

Tip for success: To retain these terms, consider their role in the criminal justice process. For example, knowing that a **defendant** is someone charged with a crime helps distinguish this term from a **plaintiff** (someone who brings a legal action).

2. Police Procedures and Actions

Understanding police procedures and terminology is critical for the **PELT B Exam**. Many questions will focus on words related to police operations, especially in areas like investigations, arrests, and searches. Some key words in this category include:

- **Interrogation**: The process of questioning a suspect or witness to gain information about a crime.
- **Surveillance**: Monitoring a person or group to gather evidence or prevent criminal activity.
- **Citation**: A written notice issued by an officer for minor infractions, such as traffic violations.
- **Misdemeanor**: A less serious crime, typically punishable by a fine or a short jail sentence.
- **Felony**: A serious crime, such as murder or robbery, typically punishable by imprisonment for more than one year.
- **Witness**: A person who has knowledge about a crime, often called to testify in court.
- **Booking**: The process of officially recording an arrest, including the suspect's personal information, fingerprints, and photograph.

- **Probation**: A court-ordered period of supervision over an offender, usually as an alternative to imprisonment.

Tip for success: Use real-world scenarios to help remember these terms. For instance, imagining the process of **booking** someone after an arrest can help cement the definition.

3. Crime-Related Vocabulary

Being able to understand and correctly use crime-related vocabulary is vital, especially when discussing crimes, evidence, and suspects. These are words you'll encounter frequently on the exam and in your professional work:

- **Burglary**: The unlawful entry into a building, typically with the intent to commit a crime like theft.
- **Robbery**: The use of force or threats to take property from another person.
- **Homicide**: The deliberate killing of one person by another.
- **Theft**: The unlawful taking of someone else's property.
- **Assault**: The intentional infliction of bodily harm on another person.
- **Vandalism**: The deliberate destruction or damage of property.
- **Forgery**: The act of making fake documents, signatures, or identification with the intent to deceive.

Tip for success: Try associating each word with a specific crime scene or real-life case you've heard of. For example, linking **robbery** with a situation involving a weapon can help you recall its definition more easily.

4. Police Equipment and Technology

Law enforcement officers rely on various tools and technologies to perform their duties. Understanding the names and functions of these tools will help you answer questions related to police equipment:

- **Patrol Car**: A police vehicle used for patrolling neighborhoods, responding to calls, and transporting suspects.
- **Body Camera**: A wearable camera used by officers to record their interactions with the public and gather evidence.
- **Radar Gun**: A device used to measure the speed of a vehicle.
- **Taser**: A stun gun used to subdue suspects without causing permanent harm.
- **Bulletproof Vest**: A piece of protective clothing designed to absorb the impact of bullets.
- **K-9 Unit**: A specialized police unit that uses trained dogs to detect drugs, explosives, or track suspects.

- **Fingerprint Scanner**: A device used to scan and record fingerprints for identification purposes.

Tip for success: Familiarizing yourself with police equipment through hands-on experience or watching law enforcement documentaries can help you better understand these terms.

Effective Strategies for Expanding Your Vocabulary

Now that you understand the types of words you'll need to know for the **PELT B Exam**, it's time to focus on effective strategies for **expanding your vocabulary**. While memorization is a part of the process, building a comprehensive vocabulary requires active learning, regular practice, and consistent exposure to new words.

1. Read Regularly and Diversely

One of the finest methods to expand your vocabulary is by reading often. Read a variety of resources, such as law enforcement reports, news stories, and books, to expose oneself to new terms and phrases. It's extremely important to read content that uses law enforcement vocabulary and associated language.

- **Law enforcement books and manuals**: Reading manuals or case studies will help you familiarize yourself with specific jargon and terminology used in the field.
- **News articles on crime and law enforcement**: Stay informed about current events in law enforcement to see how terminology is used in real-life situations.
- **Legal documents**: Reading legal documents, such as court decisions, will expose you to formal language and complex vocabulary that is commonly tested on the **PELT B Exam**.

Tip for success: Challenge yourself by reading at least one article a day that contains law enforcement or legal terminology. When you come across a new word, make sure to look it up and understand its meaning.

2. Use Flashcards

Flashcards are a time-tested strategy for enhancing vocabulary. Write the term on one side of the card and its definition on the other side. You can also add an example sentence or a relevant image to emphasize the message. Digital flashcard apps like Anki or Quizlet can be a helpful tool for on-the-go practice.

- **Word list**: Make a list of law enforcement terms that you want to memorize. Review these words regularly and test yourself on their meanings.

- **Practice daily**: Set aside a few minutes each day to go through your flashcards to reinforce your vocabulary.

Tip for success: Focus on **active recall**—try to recall the definition of a word before flipping the card over to check your answer. This improves retention and helps you recall the words more effectively.

3. Learn Word Roots, Prefixes, and Suffixes

Understanding the **roots, prefixes, and suffixes** of words can significantly boost your vocabulary. Many law enforcement terms are derived from Latin or Greek roots. By learning the meanings of these word parts, you can often deduce the meaning of unfamiliar words.

- **Prefix**: A group of letters added to the beginning of a word (e.g., **"pre-"** meaning "before" as in **"preliminary"**).
- **Suffix**: A group of letters added to the end of a word (e.g., **"-able"** meaning "capable of" as in **"enforceable"**).
- **Root word**: The base part of a word that gives it its primary meaning (e.g., **"dict"** meaning "to speak," as in **"dictate"** or **"verdict"**).

Tip for success: Whenever you encounter a difficult word, try breaking it down into its parts. Understanding the components will help you learn new words faster and recall them more easily.

4. Practice Using New Words in Sentences

To make new vocabulary stick, it's important to use the words in **real-life contexts**. Practice using new law enforcement terms in sentences, whether you're writing a report, drafting a case file, or just speaking with a colleague.

- **Write example sentences**: Take the words you're learning and create your own sentences that reflect real-life situations in law enforcement.
- **Engage in conversations**: Discussing law enforcement topics with peers or mentors will give you the opportunity to use new words and reinforce your understanding.

Tip for success: Keep a **vocabulary journal**. Every time you learn a new word, write it down along with its definition and an example sentence. Review this journal regularly to reinforce your knowledge.

5. Use Technology and Apps

Technology can be a valuable resource for expanding your vocabulary. There are numerous vocabulary-building apps and websites designed to help you learn new words and track your progress.

- **Vocabulary apps**: Apps like **Merriam-Webster**, **WordUp**, and **Vocaboly** offer exercises and quizzes to improve your vocabulary.
- **Online courses**: Many platforms, such as **Coursera** or **Udemy**, offer courses focused on expanding vocabulary, specifically tailored to law enforcement or legal terminology.

Tip for success: Set aside dedicated time each day to use vocabulary apps. Consistency is key to retention and mastery.

Building a law enforcement vocabulary is not only crucial for passing the PELT B Exam, but it is also a lasting asset in your job as a law enforcement officer. Whether you're writing reports, testifying in court, or communicating with the public, employing precise and effective language helps show professionalism and ensures clarity.

Practice Questions and Solutions: Vocabulary.

The vocabulary component of the PELT B Exam normally includes multiple-choice questions where you must identify the right meaning of a word based on its context. The key to excelling in this section is being able to understand the context in which the term is used and choose the most correct definition from the possibilities supplied.

Here are several steps to approach vocabulary questions:

1. **Read the Entire Sentence:** Never hurry to answer before reading the sentence in which the term appears. The surrounding context will often provide insights regarding the word's meaning.
2. **Look for Context Clues:** As you read, pay attention to any surrounding words or phrases that assist in explaining the unfamiliar word. These could include synonyms, antonyms, examples, or definitions embedded inside the text.
3. **Eliminate Clearly Incorrect Choices:** If an answer choice seems wholly unconnected to the context, it is usually inaccurate. Use the process of elimination to limit your possibilities.
4. **Consider Word Parts:** If the word is unfamiliar, break it down into its components—prefix, root, and suffix. Understanding how words are created can frequently provide you insights into their meanings.
5. **Select the Best Option:** After examining the context and word structure, choose the solution that best fits the definition in the context of the sentence.

Let's now go over numerous practice vocabulary questions, breaking out the reasons behind the correct and erroneous selections.

Practice Question 1

Question:
"The officer was known for his **meticulous** attention to detail, ensuring that every piece of evidence was carefully recorded."

What does the word **"meticulous"** mean?

A) Careless
B) Thorough
C) Indifferent
D) Hasty

Answer Breakdown:

- **A) Careless**: This is incorrect. If the officer were careless, he would not pay attention to the details, which is the opposite of what **"meticulous"** implies.
- **B) Thorough**: This is the correct answer. **"Meticulous"** means being extremely careful and thorough, especially with small details. This fits perfectly with the sentence describing the officer's attention to every piece of evidence.
- **C) Indifferent**: This is incorrect. **Indifferent** means showing little interest or concern, which contradicts the idea of being careful and precise.
- **D) Hasty**: This is incorrect. **Hasty** means done quickly, often without attention to detail. **"Meticulous"** implies a careful and slow approach, which is the opposite of being hasty.

Correct Answer: B) Thorough

Explanation: The context of the sentence describes the officer's **attention to detail**, which is best represented by the word **"meticulous"**. Being **meticulous** means being **very careful and precise**, especially in situations that require accuracy.

Practice Question 2

Question:
"The suspect's behavior was **erratic**, causing concern among the officers who were unsure of how he would act next."

What does the word **"erratic"** mean?

A) Predictable
B) Unsteady
C) Cooperative
D) Calm

Answer Breakdown:

- **A) Predictable**: This is incorrect. **Erratic** refers to behavior that is inconsistent and unpredictable, not predictable.
- **B) Unsteady**: This is the correct answer. **Erratic** behavior refers to something that is unpredictable, irregular, or unsteady. The officers' concern is due to the suspect's behavior being **unsteady** or fluctuating.
- **C) Cooperative**: This is incorrect. **Cooperative** means willing to work together, which doesn't match the context of behavior that is inconsistent and unpredictable.
- **D) Calm**: This is incorrect. **Calm** refers to behavior that is composed and peaceful, which is the opposite of **erratic**.

Correct Answer: B) Unsteady

Explanation: **Erratic** behavior is defined by its unpredictability and lack of consistency. In this case, the officers are concerned because the suspect's actions are unpredictable, making **unsteady** the most accurate definition.

Practice Question 3

Question:
"The officer's **unwavering** commitment to justice earned him respect from his peers and the community."

What does the word **"unwavering"** mean?

A) Uncertain
B) Steady
C) Hesitant
D) Disinterested

Answer Breakdown:

- **A) Uncertain**: This is incorrect. **Unwavering** implies a firm and resolute position, while **uncertain** suggests doubt and indecision.
- **B) Steady**: This is the correct answer. **Unwavering** means not changing or fluctuating, remaining **steady** and consistent, especially in terms of commitment or belief.
- **C) Hesitant**: This is incorrect. **Hesitant** suggests uncertainty or reluctance, which is the opposite of **unwavering**.
- **D) Disinterested**: This is incorrect. **Disinterested** means lacking interest or concern, which does not match the idea of strong and consistent commitment.

Correct Answer: B) Steady

Explanation: The word **"unwavering"** conveys firmness and consistency, especially in relation to commitment. The officer's **"unwavering commitment"** means he is **steadfast** and consistent in his dedication to justice.

Practice Question 4

Question:
"The detective asked the witness to **elucidate** the details of the suspect's appearance to help with the investigation."

What does the word **"elucidate"** mean?

A) Complicate
B) Explain
C) Conceal
D) Ignore

Answer Breakdown:

- **A) Complicate**: This is incorrect. **Elucidate** means to make something clear or explain, while **complicate** means to make something more difficult or confusing.
- **B) Explain**: This is the correct answer. **Elucidate** means to explain or clarify something, which fits perfectly with the context of asking the witness to provide clear details.
- **C) Conceal**: This is incorrect. **Conceal** means to hide or keep something secret, which is the opposite of explaining or clarifying.
- **D) Ignore**: This is incorrect. **Ignore** means to disregard, which does not align with the request for clarification.

Correct Answer: B) Explain

Explanation: **Elucidate** comes from the Latin word **"elucidare,"** meaning "to make clear." In this context, the detective is asking the witness to clarify or **explain** the details of the suspect's appearance.

Practice Question 5

Question:
"The officer's **candid** response to the investigation showed his commitment to transparency and honesty."

What does the word **"candid"** mean?

A) Dishonest
B) Deceptive
C) Honest
D) Defensive

Answer Breakdown:

- **A) Dishonest**: This is incorrect. **Candid** means truthful and open, not **dishonest**.
- **B) Deceptive**: This is incorrect. **Deceptive** means misleading or untruthful, which is the opposite of **candid**.
- **C) Honest**: This is the correct answer. **Candid** means open, truthful, and straightforward, especially in expressing thoughts or opinions.
- **D) Defensive**: This is incorrect. **Defensive** means protecting oneself from criticism or attack, which doesn't align with the meaning of **candid**.

Correct Answer: C) Honest

Explanation: **Candid** refers to being straightforward and honest, particularly when expressing one's thoughts or feelings without evasion or deceit.

Tips for Answering Vocabulary Questions

- **Context is Key**: Always pay attention to the context of the sentence to guide your understanding of the word. The surrounding text can provide crucial clues about the meaning.
- **Look for Clues in the Sentence**: Pay attention to **synonyms** or **antonyms** around the word, and use them to infer the word's meaning.
- **Eliminate Distractors**: In multiple-choice questions, eliminate options that don't fit the context. If a word seems to contradict the meaning implied in the sentence, it is likely not the correct answer.
- **Focus on Precision**: Vocabulary questions are testing your ability to understand nuances in language. Make sure the word choice fits exactly within the context.

In the vocabulary section of the PELT B Exam, your ability to assess unfamiliar terms within context is vital for success. By carefully considering the surrounding material, removing wrong choices, and applying knowledge of word meanings, you can confidently handle vocabulary questions.

With the practice questions and solutions offered in this chapter, you now have a stronger grasp of how to tackle these types of issues. Through frequent practice and use of these tactics, you will increase your vocabulary abilities and perform at your best on the PELT B Exam.

Chapter 4

Clarity in the PELLET B Exam

In law enforcement, clarity is more than just a skill—it's a key component of every element of your tasks. From preparing reports to talking with colleagues, suspects, and the public, excellent communication is the foundation of efficient law enforcement. The PELT B Exam examines this ability by examining how effectively you can detect and produce clear, coherent, and effective communication in the form of sentence structure and overall clarity.

The clarity component of the PELT B Exam examines your ability to identify the most clear and concise sentence structures while understanding how clarity affects communication in law enforcement contexts. This chapter will explain the necessity of clarity, what clarity questions assess, and the vital role clarity plays in your law enforcement activities.

We will also explain how to approach these questions on the PELT B Exam and how you can utilize clarity as a successful strategy throughout your career in law enforcement.

What Clarity Questions Assess: Sentence Structure and Communication

The clarity component of the PELT B Exam largely measures your ability to grasp and enhance sentence structure and communication. In law enforcement, being unambiguous is vital to ensuring your words are understood by coworkers, superiors, and the public. This section of the exam assesses your comprehension of how well-constructed sentences transmit a message and how to improve ambiguous or confusing language.

There are numerous major topics that clarity questions on the PELT B Exam address:

1. Sentence Structure

One of the most fundamental parts of clear communication is sentence form. In this sense, sentence structure refers to the way words, phrases, and clauses are structured within a sentence. When evaluating sentence clarity, you are sometimes asked to identify the most coherent and easily intelligible sentence. A well-structured sentence minimizes ambiguity and ensures the reader can readily understand the intended meaning.

For example, consider the following two sentences:

- **Sentence 1:** "The suspect was arrested by the officers after they witnessed him fleeing from the scene of the crime."
- **Sentence 2:** "The officers, after witnessing him fleeing the crime scene, arrested the suspect."

Both sentences convey the same information, but **Sentence 2** is clearer because the main action (the arrest) is placed early in the sentence, which makes it easier for the reader to understand. **Sentence 1**, while technically correct, creates a bit of a delay before the main action is revealed. In a law enforcement report or testimony, clarity is important to ensure that critical information is communicated as quickly and effectively as possible.

2. Avoiding Redundancy

Another part of clarity is minimizing redundancy—repeating information unnecessarily. Redundant sentences confuse the reader and obscure the intended message. For instance, take the following sentence:

- **Redundant sentence**: "The officers arrived at the scene of the crime and immediately began to begin their investigation."

Here, the phrase **"began to begin"** is repetitive. A clearer, more concise version of this sentence would be:

- **Clear sentence**: "The officers arrived at the scene of the crime and immediately began their investigation."

On the **PELT B Exam**, you may be asked to identify and correct redundant language to make sentences clearer and more direct. In law enforcement, unnecessary repetition can confuse or even mislead the reader, making it difficult to follow the sequence of events or critical details.

3. Sentence Length and Phrasing

While big sentences aren't always bad, they can sometimes become difficult to follow if they aren't well-structured. Shorter, concise phrases are generally more effective in conveying meaning, especially in high-stakes circumstances where clarity is important. The PELT B Exam measures your ability to break down too complex phrases into smaller, clearer ones that are easier for the reader to digest.

Consider this example:

- **Complex sentence**: "Despite the fact that the officer had observed the suspect acting suspiciously around the vehicle and saw him enter it quickly, he decided to approach the vehicle in a cautious manner, unsure whether the suspect's actions were merely coincidental or if he was engaged in criminal activity."
- **Simplified sentence**: "The officer observed the suspect acting suspiciously around the vehicle. After the suspect quickly entered the car, the officer decided to approach cautiously, unsure if the suspect's actions were criminal."

The second sentence is clearer because it is broken into smaller, more digestible chunks, making it easier for the reader to follow the officer's thought process and actions.

4. Word Choice

The words you use can considerably determine how clear your communication is. In law enforcement, particular terminology is essential to maintain accuracy and minimize confusion. Ambiguous or too complicated wording might make reports or remarks difficult to understand. The clarity part of the PELT B Exam examines your ability to identify the most precise and plain words to utilize in a given context.

For example, consider these two sentences:

- **Sentence 1**: "The officer was aware of the individual's **suspicious** conduct."
- **Sentence 2**: "The officer was aware of the individual's **questionable** conduct."

Both words convey a similar idea, but **"suspicious"** is a more commonly used and precise term in law enforcement contexts. The **PELT B Exam** may ask you to choose the word that best conveys meaning without introducing ambiguity.

Importance of Clear Communication in Law Enforcement Roles

Clear communication is at the heart of efficient law enforcement. The capacity to explain yourself clearly—whether in writing, verbally, or through non-verbal communication—can decide the success of an investigation, the outcome of a case, or the safety of an officer and the public. In law enforcement, the stakes are high, and misunderstanding or misinterpretation can have significant consequences.

Here are numerous reasons why clarity is vital in law enforcement roles:

1. Report Writing and Documentation

One of the most significant types of communication in law enforcement is writing reports. Officers are responsible for documenting occurrences, arrests, investigations, and other acts that occur throughout the course of their work. These reports typically become legal papers that can be used in court, therefore it is crucial that they are clear, short, and accurate.

A well-written report can help avoid misunderstandings or misinterpretations by ensuring that all relevant data are given in a clear, orderly manner. When writing reports, it is crucial to utilize clear sentence structure and accurate wording to ensure that anyone reading the report can clearly grasp the events as they happened.

2. Interacting with the Public

Law enforcement officials are generally the first point of interaction between the public and the criminal justice system. Whether giving instructions to a suspect, providing directions to a citizen, or de-escalating a tense situation, clear communication is vital for establishing authority, creating trust, and assuring safety.

For example, while explaining Miranda rights to a suspect, authorities must use straightforward language to ensure the suspect fully knows their rights. If the language used is ambiguous or unduly complex, the suspect may not fully appreciate the warnings, which could later undermine the validity of the arrest or the prosecution.

3. Court Testimonies and Legal Proceedings

Officers frequently serve as witnesses in court, where their ability to accurately describe the facts of a case can make or break the prosecution's position. Being able to narrate events in a logical and clear manner guarantees that the judge, jury, and attorneys can readily follow the story.

Testifying in court also demands an officer to stay objective and focused, avoiding superfluous details or viewpoints that could muddle the clarity of their testimony. Clear communication ensures that their testimony is focused on the facts and remains persuasive.

4. Interpersonal Communication with Colleagues

Law enforcement agents generally work in teams and need to communicate well with their colleagues. Whether it's during a briefing, a shift change, or a combined operation, clear communication among officers is crucial for ensuring that everyone is on the same page and acting in sync.

Miscommunication between police can lead to misunderstanding, blunders, or safety issues. Officers must be able to explain instructions properly, interpret directives, and exchange essential information swiftly and accurately.

5. Decision Making Under Pressure

In high-pressure situations—such as reacting to a crime in progress or handling a crisis—officers need to make decisions fast and convey those decisions properly to others. Clear communication ensures that officers can explain their objectives and actions to colleagues, superiors, and the public in a timely manner, helping to maintain order and manage issues successfully.

How to Approach Clarity Questions on the PELLET B Exam

On the PELT B Exam, clarity questions often entail identifying the most concise, clear, and logically formed text. These questions measure your comprehension of language flow, word choice, and your ability to avoid unneeded complexity or ambiguity.

1. Review the Sentence for Redundancy or Ambiguity

When reading a statement, always ask yourself if it can be simpler. Look for redundant words, unneeded sentences, or too complex structures. Simplify the language without losing its meaning, ensuring that it stays clear and direct.

2. Pay Attention to Word Choice

Choose terms that are exact and unambiguous. Avoid ambiguous or too complex language that could confuse the reader. In law enforcement, precision is vital to guarantee that your message is comprehended precisely.

3. Break Long Sentences Into Shorter Ones

If the sentence is long and difficult to follow, divide it into two or more shorter sentences. Each sentence should convey one primary point, making it easy for the reader to understand.

4. Stay Focused on the Message

The purpose of any sentence is to deliver information clearly. Focus on what is vital and avoid adding irrelevant details that could distract from the core point.

Clear communication is the backbone of law enforcement. Whether you are producing reports, communicating with the public, or testifying in court, the ability to communicate with clarity guarantees that your message is understood and that your actions are seen as professional and competent.

Identifying the Most Clearly Written Sentence

The ability to choose the most clearly written sentence from a collection of possibilities is a major skill examined on the PELT B Exam. When faced with many statements, your duty is to identify the one that is the most concise, logically formed, and free of ambiguity. Let's break down the major components to look for when analyzing sentence clarity.

1. Simple and Direct Sentence Structure

The clearest sentences are frequently the simplest ones. A well-constructed sentence often follows a straightforward subject-verb-object structure and eliminates excessive complication. When choosing the most plainly worded sentence, seek for one that is straightforward and to the point.

For example:

- **Clear sentence**: "The officer stopped the vehicle for speeding."
- **Less clear sentence**: "The officer, noticing the vehicle was speeding, decided to stop it."

While both sentences convey the same information, the first is **shorter** and **more direct**, making it the clearer option.

Tip for success: When evaluating sentences, ask yourself if the sentence can be made more concise without losing important information. If it can, that's a good indication that the sentence can be written more clearly.

2. Consistent and Logical Flow

Clear sentences follow a **logical flow**. The information should be presented in a **coherent** manner, with each part of the sentence contributing to the overall meaning. Sentences with a **disjointed flow** can confuse the reader, especially in law enforcement reports where accuracy is key.

For example:

- **Clear sentence**: "The suspect was arrested after a brief chase, during which the officer observed him throwing a bag from the vehicle."
- **Confusing sentence**: "After a brief chase, the officer observed the suspect throwing a bag from the vehicle and arrested him."

Both sentences are grammatically correct, but the first sentence presents the action in a **logical order**—the chase first, then the observation, and finally the arrest. This order makes it easier to understand the sequence of events.

Tip for success: Always ensure that the sentence presents events or actions in a **chronological or logical sequence**. This will help avoid confusion and ensure the reader follows the narrative easily.

3. Avoiding Unnecessary Details

Clarity in writing often comes down to **eliminating unnecessary details**. While it's important to include essential information, adding too many minor details can make a sentence harder to follow. When selecting the clearest sentence, avoid those with irrelevant or excessive information.

For example:

- **Clear sentence**: "The officer confiscated the weapon after the suspect was arrested."
- **Less clear sentence**: "After the suspect, who had been previously arrested for a different incident, was apprehended again for carrying a weapon illegally, the officer confiscated the weapon, which was in plain view."

The second sentence, while containing valid information, is **overly wordy** and could confuse the reader. The clearer version delivers the same information in fewer words.

Tip for success: Focus on the key points of the sentence and eliminate extraneous details that do not contribute to the main message. This will keep the sentence concise and easier to understand.

4. Correct Punctuation

Punctuation plays a key role in clarity. Proper punctuation marks, such as commas, periods, and semicolons, guide the reader through the sentence, separating ideas and ensuring that each thought is presented clearly. Misuse or absence of punctuation can lead to confusing or ambiguous sentences.

For example:

- **Clear sentence**: "The officer was careful to follow the protocol, ensuring the suspect's rights were not violated."
- **Confusing sentence**: "The officer was careful to follow the protocol ensuring the suspect's rights were not violated."

In the second sentence, the lack of a comma after "protocol" makes the sentence harder to follow, as it confuses the relationship between the two clauses.

Tip for success: Always ensure that punctuation is used correctly to **separate clauses**, clarify meaning, and prevent run-on sentences.

Common Sentence Construction Errors That Can Affect Clarity

While clarity in phrase form is vital, certain sentence construction flaws can greatly inhibit communication. On the PELT B Exam, you will be examined on your ability to identify and fix these problems, which include run-on sentences, sentence fragments, hanging modifiers, and ambiguous pronouns.

1. Run-on Sentences

A **run-on sentence** occurs when two or more independent clauses (complete sentences) are joined together without the proper punctuation or conjunction. Run-on sentences make it difficult for the reader to follow the message, as they lack the necessary breaks that separate ideas.

For example:

- **Run-on sentence**: "The officer arrived at the scene of the crime the suspect was already gone."
- **Corrected sentence**: "The officer arrived at the scene of the crime. The suspect was already gone."

In the first example, there are two independent clauses that should be separated by a period or semicolon. The second sentence, which breaks the ideas into two parts, is clearer and easier to understand.

Tip for success: Look for sentences with multiple independent clauses that aren't properly separated. Use punctuation (periods, commas, or semicolons) to break the sentence into smaller, manageable parts.

2. Sentence Fragments

A **sentence fragment** is a group of words that does not form a complete sentence. Sentence fragments often lack a subject or verb, which makes them incomplete and unclear. Fragments can be confusing because they don't express a complete thought.

For example:

- **Fragment**: "After the officers arrived at the scene."
- **Complete sentence**: "After the officers arrived at the scene, they began securing the area."

In the fragment example, there is no main clause that completes the thought. By adding a main clause, the second sentence becomes complete and clear.

Tip for success: Ensure that every sentence contains a **subject** and a **verb**, and that it expresses a complete idea.

3. Dangling Modifiers

A **dangling modifier** occurs when a descriptive phrase does not clearly or logically refer to the word it is meant to describe. This can lead to confusion or misunderstanding about the subject of the sentence.

For example:

- **Dangling modifier**: "Running quickly, the suspect was caught by the officers."
- **Corrected sentence**: "Running quickly, the officers caught the suspect."

In the first sentence, the modifier **"running quickly"** seems to describe the **suspect**, but grammatically, it's attached to the officers. The second sentence clarifies the intended meaning by rephrasing it.

Tip for success: Ensure that descriptive phrases and modifiers clearly connect to the word they are meant to describe.

4. Ambiguous Pronouns

Pronouns (such as **he**, **she**, **it**, **they**) are used to replace nouns in a sentence, but sometimes their reference can be unclear, leading to ambiguity. When multiple potential nouns could be the referent, confusion arises.

For example:

- **Ambiguous sentence**: "John was talking to Mike when he saw the suspect."
- **Clarified sentence**: "John was talking to Mike when **John** saw the suspect."

In the ambiguous sentence, it's unclear whether "he" refers to **John** or **Mike**. By replacing the pronoun with the proper noun, the second sentence is much clearer.

Tip for success: Always ensure that pronouns clearly refer to a specific noun. If there is any chance of confusion, replace the pronoun with the full noun.

How to Improve Sentence Clarity for the PELLET B Exam

Now that we've examined how to determine the most clearly written sentence and the common faults that affect clarity, let's focus on how to enhance your sentence clarity in preparation for the PELT B Exam. The capacity to compose and edit sentences with accuracy and clarity is a skill that increases with constant practice and attention to detail.

1. Practice Sentence Editing

One of the best ways to improve clarity is to practice editing sentences. Take complex, poorly written sentences and rework them for clarity. Focus on **eliminating redundancy**, **simplifying structure**, and ensuring that each sentence flows logically from one idea to the next.

- **Exercise**: Look at a passage or news article. Identify sentences that seem overly complex or confusing, then rewrite them in a simpler and clearer way.

2. Read Aloud

Reading your writing aloud can help identify areas where clarity is lacking. When you read a sentence out loud, you are more likely to hear awkward phrasing, unnecessary complexity, or sentences that don't flow smoothly. If a sentence sounds convoluted or difficult to follow, it likely needs revision.

- **Exercise**: After writing a sentence, read it aloud to yourself. Does it sound natural? Is it easy to understand? If not, revise it for clarity.

3. Focus on Active Voice

In law enforcement, clarity is often best achieved through the **active voice**. Active voice makes the sentence more direct, as it clearly shows who is doing the action and what action is being performed. In contrast, **passive voice** can create ambiguity and distance between the subject and the action.

- **Active voice**: "The officer arrested the suspect."
- **Passive voice**: "The suspect was arrested by the officer."

While passive voice isn't always incorrect, active voice tends to be clearer and more direct.

4. Review Common Grammar Rules

Improving clarity involves understanding and applying basic grammar rules. Ensure you are familiar with concepts such as **subject-verb agreement**, **correct punctuation**, and **sentence structure**. Mastering these rules will help you write clearer, more effective sentences.

---

concise communication is one of the most critical abilities in law enforcement, and the ability to produce concise sentences is a significant component of the PELT B Exam. By studying how to recognize the most clearly written sentences, how to analyze sentence structure, and how to avoid frequent construction errors, you can dramatically improve your performance on the exam and in your law enforcement career.

Tips for Enhancing Sentence Clarity

In this section, we'll delve into several established ways for boosting sentence clarity. These recommendations are aimed to help you compose sentences that are brief, effective, and simply understood, which is vital not just for the exam but also for your career in law enforcement.

1. Simplify Complex Sentences Without Losing Meaning

Often, clarity is sacrificed in favor of more intricate sentence constructions. In law enforcement reports and other official papers, it's easy to fall into the trap of utilizing long-winded words or overly complex terminology in an attempt to sound more professional or authoritative. However, this might have the reverse effect: elaborate words can confuse the reader and conceal the idea you are attempting to convey.

The idea is to simplify sentences while ensuring that all vital information is still presented properly. Here are some techniques to reduce difficult sentences without losing meaning:

- **Break long sentences into shorter ones**: One of the simplest ways to improve clarity is by dividing lengthy sentences into two or more shorter sentences. Long sentences with

multiple clauses often lose focus and become difficult to follow. Breaking them up can help the reader process the information more easily.
Example:
Complex sentence: "The suspect, who had been previously arrested for theft, was seen at the scene of the crime, and after a brief chase, he was apprehended and brought in for questioning."
Simplified sentence: "The suspect had been previously arrested for theft. He was seen at the scene of the crime. After a brief chase, officers apprehended him and brought him in for questioning."

- **Use clear subject-verb-object structures**: Sentences with a **subject-verb-object** structure are easier to understand than those with complex or passive constructions. Keeping the sentence structure simple ensures that the reader can quickly identify the subject, the action, and the object of the sentence.
Example:
Complex sentence: "Despite the fact that the officer had a clear understanding of the situation, he hesitated to act immediately due to the uncertain nature of the circumstances surrounding the suspect's behavior."
Simplified sentence: "The officer understood the situation clearly. However, he hesitated to act due to the uncertainty of the suspect's behavior."

- **Eliminate unnecessary words**: Overuse of adjectives, adverbs, and filler words can create clutter and obscure meaning. Focus on the essential parts of the sentence, eliminating any words that do not add significant value to the message.
Example:
Wordy sentence: "The officer made the decision to proceed with the arrest after carefully considering all of the available evidence and weighing the possible outcomes of the situation."
Simplified sentence: "The officer decided to proceed with the arrest after reviewing the available evidence."

Tip for success: As you write, ask yourself if each word adds value to the sentence. If it doesn't, consider removing it or replacing it with something more concise.

2. Avoiding Passive Voice

Passive voice can create confusion in a sentence by obscuring the actor (the one performing the action). In law enforcement, clear communication of actions is crucial. Passive voice makes it harder for the reader to determine who is performing the action, which can lead to misunderstandings or vagueness.

In a **passive voice** sentence, the object of the action becomes the subject of the sentence, and the actor is either omitted or less emphasized. This can make sentences harder to follow, especially in critical reports or legal documentation.

Example:

- **Passive voice**: "The report was written by the officer."
- **Active voice**: "The officer wrote the report."

In the passive voice example, the actor (the officer) is secondary to the action of writing the report. The active voice sentence makes it clearer who is performing the action.

- **Passive voice**: "The suspect was arrested by the officer after he was caught attempting to flee."
- **Active voice**: "The officer arrested the suspect after catching him attempting to flee."

Tip for success: Whenever possible, use **active voice** to make your sentences clearer and more direct. In an active voice, the subject performs the action, making the sentence more dynamic and easier to understand. **Active voice** should be your default choice in law enforcement writing.

3. Avoiding Redundancy

Redundancy arises when the same notion is repeated needlessly within a sentence or paragraph. This can confuse the reader and make your text overly long. In law enforcement, concise writing is necessary, especially when capturing critical incidents or creating reports. Redundant sentences can lessen the effect of your message and waste time.

For example:

- **Redundant sentence**: "The suspect was arrested for the crime of theft after he was apprehended for taking the property unlawfully."
- **Clear sentence**: "The suspect was arrested for theft after taking the property unlawfully."

In the first sentence, the phrase "the crime of theft" is unnecessary, and "apprehended for taking the property unlawfully" repeats the concept of theft.

- **Redundant sentence**: "The officer approached the scene of the crime and then proceeded to investigate the area, beginning his investigation right away."
- **Clear sentence**: "The officer arrived at the scene and began his investigation immediately."

Here, the second sentence is cleaner and more effective because it eliminates the unnecessary repetition of the idea that the officer was investigating.

Tip for success: When writing, review each sentence to ensure that there's no repeated information. If a word or phrase is unnecessary, eliminate it to improve clarity and conciseness.

4. Using Clear and Direct Language

Another technique to boost clarity is by choosing clear and plain language. Avoid using extremely sophisticated vocabulary, jargon, or unclear terms that could confuse the reader. While technical language may be appropriate in some instances, law enforcement communication should stress clarity and accessibility. When communicating, whether in a report, a statement, or testimony, your goal is to ensure that your message is clearly understood by anyone reading it—whether they be fellow officers, the public, or a court.

Example:

- **Unclear sentence**: "The officer sought to ascertain whether the suspect was in violation of any laws."
- **Clear sentence**: "The officer checked if the suspect had broken any laws."

In the second sentence, the use of **"checked"** is more straightforward and avoids the complex phrasing of "sought to ascertain."

Tip for success: Use words that are **simple** and **direct**. If a more straightforward term conveys the same meaning, prefer that over a more complex word.

5. Organizing Information Logically

Organizing your ideas logically is a crucial aspect of clear writing. Especially in law enforcement, where your writing may be evaluated for legal or procedural objectives, presenting material in a logical sequence is vital. Readers must be able to follow the narrative or explanation without getting lost or confused.

For example:

- **Confusing sentence**: "The suspect, after being stopped by the officer, attempted to flee and was pursued. He was finally apprehended when the officer tackled him."
- **Logical sentence**: "The officer stopped the suspect, who attempted to flee. The officer pursued him and apprehended him after tackling him."

In the second example, the information is presented logically—first, the officer stops the suspect, then the suspect flees, followed by the pursuit and arrest. This order allows the reader to follow the sequence of events easily.

Tip for success: When organizing your sentences, make sure each part of the sentence flows logically. Use **transition words** or phrases to guide the reader through the sequence of events or actions.

How to Practice Sentence Clarity

To increase your ability to create coherent sentences, you need to practice consistently. The more you work on simplifying your writing, reducing superfluous complexity, and ensuring logical flow, the better you will get at generating clear, concise, and effective phrases. Here are some helpful activities to help you enhance clarity:

1. Sentence Revision Exercises

Take a paragraph or an example sentence and practice editing it for clarity. Focus on reducing difficult language structures and eliminating redundancy. Afterward, compare your improved version to the original and judge how much clearer your version is.

2. Peer Review and Feedback

Sharing your work with a colleague, mentor, or peer can help you discover places where clarity may be lacking. Ask for specific input regarding confusing or overly complicated sentences, and utilize that feedback to better your work.

3. Practice Writing Reports

Law enforcement officers routinely write reports, and exercising this skill can assist enhance your sentence clarity. Write practice reports using real-life scenarios or occurrences you've encountered. Focus on structuring material logically, using active voice, and eliminating needless detail.

Whether you are preparing a report, presenting testimony, or simply dealing with the public, clarity guarantees that your message is understood without ambiguity. The techniques and strategies provided in this chapter will help you enhance your sentence clarity for the PELT B Exam and beyond.

By shortening difficult phrases, minimizing passive voice, eliminating repetition, and adopting simple, direct language, you can boost the clarity of your writing and communication. Regular practice and self-reflection on your writing will lead to constant growth, making you a more successful communicator in your law enforcement job.

Practice Questions and Solutions: Example Clarity Questions

Example Question 1

Question:
Which of the following sentences is the clearest and most concise?

A) "The suspect, who was wearing a blue jacket, was arrested after the officers saw him running away from the scene of the crime."
B) "The suspect was arrested after the officers, who had witnessed him running from the crime scene, saw him wearing a blue jacket."
C) "The officers observed the suspect running away from the crime scene, and then they saw that he was wearing a blue jacket, so they arrested him."
D) "After the officers saw the suspect running from the crime scene, they arrested him and noticed that he was wearing a blue jacket."

Answer Breakdown:

- **A) "The suspect, who was wearing a blue jacket, was arrested after the officers saw him running away from the scene of the crime."**
  This sentence is somewhat clear but can be improved. The clause **"who was wearing a blue jacket"** unnecessarily interrupts the main message and makes the sentence longer than it needs to be.
- **B) "The suspect was arrested after the officers, who had witnessed him running from the crime scene, saw him wearing a blue jacket."**
  This sentence is wordy and awkwardly structured. It introduces **redundancy** with **"who had witnessed"** and **"saw him"**, both implying that the officers observed the suspect's actions. It's also a bit confusing due to the passive construction of the sentence.
- **C) "The officers observed the suspect running away from the crime scene, and then they saw that he was wearing a blue jacket, so they arrested him."**
  This sentence is **too long** and has unnecessary clauses. The **"and then they saw"** and **"so they arrested him"** add more information than necessary. The sentence could be more concise.
- **D) "After the officers saw the suspect running from the crime scene, they arrested him and noticed that he was wearing a blue jacket."**
  This is the clearest and most concise option. It eliminates unnecessary words while keeping the essential information intact. The **"after the officers saw"** sets the sequence clearly, and the arrest is immediately followed by the detail about the jacket. The sentence flows logically.

Correct Answer: D

Explanation: Sentence D is the most concise and clear. It conveys the sequence of events effectively while avoiding redundancies and unnecessary complexity. It sticks to the core actions and provides the relevant details in a clear, straightforward manner.

Example Question 2

Question:
Which sentence is more clearly written?

A) "Given the circumstances, it was essential that the officer, who had been trained in emergency protocols, reacted quickly to the dangerous situation that had developed."
B) "It was important that the officer reacted quickly to the dangerous situation, given the fact that he had been trained in emergency protocols."
C) "The officer, trained in emergency protocols, quickly reacted to the dangerous situation that had developed."
D) "The officer, who was trained in emergency protocols, immediately reacted to the dangerous situation, which had developed due to the circumstances."

Answer Breakdown:

- **A) "Given the circumstances, it was essential that the officer, who had been trained in emergency protocols, reacted quickly to the dangerous situation that had developed."**
  This sentence has **redundant phrasing** and a complicated structure. **"Given the circumstances"** and **"that had developed"** are unnecessary details that clutter the sentence. The use of **"essential"** is also a bit excessive when describing the importance of the officer's reaction.
- **B) "It was important that the officer reacted quickly to the dangerous situation, given the fact that he had been trained in emergency protocols."**
  This sentence could be clearer. **"Given the fact that"** is a **redundant** phrase. The sentence could be shortened to improve clarity and impact.
- **C) "The officer, trained in emergency protocols, quickly reacted to the dangerous situation that had developed."**
  This sentence is concise and clear. It places the most important information at the beginning and provides relevant details without overcomplicating the structure. The sentence is straightforward, clear, and direct.
- **D) "The officer, who was trained in emergency protocols, immediately reacted to the dangerous situation, which had developed due to the circumstances."**

While not a terrible sentence, **D** is a bit wordier than **C**. The phrase **"which had developed due to the circumstances"** adds unnecessary complexity without providing additional value.

Correct Answer: C

Explanation: Sentence C is the most concise, clear, and direct. It places the most relevant details up front and avoids extra wording or redundancy. The phrasing **"trained in emergency protocols"** and **"quickly reacted"** are clear and to the point.

Example Question 3

Question:
Which sentence is the clearest?

A) "In the event that the suspect does not comply with the officer's orders, the officer should, without delay, take appropriate action in accordance with the law."
B) "If the suspect does not comply with the officer's orders, the officer should immediately take the necessary action according to the law."
C) "If the officer's orders are not followed by the suspect, the officer should take action immediately and in accordance with the law."
D) "The officer should take action, without delay, if the suspect does not comply with the orders, ensuring that the action taken is in accordance with the law."

Answer Breakdown:

- **A) "In the event that the suspect does not comply with the officer's orders, the officer should, without delay, take appropriate action in accordance with the law."**
  This sentence is **overcomplicated** with the phrase **"In the event that"** and **"appropriate action in accordance with the law"**. The sentence could be more direct and concise.
- **B) "If the suspect does not comply with the officer's orders, the officer should immediately take the necessary action according to the law."**
  This sentence is much clearer. It's concise and direct, using **"immediately"** to emphasize urgency while removing unnecessary wording like **"in the event that"**.
- **C) "If the officer's orders are not followed by the suspect, the officer should take action immediately and in accordance with the law."**
  While this sentence is still clear, it introduces some unnecessary complexity with the passive phrasing of **"the officer's orders are not followed by the suspect."** Using the active voice makes the sentence clearer.

- **D)** "The officer should take action, without delay, if the suspect does not comply with the orders, ensuring that the action taken is in accordance with the law."
  This sentence is a bit wordy, particularly with the phrase **"ensuring that the action taken is in accordance with the law."** It could be shortened without losing any meaning.

Correct Answer: B

Explanation: Sentence B is the clearest and most concise. It conveys the necessary information in a direct and easy-to-understand manner, with no extra phrases or redundant wording.

Tips for Answering Clarity Questions on the PELLET B Exam

- **Look for the Most Direct Option**: Choose sentences that communicate the message in a straightforward, **direct** manner. Avoid unnecessary phrases or wordy constructions.
- **Avoid Passive Voice**: In general, **active voice** is clearer and more direct. Choose sentences where the subject actively performs the action.
- **Eliminate Redundancies**: Watch for unnecessary repetition of information. The simpler the sentence, the clearer the message.
- **Consider Logical Flow**: Sentences should follow a **logical sequence** of events. Avoid confusing or disjointed phrasing.
- **Be Concise**: Don't add extra words that don't contribute meaningfully to the sentence. Each word should serve a purpose.

Clarity is essential in law enforcement, as it ensures that your communication—whether written or verbal—is understood by all involved parties. Whether you're preparing for the **PELT B Exam** or applying these principles in your day-to-day law enforcement duties, mastering clarity in your writing will significantly enhance your effectiveness.

Common Pitfalls in Clarity Questions

The clarity section of the PELT B Exam generally includes questions that demand you to evaluate the usefulness of a sentence. Test-takers typically fall into certain pitfalls when answering these questions. Recognizing these faults and understanding how to prevent them will not only help you succeed in the PELT B Exam, but also boost your communication skills as a law enforcement officer.

1. Overuse of Passive Voice

One of the most typical errors in clarity questions is the overuse of passive voice. In passive voice, the subject of the phrase receives the action rather than executing it. While passive voice isn't necessarily incorrect, it can often make sentences more complicated and less direct.

For example:

- **Passive voice**: "The suspect was arrested by the officers after being observed fleeing the scene."
- **Active voice**: "The officers arrested the suspect after observing him fleeing the scene."

In the passive voice example, the focus is on the action (the arrest), and it takes longer to get to the point. The active voice is much clearer and more direct, as it places emphasis on the officer's actions rather than the suspect's.

Why this is a problem: Passive voice tends to create ambiguity, as it often obscures the identity of the actor (in this case, the officers). In law enforcement communication, clarity is essential, and the active voice makes the sentence easier to follow.

How to avoid it: Focus on using the **active voice**, where the subject (the doer of the action) performs the verb (the action). This provides clarity by making the sentence more direct and reducing unnecessary words.

---

2. Redundancy and Wordiness

Another typical mistake is redundancy—using more words than necessary to communicate an idea. Redundant phrases generally repeat the same information or use many words to explain the same topic. This not only adds length to your writing but can also make the message tougher to follow.

For example:

- **Redundant**: "The officer made the decision to arrest the suspect after realizing he had committed a crime."
- **Clearer**: "The officer arrested the suspect after realizing he had committed a crime."

In the redundant sentence, the phrase "made the decision to arrest" can be simplified to just "arrested." Both phrases mean the same thing, but the redundant version adds unnecessary complexity.

Why this is a problem: Redundant sentences dilute the main point and waste valuable time and space. In law enforcement, where efficiency is key, you want to communicate quickly and clearly.

How to avoid it: Look for words or phrases that repeat the same idea. Eliminate unnecessary qualifiers and adjectives that don't add value to the meaning of the sentence. Aim to keep your sentences concise without omitting important details.

---

3. Misplaced Modifiers

Misplaced modifiers occur when descriptive phrases are positioned incorrectly in a sentence, leading to confusion or misinterpretation of the intended meaning. When a modifier is misplaced, it creates ambiguity about what it is meant to describe.

For example:

- **Misplaced modifier**: "The officer saw the suspect fleeing from the scene in his patrol car."
- **Corrected**: "In his patrol car, the officer saw the suspect fleeing from the scene."

In the first example, the phrase **"in his patrol car"** seems to modify **"the suspect,"** making it sound like the suspect is in the patrol car, which is clearly not the case. In the second sentence, the modifier is placed in a clearer position, making it clear that it's the officer, not the suspect, in the patrol car.

Why this is a problem: Misplaced modifiers confuse the reader and make the meaning unclear. In law enforcement, where accuracy is paramount, such errors can lead to misinterpretations of facts.

How to avoid it: Ensure that the descriptive phrase or modifier is placed directly next to the word it is intended to describe. This keeps the meaning clear and prevents ambiguity.

---

4. Lack of Logical Flow

Another common problem in clarity questions is the lack of logical flow. When sentences are not structured in a clear, coherent manner, they can confuse the reader. A lack of logical flow makes it difficult for the reader to follow the movement of ideas, which can be damaging in law enforcement writing when exact information needs to be delivered in an ordered manner.

For example:

- **Lack of logical flow**: "The suspect was apprehended, and the officers secured the area. The officers had already set up a perimeter, and they were conducting a search for evidence."
- **Improved flow**: "The officers set up a perimeter and began conducting a search for evidence. The suspect was apprehended after the search."

In the first example, the events are presented in a somewhat disorganized way, making it harder to follow the sequence of actions. In the improved sentence, the sequence is more straightforward, allowing the reader to easily follow the officers' actions.

Why this is a problem: Disorganized sentences create confusion and force the reader to work harder to piece together the information. In law enforcement, where clarity is essential, the logical flow of information is critical.

How to avoid it: Present ideas in a **logical order**, starting with the most important or immediate action and progressing to the next steps. Avoid jumping between unrelated events or actions, and make sure each sentence connects smoothly to the next.

---

5. Overuse of Complex or Uncommon Words

Using needlessly complex vocabulary or technical jargon might make a sentence tougher to grasp. While legal and law enforcement writing typically requires precise vocabulary, misuse of sophisticated or rare phrases can generate unnecessary confusion, especially for readers who may not be familiar with the terminology.

For example:

- **Complex/unclear**: "The suspect demonstrated an **inordinate** amount of **perseverance** during his attempt to evade capture."
- **Simplified**: "The suspect showed great determination in his attempt to escape."

In the first example, words like **"inordinate"** and **"perseverance"** could be replaced with simpler words that convey the same meaning more clearly. The second sentence is easier to understand while still conveying the same idea.

Why this is a problem: Using unnecessarily complex or uncommon words can make your writing inaccessible or unclear. In law enforcement, the goal is always to ensure that your message is understood by a wide audience, including individuals with varying levels of expertise.

How to avoid it: Strive for clarity and simplicity in your writing. Use words that are easily understood by the average reader while still maintaining accuracy. If a simpler word can convey the same meaning as a more complex one, opt for the simpler choice.

---

6. Confusing or Vague Pronouns

Pronouns are meant to replace nouns, but when they are used unclearly, they can lead to confusion. The most common issue occurs when a pronoun does not have a clear antecedent, meaning it is not immediately obvious what the pronoun refers to.

For example:

- **Vague pronoun**: "The officer spoke to the suspect before he was taken to the station."
- **Clear pronoun**: "The officer spoke to the suspect before **the suspect** was taken to the station."

In the first example, the pronoun **"he"** could refer to either the officer or the suspect, creating ambiguity. In the second example, replacing the pronoun with **"the suspect"** makes the sentence clear.

Why this is a problem: Ambiguous pronouns confuse the reader, making it unclear who or what the sentence is referring to. In law enforcement writing, clarity is paramount, and any confusion can lead to misinterpretations.

How to avoid it: Always ensure that pronouns clearly refer to a specific noun. If there is any chance of ambiguity, replace the pronoun with the noun to clarify the reference.

How to Avoid These Pitfalls on the PELT B Exam

Recognizing and avoiding these common pitfalls is crucial for success on the **PELT B Exam**. Here are some strategies to help you overcome these challenges:

1. **Read Carefully**: Before answering clarity questions, take the time to carefully read the sentence. Look for redundancies, misplaced modifiers, or instances of passive voice.
2. **Use Active Voice**: Where possible, use active voice to make your sentences more direct and clear.

3. **Practice Writing**: Regularly practice writing clear, concise sentences. Pay attention to the structure, flow, and clarity of each sentence.
4. **Eliminate Unnecessary Words**: Look for opportunities to shorten sentences by eliminating unnecessary words or phrases.
5. **Ask for Feedback**: Have others read your writing and point out areas where clarity can be improved. This will help you identify patterns in your writing and allow you to correct common errors.

Clarity is vital for success on the PELT B Exam and in your law enforcement job. By recognizing and eliminating typical mistakes such as passive voice, redundancy, incorrect modifiers, and wordiness, you can dramatically increase the clarity of your writing.

Effective communication is an essential ability in law enforcement, and learning the art of clear writing will not only help you score well on the exam but also make you a more effective officer in the field.

With consistent practice, attention to detail, and an emphasis on clarity, you will be well-prepared to tackle clarity issues on the PELT B Exam and communicate more effectively in your professional life.

Chapter 5

Reading Comprehension in the PELLET B Exam

Reading comprehension is more than just understanding written words; it's about being able to absorb, analyze, and apply the information you read in real-world circumstances. This talent is crucial in law enforcement, because officers must process huge amounts of textual material, from legal documents and evidence reports to witness testimony and criminal records. In fact, reading comprehension is a crucial talent that directly affects the quality of decision-making, investigative procedures, and even the ability to perform basic law enforcement activities.

The PELT B Exam, utilized in California to assess the competence of law enforcement candidates, has a high emphasis on reading comprehension. As an officer, the ability to comprehend and swiftly grasp vital data from written sources is crucial for proper decision-making and ensuring that justice is administered. Whether you are reading an officer's report, a search warrant, a court order, or a suspect's statement, being able to understand and analyze such material quickly and efficiently is crucial to your work.

In this chapter, we will analyze the role of reading comprehension in law enforcement decision-making, its relationship to critical thinking abilities, and present an overview of how the PELT B Exam measures this skill. By the end of this chapter, you will understand the importance of reading comprehension and how it plays a crucial part in the tasks you will accomplish as a law enforcement officer.

Overview of Reading Comprehension in the PELLET B Exam

The PELT B Exam is designed to assess the core abilities needed for a career in law enforcement. Among these skills, reading comprehension has a very significant place. The reading comprehension component of the exam measures your ability to read a piece and understand its content, identify essential features, and make inferences based on the material.

Typically, a reading comprehension question gives you a passage, followed by numerous questions that test your grasp of the subject. These questions might range from easy data recall to more complicated activities that need you to analyze the underlying meaning, tone, and intent behind the paragraph.

The importance of reading comprehension on the PELT B Exam is multifaceted:

1. **Identifying Key Information:** Officers need to identify essential bits of information in a report, statement, or direction, much like they would need to recognize key facts when responding to a crime scene or drafting a report.
2. **Understanding Context:** Law enforcement agents are typically expected to read and analyze legal papers, witness statements, and various kinds of communication. The ability to understand these documents' context allows officers to make informed decisions regarding actions to take.
3. **Evaluating Information:** A vital part of reading comprehension is the capacity to not just read but assess the information. Officers typically have to make decisions fast based on written material. The ability to appraise the significance of the information supplied is a major aspect of this talent.
4. **Synthesizing and Applying Information:** After understanding and assessing the content, officers must be able to synthesize that information and apply it to real-life scenarios. Whether it's using the specifics of a report to conduct an investigation or reviewing legal terminology in a warrant to identify the next steps, the ability to apply understanding effectively is vital.

Statistics and Facts

Research into the cognitive aspects of reading comprehension reveals that those who score well in this area can process and remember information more effectively. According to a survey by the National Center for Education Statistics (NCES), children who score high on reading comprehension examinations tend to display better critical thinking ability, especially when dealing with complicated or abstract information. In law enforcement, this talent is particularly crucial as police routinely deal with dense, technical, and sophisticated information on a regular basis.

In law enforcement, clear communication is crucial, and reading comprehension enables officers to understand the intricacies of a case, follow protocols accurately, and make suitable conclusions. Understanding the ins and outs of reports, interrogations, legal documents, and other written information is crucial for preventing errors, especially in high-stakes scenarios.

The Role of Reading Comprehension in Law Enforcement Decision-Making

The link between reading comprehension and decision-making is crucial in the setting of law enforcement. Officers sometimes rely on written reports, incident logs, witness accounts, and legal papers to guide their actions. The clearer the comprehension, the more efficient and correct the decisions made.

1. Interpreting Reports and Statements

Officers spend a considerable percentage of their time reading reports, whether those produced by colleagues, other law enforcement officials, or the public. These reports contain crucial information, such as crime details, witness testimony, and forensic evidence. A thorough knowledge of the report can help officers select the next line of action.

For example, when reviewing a witness statement, an officer needs to distinguish between factual details, views, and possibly deceptive material. This needs not only basic reading comprehension abilities but also the capacity to critically analyze and assess the reliability of the material being provided.

2. Legal Documents and Court Orders

Law enforcement agents are routinely expected to read and follow legal documents, including search warrants, subpoenas, court orders, and Miranda rights cautions. These agreements often contain specific legal language that demands careful reading and a comprehensive comprehension.

If an officer misinterprets a legal document, it could result in improper acts, such as unlawful searches or arrests, thereby undermining the integrity of an investigation. For instance, failing to properly appreciate the legal criteria of a search warrant could lead to a breach of a suspect's rights, causing evidence to be inadmissible in court.

3. Real-Time Decision-Making

Reading comprehension is not just necessary in evaluating materials; it is also critical in real-time decision-making during an incident. For example, cops may be expected to swiftly read and understand incoming radio messages or emergency warnings, which typically contain important facts about a situation.

The capacity to comprehend and understand information rapidly in high-pressure situations is crucial for making informed decisions. Whether responding to a crime in progress, a disturbance, or a medical emergency, police must absorb vital details from numerous sources and apply that information swiftly to assess the situation and act accordingly.

4. Communicating with Colleagues and the Public

Clear understanding helps police to interpret and respond to written or spoken information in a precise and effective manner. This competence is extremely useful when speaking with coworkers, superiors, or the public. Misunderstanding a piece of essential information can lead to miscommunication, which could affect the outcome of an inquiry or the handling of a situation.

For example, if a dispatcher gives an officer crucial information regarding a suspect's position, but the officer doesn't completely understand the message due to a lack of reading comprehension, it could delay the officer's reaction and potentially jeopardize lives.

5. Assessing the Legal Impact of Decisions

Reading comprehension also plays a significant part in understanding the legal ramifications of actions made during law enforcement operations. For example, when officers are involved in interrogations or arrest operations, they must be aware of the legal constraints in which they operate, which are often stated in legal documentation.

Understanding Miranda rights, court orders, and due process is vital to prevent abuses of constitutional rights. Officers must read and understand these materials accurately, ensuring they act within the law.

How Reading Comprehension Relates to Critical Thinking Skills

Critical thinking is a vital talent in law enforcement. It involves the ability to evaluate, analyze, and draw conclusions based on existing information. Reading comprehension and critical thinking are closely related—strong comprehension abilities allow you to absorb information, while critical thinking allows you to examine its meaning, relevance, and applicability.

1. Analyzing Information for Relevance

Reading comprehension is the initial stage in analyzing information. Once you understand the topic, critical thinking abilities enable you to judge its relevance to the issue at hand. For example, when reviewing witness testimonies or investigative reports, you must be able to determine if the information supports your inquiry or requires more verification.

Example: If an officer reads a suspect's statement, comprehension alone would allow the officer to grasp the words. However, critical thinking is required to judge if the statement is trustworthy, consistent with other evidence, and beneficial in progressing the investigation.

2. Making Informed Decisions

Once information is comprehended, critical thinking comes into play when making judgments based on that information. In law enforcement, personnel regularly make judgments that can have catastrophic implications. For example, an officer could need to decide whether to follow a suspect, detain a witness, or obtain additional evidence. These decisions are based not just on the facts supplied in reports and statements but also on the officer's ability to assess the context and ramifications of the event.

Critical thinking entails examining many views and analyzing probable outcomes before making a choice. Officers need to grasp the context of the information they read—whether it's a report, a legal document, or a witness statement—and analyze it within the broader perspective of the investigation or situation.

3. Drawing Logical Conclusions

Critical thinking also entails forming logical conclusions from the facts at hand. Officers must use their grasp of a situation to make decisions that correspond with legal requirements, departmental protocols, and ethical considerations. A well-read officer who utilizes critical thinking is able to appraise a situation and identify the best course of action, especially when faced with insufficient or unclear information.

Example: When reading a police report that involves conflicting witness testimonies, critical thinking allows an officer to sift through the information and make a judgment about which parts of the testimony are more believable or likely to be accurate, based on available data.

4. Evaluating Arguments and Contradictions

Critical thinking also entails the ability to notice and analyze discrepancies or biases within the information being provided. This is particularly essential when analyzing witness statements, reports, or even suspect admissions. An officer must analyze whether the material is rational, whether it corresponds with other evidence, and whether there are any gaps or discrepancies that need to be addressed.

Improving Reading Comprehension for the PELT B Exam

Improving your reading comprehension skills for the PELT B Exam involves practice and active engagement with reading materials. Here are various techniques to help you develop your reading comprehension and critical thinking skills:

1. Regularly Read Law Enforcement and Legal Materials

The more you expose yourself to law enforcement-related information, the better you will get at comprehending and interpreting them. Read reports, case studies, and legal documents periodically to acquaint yourself with the language and organization of these items.

- **Tip**: Set aside time each week to read a combination of police reports, legal texts, and news articles related to law enforcement. Practice summarizing key points and making connections between different pieces of information.

2. Practice Active Reading

Active reading involves more than just reading the words; it's about engaging with the material. As you read, ask yourself questions like:

- What is the main point of this passage?
- What details are most important?
- How does this information connect to what I already know?
- Are there any biases or contradictions in the material?

By practicing active reading, you develop your ability to understand and analyze information more effectively.

3. Enhance Your Vocabulary

A strong vocabulary is essential for effective reading comprehension. By expanding your vocabulary, you will be able to understand more complex materials and grasp the meaning of words in context.

- **Tip**: Make a list of unfamiliar terms you come across while reading, and take time to learn their meanings. Focus on words that are commonly used in legal and law enforcement contexts.

4. Practice Reading Comprehension Questions

The best way to prepare for the **PELLET B Exam** is by practicing reading comprehension questions. Use practice exams and reading materials to simulate the test environment and improve your ability to answer comprehension questions quickly and accurately.

- **Tip**: After answering a question, review the passage again and try to explain why the correct answer is right and why the other options are wrong. This practice helps you improve both your comprehension and critical thinking skills.

Reading comprehension is a key skill in law enforcement, and it plays a central part in the PELT B Exam. The capacity to understand, analyze, and apply information from written documents is crucial for effective decision-making and communication in your role as an officer. By establishing good reading comprehension abilities, you not only improve your score on the exam but also strengthen your ability to make educated judgments and communicate effectively in your job.

Strategies for Efficient Reading

In the fast-paced workplace of law enforcement, time is often of the essence. Officers must swiftly process vast amounts of information, whether it's in the form of reports, witness statements, or legal paperwork. Reading efficiently is therefore crucial—being able to retrieve key information quickly without sacrificing comprehension.

One of the most effective ways to improve reading comprehension is to employ the appropriate reading strategies for the work at hand. Skimming and thorough reading are two typical approaches that serve various reasons. Understanding when to utilize each strategy will help you go through reading comprehension questions more rapidly and accurately, particularly in high-stakes contexts like the PELT B Exam.

1. Skimming: When and How to Use It

Skimming involves quickly reading a passage to get a general sense of the content without focusing on every single detail. The goal is to understand the main ideas and structure of the passage. This technique is particularly useful when you need to get an overview of the material in a short amount of time.

When to Use Skimming:

- **Time Constraints**: If you are pressed for time, skimming allows you to get a sense of the passage's content quickly, enabling you to identify key points and focus your attention on the most relevant information.
- **Previewing Material**: Skimming is useful when you are previewing the material to understand its general structure and content. For example, before diving into a complex report or witness statement, you might skim it to familiarize yourself with the main topics.
- **Finding Specific Information**: If you are looking for a specific fact or detail (such as a date, location, or name), skimming helps you locate it quickly without reading the entire passage in detail.

How to Skim Effectively:

- **Focus on Headings and Subheadings**: If the passage has headings or subheadings, pay attention to them. They often provide insight into the structure of the passage and highlight the key points.
- **Read the First and Last Sentences of Each Paragraph**: The first sentence often introduces the main idea of the paragraph, and the last sentence may summarize the key takeaway. This technique helps you get a general sense of the content without reading every word.

- **Look for Keywords**: Pay attention to keywords or phrases that are repeated throughout the passage, as they are often central to the topic.
- **Ignore Non-Essential Information**: Skip over descriptive details, examples, and minor elaborations unless they are essential to understanding the main point.

Example of Skimming:

Imagine you are skimming a report on a robbery. The report includes detailed descriptions of the scene, suspect, and witness testimonies. By focusing on the headings ("Suspect Description," "Crime Scene Investigation," "Witness Statements"), the first and last sentences of paragraphs, and keywords like "robbery," "suspect," and "witness," you can quickly identify the core aspects of the incident without getting bogged down in unnecessary details.

2. Detailed Reading: When and How to Use It

Detailed reading is a more in-depth strategy where you carefully read every word and examine the significance of the piece. This strategy is essential when you need to completely understand the material and when accuracy is critical—such as when working with legal documents or complex reports. Detailed reading guarantees you don't miss any vital information and allows you to engage with the book on a deeper level.

When to Use Detailed Reading:

- **Complex Material**: When the passage is dense or complex, such as a legal document, detailed reading is necessary to fully comprehend the content. Law enforcement officers frequently deal with complex documents, such as search warrants, criminal statutes, or court rulings, which require careful attention.
- **Understanding Context and Inferences**: Detailed reading helps you identify nuances in the text and understand not just the surface information but also any underlying meanings or implications.
- **Answering Specific Questions**: For some reading comprehension questions, you may need to recall specific details from the text, such as the sequence of events or the exact wording of a statement. Detailed reading ensures you don't miss these key elements.

How to Read in Detail:

- **Read Every Sentence Carefully**: Take your time to understand each sentence. If a sentence is unclear, go back and re-read it until you fully comprehend its meaning.
- **Highlight or Take Notes**: If you're working with a printed passage, use a highlighter to mark key phrases or sentences that you want to return to later. You can also take notes to summarize important points.

- **Pay Attention to Details**: In detailed reading, every word counts. Look for dates, times, names, locations, and other specific details that might be important for answering comprehension questions.
- **Look for Relationships Between Ideas**: Detailed reading allows you to connect different pieces of information and understand how they relate to one another. For instance, in a report, understanding the relationship between the suspect's actions and the officer's response may be crucial.

Example of Detailed Reading:

Imagine you are reading a witness statement in a case where a defendant has been accused of theft. A careful reading would require scrutinizing every component of the statement—who the witness is, the timing of events, the demeanor of the suspect, and the particular acts the witness did. You would pay special attention to the wording to ensure you fully comprehend the meaning and ramifications of the statement.

Identifying the Main Idea, Supporting Details, and Inferences

Reading comprehension isn't just about recognizing individual words—it's about understanding the larger message conveyed by the passage. Being able to identify the **main idea**, **supporting details**, and **inferences** is essential for answering comprehension questions effectively, especially on the **PELT B Exam**.

1. Identifying the Main Idea

The **main idea** of a passage is the central point the author is trying to convey. It's the primary concept or argument that the entire passage is focused on. In law enforcement, identifying the main idea is crucial for understanding the broader context of a situation. Whether reading a report, witness statement, or legal document, grasping the main idea helps you make informed decisions and assess the significance of the information provided.

How to Identify the Main Idea:

- **Look at the Title**: The title often provides a clue about the main idea of the passage. For example, if the title of a report is "Suspect Arrested After Robbery," you can reasonably assume the main idea will focus on the arrest and the crime committed.
- **Read the First Paragraph**: The main idea is often introduced in the first paragraph or sentence of the passage. In longer passages, the first few sentences usually provide a summary of what's to come.
- **Summarize the Passage**: After reading the passage, try to summarize it in one sentence. This will help you pinpoint the central theme or idea.

Example:

If you are reading a report about a suspect's arrest, the **main idea** might be something like: "Officers arrested the suspect after a high-speed chase following a robbery." This summarizes the central focus of the passage.

2. Identifying Supporting Details

Once you've identified the main idea, the next step is to understand the **supporting details**. These are the facts, examples, or evidence that back up the main idea. Supporting details provide context and clarify the message the author is trying to convey. In law enforcement, these details are crucial for building a case, following procedures, and making informed decisions.

How to Identify Supporting Details:

- **Look for Facts and Examples**: Supporting details often come in the form of **facts** (such as names, dates, locations) or **examples** (such as specific actions or behaviors).
- **Pay Attention to Transitions**: Words like **"for example"**, **"in addition"**, or **"furthermore"** signal that supporting details are about to be introduced.
- **Focus on Evidence**: In investigative reports or witness statements, the supporting details will typically include evidence or observations that reinforce the main idea.

Example:

In a report about a robbery, the **supporting details** might include the **time** of the robbery, **description of the suspect**, and **statements from witnesses**. These details reinforce the central point of the robbery and support the conclusions drawn in the report.

3. Making Inferences

Inferences are conclusions that you draw based on the information provided in the passage. They are not directly stated but can be reasonably inferred from the context. In law enforcement, the ability to make accurate inferences is crucial for understanding motives, predicting outcomes, and taking appropriate actions.

How to Make Inferences:

- **Look for Hints or Clues**: Inferences are often based on subtle clues or hints in the text. For example, if a witness mentions that a suspect was "acting nervous and looking around," you might infer that the suspect was trying to avoid being seen.
- **Consider the Bigger Picture**: Sometimes, making an inference involves looking at the passage as a whole and considering how the details fit together. For example, if a report mentions a series of escalating incidents, you might infer that the situation is likely to escalate further if not addressed.

- **Use Your Prior Knowledge**: In some cases, your own knowledge of law enforcement procedures, criminal behavior, or general logic can help you make informed inferences from the material.

Example:
If a report describes a suspect being observed near a stolen vehicle and acting suspiciously, you might infer that the suspect is likely involved in the theft, even though the report does not explicitly state this.

Now, we've studied tactics for efficient reading, including when to utilize skimming vs. deep reading. Both approaches are crucial for reading comprehension, but knowing when and how to apply them effectively will help you digest information more quickly and properly. Additionally, understanding how to recognize the main idea, supporting details, and inferences is crucial to mastering reading comprehension on the PELT B Exam and thriving in law enforcement decision-making.

Understanding Fact-Based vs. Inference-Based Questions

Reading comprehension questions can often be classified into two categories: fact-based questions and inference-based questions.

Understanding the distinction between these two sorts of questions is vital for picking the correct response and understanding the passage accurately. Let's go into each type and see how to tackle them.

Fact-Based Questions

Fact-based questions ask you to recall specific details from the passage. These questions are designed to test your ability to extract **concrete information** and **facts** presented in the text. They focus on details that are directly stated, such as names, dates, locations, or events. These questions are typically straightforward, requiring you to find information that is clearly presented in the passage.

Example of a Fact-Based Question:

Passage excerpt:
"The suspect, John Doe, was seen leaving the scene of the crime at approximately 10:15 PM. He was wearing a black hoodie and carrying a duffel bag."

Question:
What time was the suspect seen leaving the scene?

Answer:
10:15 PM.

How to Approach Fact-Based Questions:

- **Read the Question Carefully**: Pay close attention to the question to ensure you're looking for the right detail. Fact-based questions often ask for specific information, such as dates, times, names, or locations.
- **Go Back to the Passage**: After reading the question, locate the section of the passage that directly answers the question. The answer should be explicitly stated in the text.
- **Do Not Overthink**: Fact-based questions are generally straightforward. Stick to the information that is directly presented, and avoid making assumptions.

Tips for Success:

1. **Highlight Key Information**: While reading the passage, underline or highlight important facts. This will help you quickly locate key details when answering fact-based questions.
2. **Look for Dates, Names, and Locations**: Fact-based questions often involve specific details like dates, names, or places. Be sure to pay attention to these elements in the passage.
3. **Eliminate Distractors**: Sometimes, reading comprehension questions will include distractors—answer choices that seem correct but are irrelevant or incorrect. Focus on the key facts to avoid getting misled by these options.

Inference-Based Questions

Inference-based questions go beyond the surface details of the passage. These questions require you to **read between the lines** and draw conclusions based on the information presented. Inference-based questions test your ability to interpret the meaning or implications of the passage, rather than simply recalling facts. The answer to an inference-based question may not be directly stated, but it can be logically deduced from the text.

Example of an Inference-Based Question:

Passage excerpt:
"After the suspect was apprehended, he was observed sweating profusely and constantly looking over his shoulder. Despite being asked about the crime, he remained silent and avoided eye contact."

Question:
What can be inferred about the suspect's behavior during questioning?

Answer:
The suspect is likely nervous or trying to hide something.

How to Approach Inference-Based Questions:

- **Look for Contextual Clues**: Inference questions require you to analyze the broader context of the passage. Pay attention to the tone, the actions of the characters, and the setting. These elements often provide clues about the underlying meaning.
- **Consider What Is Implied**: Ask yourself what the author is trying to suggest indirectly. In many cases, inference-based questions rely on **indirect language**—the passage doesn't say exactly what is happening, but the clues point to a particular conclusion.
- **Eliminate Obvious Answers**: Inference questions may include answers that seem correct but don't fit the overall context of the passage. Eliminate choices that don't align with the subtle clues in the text.

Tips for Success:

1. **Pay Attention to Tone and Body Language**: In passages that describe people's actions or behavior, body language and tone can be powerful indicators of unspoken emotions or motivations.
2. **Focus on Implications**: Think about what the author is implying, rather than what is explicitly stated. For example, a character's actions, facial expressions, or reactions may suggest something about their feelings or intentions.
3. **Practice Critical Thinking**: The key to mastering inference questions is to practice critical thinking. Analyze the details and draw conclusions that make sense based on the evidence provided.

How to Approach Questions That Ask for the Meaning of a Passage

Some reading comprehension questions urge you to determine the meaning or purpose of the passage as a whole. These questions often ask you to interpret the core subject, the tone, or the author's aim. Unlike fact-based questions, which focus on specific details, these questions demand you to examine the overall message and underlying meaning of the text.

Example of a Question Asking for the Meaning of a Passage:

Passage excerpt:
"The officers moved cautiously through the dark alley, their senses heightened. Every creak of

the wooden fence, every rustle of leaves, heightened their suspicion that they weren't alone. Despite the tense atmosphere, they maintained their focus, prepared for whatever they might encounter."

Question:
What is the main idea of the passage?

Answer:
The passage describes the officers' vigilance and heightened awareness as they search a potentially dangerous area.

How to Approach Meaning-Based Questions:

- **Identify the Central Theme**: Start by identifying the core message of the passage. What is the author trying to communicate about the situation or the characters? In law enforcement passages, the theme could involve actions like **patrolling, responding to a crime**, or **investigating a scene**.
- **Look for the Author's Purpose**: Determine why the passage was written. Is it to describe an event, explain a situation, or convey a message about behavior or attitudes? Understanding the purpose helps you grasp the broader meaning of the passage.
- **Analyze the Tone and Language**: The tone of the passage (serious, humorous, formal, etc.) often provides clues about the author's intent. For example, a passage describing a tense situation with **heightened suspicion** might suggest an underlying **danger** or **uncertainty**.
- **Consider the Bigger Picture**: When answering these types of questions, avoid getting lost in the small details. Instead, focus on the overall message the passage conveys. What can you infer about the broader situation based on the language and context provided?

Tips for Success:

1. **Read for the Main Idea First**: Before diving into the details, get a general sense of the passage's message. What's the passage about at a high level? What's the tone or mood of the passage?
2. **Consider the Entire Passage**: Meaning-based questions require you to evaluate the passage as a whole. Read the entire text carefully, considering how each section contributes to the overall message.
3. **Practice Summarizing**: After reading a passage, try to summarize it in one sentence. This will help you hone your ability to identify the key themes and ideas quickly.

Combining Fact-Based and Inference-Based Approaches

To be successful in reading comprehension, particularly on the **PELT B Exam**, it's important to integrate both **fact-based** and **inference-based** strategies. Each type of question requires a different way of thinking, but both are essential for fully understanding and engaging with the material.

- **Fact-Based Questions**: Focus on finding specific, verifiable details from the passage. Read for clarity and precision, and refer back to the passage as often as needed.
- **Inference-Based Questions**: Focus on drawing conclusions based on context and clues. Use critical thinking to evaluate the text and assess its implications.
- **Meaning-Based Questions**: Focus on understanding the overall message, tone, and purpose of the passage. Look at how the passage fits within the broader context.

By practicing both approaches, you'll be prepared to tackle a variety of reading comprehension questions with confidence.

By learning the capacity to discriminate between fact-based and inference-based questions, and understanding how to approach questions regarding the meaning of a text, you may enhance both your exam performance and your overall reading comprehension skills.

Understanding the Importance of Speed and Retention

Reading speed and retention are related. Simply reading rapidly without comprehending the material is unproductive, especially in law enforcement, where detail is often crucial. However, reading too slowly can be just as hazardous, especially when dealing with time-sensitive jobs such as analyzing reports or responding to emergencies.

Reading speed relates to the rate at which you digest and assimilate information from a text. Increasing reading speed without sacrificing understanding is crucial when you need to process big volumes of data under time limitations. On the PELT B Exam, time is limited, and questions are designed to challenge your ability to grasp and process information fast.

Retention relates to your capacity to recall significant information, ideas, and details from the text after reading it. The more effectively you retain material, the better you'll be able to answer questions on the PELT B Exam and apply the information in real-world scenarios.

Improving both your reading speed and retention can help you become more efficient at processing written content, ensuring that you can handle even the most time-sensitive activities with accuracy and confidence.

Improving Reading Speed Under Time Pressure

Time constraint is one of the most critical obstacles of the PELT B Exam and many law enforcement activities. Officers often need to read rapidly to assess circumstances, analyze records, or respond to emergencies. Improving your reading speed doesn't entail abandoning comprehension—it's about improving the efficiency of your reading process.

1. Preview the Material Before Reading

Before you get into the material, spend a little time previewing it. This stage helps you gain an idea of what the passage is about, allowing you to select significant areas that will likely include important information. Previewing the material gives you a mental foundation for understanding the text.

How to Preview:

- **Read the Title and Subheadings**: Titles and subheadings can give you a general sense of what the passage is about. For example, if the subheading is "Suspect Description," you can predict that the section will contain information about the suspect's physical appearance or behavior.
- **Scan for Keywords**: Before fully reading the passage, quickly scan the text for **keywords** or **important phrases**. These might include names, dates, or locations that will help you understand the context and importance of the material.
- **Look for Bullet Points or Lists**: If the text contains bullet points or numbered lists, these often highlight key facts or steps. These are usually easier to scan for important details than large blocks of text.

By previewing the material, you can focus your attention on the most relevant parts of the passage, reducing the time spent reading extraneous details.

2. Practice Speed Reading Techniques

Speed reading strategies are designed to help you read quicker without sacrificing comprehension. While you may not be able to read as quickly as a professional speed reader, using these tactics will help you read quicker and more efficiently under time pressure.

Speed Reading Techniques:

- **Minimize Subvocalization**: **Subvocalization** refers to the habit of silently "saying" each word in your head as you read. While this can be helpful for comprehension, it can significantly slow you down. Try to minimize subvocalization by focusing on reading groups of words instead of individual words.
- **Use Your Finger or a Pen**: **Guiding your eyes** with your finger or a pen can help you focus and maintain a steady reading pace. By moving your finger along the lines of the text, you prevent your eyes from wandering and help your brain process information more efficiently.
- **Avoid Re-reading**: Re-reading text can slow you down and disrupt your flow. Try to focus on understanding the material the first time through. If you don't understand a sentence, skip ahead and come back to it later if necessary.
- **Expand Your Peripheral Vision**: Rather than reading word by word, try to read in chunks. Your peripheral vision can capture several words at once, allowing you to process information faster.

Practice Speed Reading: Speed reading is a skill that improves with practice. Set aside time each day to practice reading quickly. Start with easier material, then gradually work up to more complex passages.

3. Eliminate Distractions

To read more efficiently, you need to create an environment that minimizes distractions. Whether you're preparing for the **PELT B Exam** or reviewing case files at the station, a distraction-free environment will help you focus and increase your reading speed.

How to Eliminate Distractions:

- **Find a Quiet Environment**: Try to find a quiet space where you can read without interruptions. This will help you focus and retain the information better.
- **Turn Off Notifications**: If you're using a digital device to read, turn off notifications or set your phone to silent. Constant interruptions can break your concentration and slow down your reading speed.
- **Set a Time Limit**: Set a specific time limit for reading a section of material. By creating a sense of urgency, you will train yourself to focus more intensely and read faster.

4. Read with a Purpose

When you read with a specific purpose in mind, you are more likely to read efficiently. Whether you are reading a report, a legal document, or a training manual, having a clear goal helps you focus on extracting the relevant information.

How to Read with Purpose:

- **Identify Your Goal**: Before reading, ask yourself what information you are trying to extract. Are you looking for a specific fact? Are you trying to understand a particular concept or argument?
- **Focus on Key Details**: With your goal in mind, focus on extracting the details that will help you answer questions or make decisions. Skim over less important parts of the text.

Improving Retention Through Active Reading

In addition to reading faster, it's vital to retain the information you read. Retention permits you to recall key data and details when answering inquiries, solving problems, or making judgments. Active reading is a strategy that helps you engage with the material, enhancing both your understanding and recall.

1. Annotate and Take Notes

One of the most effective ways to improve retention is by actively engaging with the text. **Annotating** the material and taking notes forces you to process the information and reinforces your understanding.

How to Annotate and Take Notes:

- **Highlight Key Points**: As you read, underline or highlight key facts, concepts, or phrases that you think are important.
- **Write Summaries**: After each section or paragraph, write a brief summary of what you just read. This will help reinforce the material and ensure that you understand it.
- **Make Connections**: As you read, try to make connections between the new information and what you already know. Linking new knowledge to existing knowledge helps strengthen memory retention.

Active Note-Taking: Write down important points or questions you may have as you go through the passage. This can also help you stay engaged with the material.

2. Visualize the Material

Visualizing what you're reading is another powerful retention technique. By forming mental images of the information, you can create a stronger connection to the material and make it easier to recall later.

How to Visualize:

- **Create Mental Pictures**: When reading descriptions of events, places, or people, try to visualize them in your mind. For example, if a report describes a suspect's appearance, imagine what the suspect looks like based on the details provided.
- **Use Diagrams or Charts**: For complex information, such as data or procedural steps, draw diagrams or flowcharts to represent the material visually. This will help organize the information and make it easier to recall.

3. Teach What You've Learned

One of the best ways to solidify what you've read is by teaching it to someone else. When you explain the material to others, you reinforce your understanding and help commit it to memory.

How to Teach What You've Learned:

- **Discuss with Peers**: After reading a section, discuss it with a study partner or colleague. Try to explain the main ideas and key details from memory.
- **Practice Explaining**: If you don't have anyone to talk to, try explaining the material out loud to yourself. This helps reinforce the information and test your understanding.

4. Review Regularly

Reviewing the material regularly is essential for long-term retention. The more frequently you revisit the material, the more likely you are to retain it.

How to Review:

- **Daily Review**: Set aside time each day to review the material you've read. This could be a brief summary or a deeper dive into specific sections.
- **Spaced Repetition**: Use the spaced repetition method, where you review the material at increasing intervals. This technique has been shown to improve memory retention over time.

Improving your reading speed and retention is vital for success on the PELT B Exam and in your law enforcement career. By learning tactics such as skimming, active reading, and effective note-taking, you can read more rapidly while remembering crucial information. Whether you're preparing for the exam or reviewing a report, these approaches will help you process content more rapidly and use it effectively in your work.

Through constant practice, you can build the abilities to read and absorb material under time pressure without losing accuracy or understanding. The capacity to retain and recall crucial data will not only increase your exam performance but will also boost your effectiveness as an officer, enabling you to make educated judgments, respond promptly to circumstances, and communicate properly with others.

Practice Passages And Questions: Reading Comprehension.

Before digging into the practice passages and questions, let's briefly discuss the format of reading comprehension questions on the PELT B Exam. These questions are designed to test several fundamental components of reading:

1. **Fact Recall**: Questions that test your ability to identify specific details, such as names, dates, or locations.
2. **Main Idea**: Questions that ask you to identify the central theme or purpose of the passage.
3. **Supporting Details**: Questions that ask you to extract additional details that support the main idea or argument.
4. **Inferences**: Questions that ask you to draw conclusions based on information that is not explicitly stated in the passage.
5. **Tone and Purpose**: Questions that ask you to evaluate the author's intent or the emotional tone of the passage.

Reading comprehension on the **PELT B Exam** doesn't simply focus on regurgitating information; it evaluates your ability to process and apply what you read. This is why practicing with sample passages and questions will help improve both your speed and accuracy in answering these types of questions.

Sample Passage 1: Crime Report Analysis

Passage:

On the evening of May 5, 2025, officers were dispatched to a disturbance call at 2200 Elm Street. Upon arrival, officers observed a group of individuals standing outside a house. The group appeared to be arguing, and one individual, later identified as James Tyler, was seen gesturing aggressively and shouting at the others. Officers approached the group and separated Tyler from the others. After a brief conversation, Tyler was arrested for public intoxication and disorderly conduct. No physical altercation occurred, but the situation remained tense. Officers issued Tyler a citation and advised him to refrain from further disruptive behavior. The situation was cleared without further incident.

Question 1: What was the reason for James Tyler's arrest?

A) Assault
B) Public intoxication and disorderly conduct
C) Disturbing the peace
D) Vandalism

Answer Breakdown:

- **A) Assault**: This is incorrect. While the passage mentions a tense situation, there is no indication that Tyler physically attacked anyone or engaged in assaultive behavior.
- **B) Public intoxication and disorderly conduct**: This is correct. The passage explicitly states that Tyler was arrested for these offenses, which is the primary reason for his arrest.
- **C) Disturbing the peace**: While Tyler's actions may have contributed to a disturbance, this is not the specific charge mentioned in the passage.
- **D) Vandalism**: This is incorrect. Vandalism is not mentioned as part of the incident described in the passage.

Correct Answer: B
Explanation: The passage specifically states that James Tyler was arrested for **public intoxication and disorderly conduct**, making option B the correct choice.

Sample Passage 2: Legal Document Interpretation

Passage:

Under California Penal Code Section 245, assault with a deadly weapon is defined as an unlawful attempt to commit a violent injury on another person using a weapon that is capable of inflicting substantial harm.

The weapon may include firearms, knives, or blunt instruments, and the intent to cause harm must be proven. A conviction under this statute can result in imprisonment for up to four years, depending on the circumstances and the severity of the offense. Defendants charged under Section 245 may be offered a plea bargain, depending on prior offenses and the nature of the weapon used.

Question 2: What must be proven for a conviction under Penal Code Section 245?

A) That the defendant used a firearm
B) That the defendant had the intent to cause harm
C) That the defendant caused injury
D) That the defendant was armed with a knife

Answer Breakdown:

- **A) That the defendant used a firearm**: This is incorrect. The passage mentions that the weapon could be a firearm, knife, or blunt instrument, but it does not specify that a firearm must be used to prove a conviction.
- **B) That the defendant had the intent to cause harm**: This is correct. The passage clearly states that **intent to cause harm** must be proven for a conviction under Section 245.
- **C) That the defendant caused injury**: This is incorrect. While the passage discusses an attempt to commit injury, it does not require that injury be caused to prove the offense.
- **D) That the defendant was armed with a knife**: This is incorrect. While the passage mentions knives as an example of a weapon, the weapon itself is not the sole factor. The intent to cause harm is what must be proven.

Correct Answer: B
Explanation: The passage explicitly states that the key element for a conviction under **Penal Code Section 245** is **the intent to cause harm**, making option B the correct choice.

Sample Passage 3: Officer's Testimony

Passage:

During his testimony, Officer Hernandez explained that he approached the suspect, who was parked in a vehicle in a known drug-dealing area. Upon contacting the suspect, Officer Hernandez noticed the suspect's nervous behavior and the smell of marijuana coming from the car. After asking the suspect for identification, the officer observed a small bag of what appeared to be marijuana on the passenger seat.

The officer then conducted a search of the vehicle and found more marijuana and paraphernalia hidden in the trunk. The suspect was arrested and charged with possession of controlled substances.

Question 3: What evidence led to the suspect's arrest?

A) The officer's suspicion alone
B) The smell of marijuana and the bag in the vehicle
C) The suspect's nervous behavior
D) The officer's search of the suspect's home

Answer Breakdown:

- **A) The officer's suspicion alone**: This is incorrect. While suspicion may have played a role, the passage indicates that concrete evidence—specifically the smell of marijuana and the discovery of the bag—led to the arrest.
- **B) The smell of marijuana and the bag in the vehicle**: This is correct. The passage describes how the officer noticed the **smell of marijuana** and found a **bag of marijuana** in the vehicle, both of which were key pieces of evidence for the arrest.
- **C) The suspect's nervous behavior**: While the suspect's nervous behavior was noted, it was not the sole factor leading to the arrest. The evidence of marijuana in the car was more significant.
- **D) The officer's search of the suspect's home**: This is incorrect. The passage mentions a search of the **vehicle**, not the suspect's home.

Correct Answer: B

Explanation: The arrest was based on **the smell of marijuana** and the discovery of a **bag** in the vehicle, which were concrete pieces of evidence linking the suspect to the offense.

Sample Passage 4: Witness Statement

Passage:

Witness Maria Johnson stated that she saw the suspect enter the convenience store at around 8:00 PM. She described the suspect as wearing a black hoodie and carrying a backpack. Johnson said she noticed the suspect acting nervously as he moved towards the cashier and looked around the store.

At one point, the suspect's hand went into his backpack, and Johnson immediately felt uneasy. She left the store shortly after and called 911 to report a suspicious individual. Later, the police apprehended the suspect as he exited the store. Inside his backpack, officers found stolen merchandise from the store.

Question 4: What did the witness notice that caused her to feel uneasy?

A) The suspect's clothing
B) The suspect's nervous behavior and actions
C) The store's security cameras
D) The suspect's conversation with the cashier

Answer Breakdown:

- **A) The suspect's clothing**: This is incorrect. While the passage mentions the suspect's clothing (black hoodie and backpack), it was the suspect's behavior and actions that caused the witness to feel uneasy.
- **B) The suspect's nervous behavior and actions**: This is correct. The passage specifically notes that the witness felt uneasy due to the **suspect's nervous behavior** and **actions**—specifically, when the suspect's hand went into his backpack.
- **C) The store's security cameras**: This is incorrect. There is no mention of the store's security cameras affecting the witness's feelings.
- **D) The suspect's conversation with the cashier**: This is incorrect. The passage does not describe any conversation between the suspect and the cashier. The witness's unease was due to the suspect's behavior, not his interactions with the cashier.

Correct Answer: B
Explanation: The witness felt uneasy due to the **nervous behavior** and **actions** of the suspect, specifically when he placed his hand in his backpack, making option B the correct choice.

Tips for Answering Reading Comprehension Questions

1. **Focus on Key Details**: Pay attention to the main facts, key details, and supporting information in the passage. When answering questions, refer directly to these elements.
2. **Look for Context Clues**: For inference-based questions, analyze the context to draw conclusions that may not be explicitly stated in the text.
3. **Eliminate Distractors**: Often, reading comprehension questions will include distractor answers—choices that may seem plausible but are irrelevant or incorrect. Use your understanding of the passage to eliminate these options.
4. **Review the Passage**: If you're unsure about an answer, go back to the passage. Don't just rely on memory—revisit the text to find the most accurate answer.
5. **Read Carefully**: Many reading comprehension questions are designed to test your ability to understand subtle differences in wording. Read the question and passage carefully to ensure that you're not misinterpreting any part of the text.

Mastering reading comprehension is vital for success on the PELT B Exam and in law enforcement. By practicing with example passages and understanding how to approach different types of questions—whether fact-based, inference-based, or meaning-based—you'll build the skills needed to read efficiently, comprehend crucial information, and make well-informed decisions.

The practice passages in this chapter have provided insight into how reading comprehension questions are structured, and the breakdowns of each answer choice will help you refine your test-taking skills. By strengthening your capacity to quickly process and retain knowledge, you'll be better prepared for the PELT B Exam and ready to flourish in your law enforcement profession.

Common Challenges in Reading Comprehension

Reading comprehension can be tough for a variety of reasons. The portions in the PELT B Exam may feature complex information, abstract terminology, or subtle subtleties that can make deciphering the subject more challenging. Furthermore, the questions themselves can be challenging, requiring a profound comprehension of the material and its context. Here are some frequent issues candidates find when studying for the PELT B Exam:

1. Complex Language and Vocabulary

One of the biggest challenges in reading comprehension is encountering complex or new terminology. Law enforcement-related texts may contain technical jargon, legal terminology, or formal language that might make understanding the information more complex. As an officer, you will need to be conversant with legal and procedural words, as these phrases are commonly part of the texts you'll see in your everyday work.

How to overcome this challenge:

- **Practice Regularly**: The more you expose yourself to complex language and vocabulary, the more familiar you will become with it. Read law enforcement-related texts such as **case reports, legal documents**, and **incident reports** to familiarize yourself with common terminology.
- **Contextual Clues**: Often, the meaning of a word or phrase can be inferred from the context in which it is used. Pay attention to surrounding sentences or paragraphs to understand unfamiliar words.

- **Use a Dictionary**: When encountering unfamiliar words, take the time to look them up. Familiarity with a broader range of vocabulary will help improve your comprehension skills.

2. Misleading or Ambiguous Questions

Reading comprehension questions can sometimes be tough, with response choices that sound plausible but are not correct. Some questions are designed to mislead you, requiring careful attention to the wording and phrasing of the passage. Misleading or ambiguous questions typically challenge your ability to avoid leaping to conclusions or making assumptions based on limited facts.

How to overcome this challenge:

- **Read Carefully**: Pay close attention to the specific wording of each question. Be aware of words like "always," "never," "most likely," or "except," as these can significantly change the meaning of the question.
- **Look for Specific Information**: Make sure you refer directly to the passage to find the most accurate answer. Avoid relying on memory or assumptions about what you've read.
- **Eliminate Wrong Answers**: In many cases, there will be at least one or two answer choices that can be ruled out as incorrect. Eliminate these first to narrow your options and increase the chances of selecting the correct answer.

3. Identifying the Main Idea vs. Supporting Details

Many reading comprehension questions need you to discern between the primary idea of a text and the supporting details that are used to expound on it. This can be particularly tough when the chapter contains a lot of detailed information that may appear relevant but isn't central to the broader message of the text.

How to overcome this challenge:

- **Read the First and Last Sentences**: The main idea is often introduced in the first sentence and concluded in the last sentence of the paragraph or passage. Focus on these key sentences to identify the overall message.
- **Identify Key Terms**: Look for terms or phrases that are repeated throughout the passage. These often point to the main idea or central theme.
- **Summarize the Passage**: After reading, try to summarize the passage in your own words in one or two sentences. This will help you pinpoint the main idea and understand the supporting details in relation to it.

4. Making Inferences Based on Implicit Information

Another challenge in reading comprehension is making inferences from implicit information. Inferences are conclusions you draw based on the text that are not explicitly stated but can be deduced from the context. These types of questions require you to think critically and apply logic to understand the broader implications of the passage.

How to overcome this challenge:

- **Look for Clues**: Inference-based questions often rely on clues that are hidden in the passage. Pay attention to the tone, word choice, and subtle details that may hint at the broader meaning.
- **Read Between the Lines**: In some cases, you'll need to think about what the author is implying rather than what is directly stated. Consider the context and the likely motivations of the characters or individuals involved.
- **Consider the Bigger Picture**: Don't just focus on the surface-level details—consider the passage as a whole and how the different pieces of information fit together.

5. Time Pressure and Reading Efficiency

Time constraint can be one of the most significant obstacles of the PELT B Exam. With a limited amount of time to read and answer questions, it might be challenging to comprehend and recall all the information you need. Speed and efficiency are critical, but it's also important to ensure that you don't speed through the questions and miss key details.

How to overcome this challenge:

- **Practice with Timed Tests**: The best way to improve your reading speed and efficiency is to practice under timed conditions. This will help you get used to working within the time constraints and increase your comfort level with reading quickly.
- **Use Skimming and Scanning Techniques**: For passages with a lot of information, practice skimming for the main ideas and scanning for specific details. This will help you process information faster while still retaining the most important facts.
- **Focus on Key Questions**: Some questions are more difficult than others. If you're running out of time, don't dwell too long on any one question. Focus on the easier questions first, and if necessary, come back to the more difficult ones later.

Tips for Avoiding Misinterpretation of Complex Passages

Complex passages, especially those incorporating technical terminology, complex ideas, or different views, might lead to misinterpretations. Law enforcement records, in particular, can be voluminous and tough to comprehend. Learning how to tackle these types of passages effectively is vital for scoring well on the PELT B Exam.

1. Break Down Complex Sentences

Complex sentences can often contain multiple clauses, making them difficult to follow. Breaking these sentences down into smaller parts can help you better understand the meaning.

How to break down complex sentences:

- **Identify the Subject and Verb**: Focus on the core subject and verb of each sentence. This will help you understand the primary action or statement being made.
- **Simplify Subordinate Clauses**: Look for subordinate clauses (e.g., phrases that begin with "although," "because," "despite") and isolate them. By focusing on the main clause first, you can better understand the sentence as a whole.
- **Paraphrase the Sentence**: After breaking it down, try rephrasing the sentence in simpler terms. This will help you internalize the information and ensure you understand the key message.

2. Focus on Context and Purpose

When reading a complex passage, it's important to focus on the **context** and **purpose** of the text. Understanding the overall goal of the passage will help you interpret individual details more effectively.

How to focus on context:

- **Identify the Author's Intent**: Think about why the passage was written. Is it trying to inform, persuade, or describe? Understanding the purpose will guide your interpretation of the details.
- **Analyze the Setting**: Pay attention to the time, place, and circumstances described in the passage. The context will often provide crucial information for answering questions correctly.
- **Assess the Tone**: The tone can reveal the author's attitude toward the subject. Whether it's serious, sarcastic, or neutral, the tone will affect how you interpret the information.

3. Identify Unnecessary Information

In some passages, especially longer ones, there may be information that is not essential to answering the questions. **Unnecessary details** can distract you and lead to confusion.

How to identify unnecessary information:

- **Look for Irrelevant Facts**: Focus on the facts that directly support the main idea or the question being asked. Disregard tangential details that do not add to the understanding of the main topic.
- **Avoid Overanalyzing**: In complex passages, it's easy to get lost in the details. Stick to the essential points and avoid spending too much time on aspects that don't contribute to answering the question.

4. Use Active Reading Strategies

Active reading involves engaging with the material as you read. This means not just passively reading the words but actively interacting with the content to ensure you understand it deeply.

How to read actively:

- **Ask Questions**: As you read, ask yourself questions about the material. What is the author trying to convey? What are the key points? What is the author's perspective on the subject?
- **Take Notes**: Jot down important ideas, facts, or any points that stand out. Writing notes helps you engage with the material and reinforces your understanding.
- **Highlight Key Information**: Mark important facts or phrases that seem relevant to the main idea. This will help you refer back to these points quickly when answering questions.

Reading comprehension is a skill that needs time and practice to acquire, especially while preparing for the PELT B Exam. The ability to detect frequent challenges—such as difficult language, misleading questions, and the need to discriminate between core ideas and supporting details—will help you approach each section with confidence. By implementing the tactics presented in this chapter, you can improve your ability to digest information efficiently, avoid misinterpretation, and enhance your overall performance.

Remember, reading comprehension on the PELT B Exam is not only about reading rapidly; it's about reading with purpose, connecting with the subject, and retaining the vital information. With regular preparation and by following these tactics, you will be well-equipped to face the problems of reading comprehension on the exam and flourish in your law enforcement career.

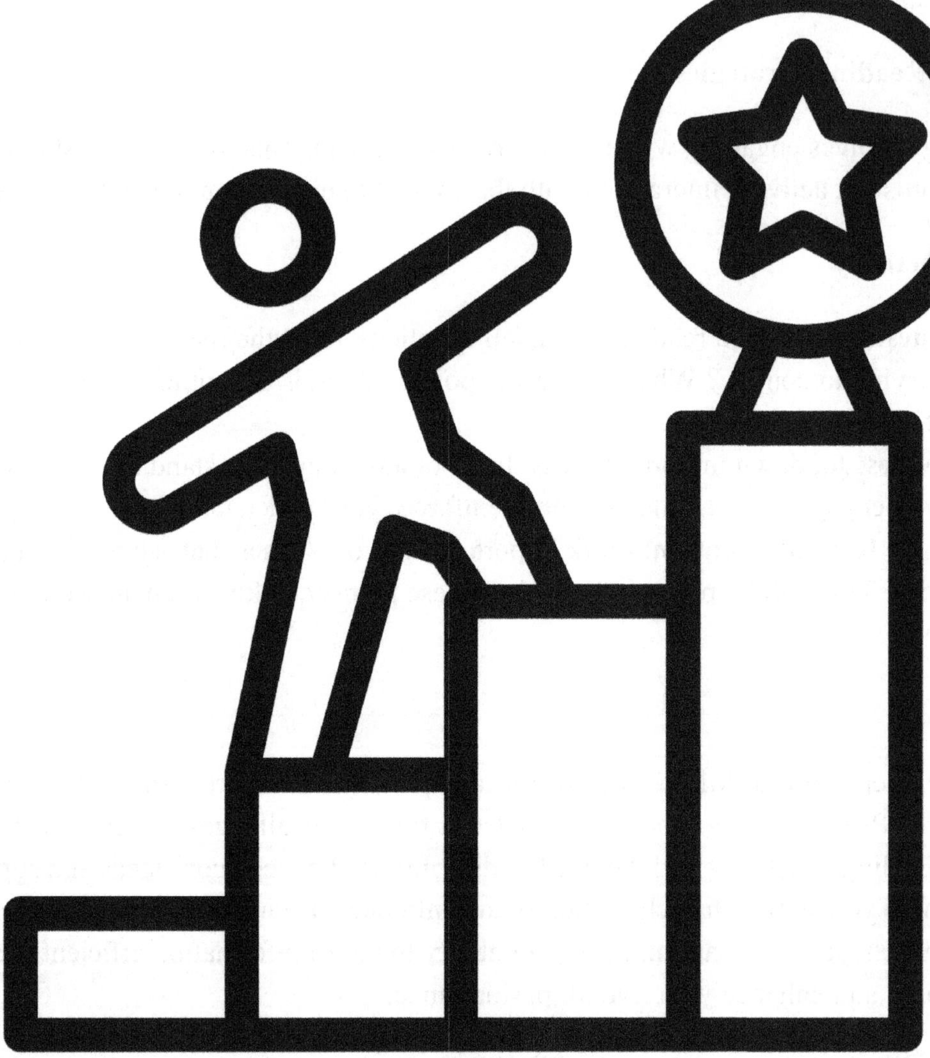

Chapter 6

Strategies for Success

The route to passing the PELT B Exam can seem overwhelming, but with the appropriate techniques, you can set yourself up for success. Whether you're preparing for the exam as part of your entry into law enforcement or simply looking to expand your knowledge, the key to success rests in how you arrange and approach your study time. Just like physical training for a police academy, efficient preparation for the PELT B Exam demands a planned method, constant practice, and a balance between hard effort and self-care.

The PELT B Exam measures numerous fundamental skills that are required for law enforcement professionals, such as reading comprehension, vocabulary, spelling, and sentence clarity. The breadth and diversity of the content can be overwhelming, but with efficient study techniques, you can tackle these problems with confidence. In this chapter, we will explore how to structure your study sessions for optimum retention, employ spaced repetition and active recall to boost your learning, and present recommendations for balancing your study time with breaks and self-care to avoid burnout.

Effective Study Techniques for Maximum Retention

Effective studying isn't just about putting in the hours—it's about how you employ that time. The purpose of studying isn't only to learn content, but to remember and utilize that knowledge when you need it most. Here are some great tactics that will help you maximize your study sessions and retain the knowledge better for the PELT B Exam.

1. Organizing Your Study Sessions

The first step in obtaining optimum retention is adopting an organized study strategy. Simply plunging into the content without a defined structure can lead to frustration, overwhelm, and poor learning. Instead, organize your study periods into small portions with clear goals and objectives.

How to organize your study sessions:

- **Break Down the Material**: The **PELT B Exam** covers several different areas—spelling, vocabulary, reading comprehension, and clarity. To avoid feeling overwhelmed, break the

material down into smaller sections and focus on one area at a time. This will allow you to approach the material methodically and help you track your progress.
- **Set Specific Goals**: Instead of saying "I'm going to study for an hour," set specific goals for each study session. For example, you might set the goal of completing **10 spelling exercises**, reviewing **20 vocabulary words**, or finishing **one practice reading passage** within the hour. Having specific goals ensures that your study session remains focused and productive.
- **Use a Study Calendar**: Plan out your study sessions in advance. Allocate time each day for study and create a weekly or monthly calendar that includes the topics you plan to cover. This will help you manage your time effectively and make sure you are reviewing all necessary material before the exam.

2. Active Learning for Maximum Retention

One of the most efficient study approaches for enhancing recall is active learning. This entails engaging with the content in ways that foster greater knowledge, rather than passively reading or memorizing data. Active learning can include actions such as practicing problems, teaching the topic to someone else, and testing yourself periodically.

How to incorporate active learning:

- **Self-Testing**: One of the most effective ways to retain information is to test yourself regularly. This can be done through practice questions, flashcards, or even by summarizing the material from memory. Self-testing not only helps you assess what you've learned but also reinforces the material in your brain, making it easier to recall when needed.
- **Teach What You've Learned**: Teaching someone else what you've learned is a powerful method for reinforcing your understanding of the material. Even if you don't have a study partner, you can explain concepts out loud to yourself, or write out explanations as if you were teaching a class. This will help you solidify the information in your mind and uncover any areas you might need to review further.
- **Engage in Active Note-Taking**: Instead of simply reading through your notes, engage in active note-taking. Summarize information in your own words, highlight key points, and organize your notes in a way that helps you understand and remember the material. You can also create **mind maps** or **diagrams** that visually represent the connections between concepts.

Utilizing Spaced Repetition for Optimal Learning

Spaced repetition is a well-researched learning approach that involves revisiting content at increasing intervals over time. This strategy capitalizes on the brain's natural tendency to forget knowledge over time, urging you to review the topic before it's fully lost. By doing so, you reinforce your knowledge and ensure that it stays in your long-term memory.

1. The Science Behind Spaced Repetition

Research has demonstrated that spaced repetition promotes retention by taking use of the spacing effect—the phenomenon where knowledge is more easily remembered if it is revisited at increasing intervals. Studies have revealed that reviewing content immediately before forgetting it helps consolidate it in your memory. In contrast, cramming (studying vast quantities of material in a short period) is less beneficial for long-term recall.

How to use spaced repetition effectively:

- **Use Spaced Repetition Software**: There are numerous apps and programs available that utilize spaced repetition algorithms to help you review material at optimal intervals. Tools like **Anki** or **Quizlet** allow you to create digital flashcards and automatically schedule reviews based on your progress. These tools are particularly helpful for vocabulary words and key facts, which you need to retain for the **PELT B Exam**.
- **Review at Increasing Intervals**: Start by reviewing material soon after you learn it, then gradually increase the time between reviews. For example, review new material after 1 hour, then 1 day, 3 days, 1 week, 2 weeks, and so on. This spaced approach strengthens your recall of the material.
- **Be Consistent**: Consistency is key with spaced repetition. Set aside time each day to review past material, even as you continue to study new material. This consistency helps you maintain and reinforce your knowledge, reducing the chance of forgetting important information.

2. Creating a Spaced Repetition Schedule

To incorporate spaced repetition into your study routine, create a schedule that breaks down the material into manageable segments. For example, you can divide your study materials into weekly units and review them as follows:

- **Week 1**: Study new material (vocabulary, reading comprehension strategies, etc.) and review it after 1 hour, 1 day, 3 days, and 1 week.
- **Week 2**: Review the material from Week 1 while studying new content from Week 2. Continue reviewing past material at increasing intervals.

This combination of regular study and spaced reviews will help you reinforce your learning and improve your long-term retention of the material.

Active Recall: Testing Your Knowledge for Better Retention

Active recall is a powerful approach that includes actively recalling information from memory rather than merely re-reading or passively reviewing content. Research repeatedly reveals that actively recalling knowledge strengthens the brain connections linked with memory, making it easier to access the information when needed.

1. How Active Recall Works

When you engage in active recall, you challenge yourself to retrieve knowledge from memory without glancing at your notes or the content. This procedure requires your brain to work harder, which promotes memory retention.

For example, instead of merely going over vocabulary lists, you might try to recall the definitions of terms from memory. The more effort you put into obtaining the information, the better you will remember it.

How to use active recall effectively:

- **Use Flashcards**: Flashcards are a great tool for active recall. Write a question or prompt on one side and the answer on the other. Test yourself by trying to recall the answer before flipping the card over.
- **Practice Retrieval**: After studying a section, close your book or notes and try to recall as much information as possible. Don't just look at the material again right away—force yourself to actively recall the information first. This strengthens the connections in your brain and enhances retention.
- **Teach What You've Learned**: As mentioned earlier, teaching someone else what you've learned is an excellent form of active recall. Explaining concepts out loud or writing summaries helps solidify your understanding and memory.

Tips for Balancing Study Time with Breaks and Self-Care

While focused study sessions are necessary, it's as important to balance study time with relaxation and self-care. Overloading yourself with hours of non-stop studying can lead to fatigue and limit your ability to retain material properly. Taking regular breaks and creating time for relaxation and exercise is vital for sustaining your mental and physical well-being.

1. The Pomodoro Technique: Structured Study with Breaks

The **Pomodoro Technique** is a popular time management method that involves studying in short, focused intervals, followed by short breaks. The standard Pomodoro cycle consists of **25 minutes of studying** followed by a **5-minute break**, and after four cycles, you take a **longer break** (usually 15-30 minutes). This technique helps you maintain focus and prevents mental fatigue.

How to use the Pomodoro Technique:

- **Set a Timer**: Set a timer for 25 minutes and focus entirely on studying during that time. Avoid distractions such as checking your phone or social media.
- **Take Short Breaks**: After each 25-minute interval, take a 5-minute break to relax, stretch, or hydrate. These short breaks help refresh your mind and body.
- **Take Longer Breaks**: After completing four study sessions, take a longer break to recharge fully. Use this time to engage in a relaxing activity, such as walking, meditating, or listening to music.

2. Prioritize Rest and Sleep

Your brain processes and consolidates memories during sleep, so it's important to prioritize rest, especially in the weeks leading up to the exam. Aim for **7-9 hours of sleep** each night to ensure your brain has adequate time to store and strengthen the information you've studied during the day.

How to prioritize rest:

- **Stick to a Sleep Schedule**: Go to bed and wake up at the same time each day to maintain a regular sleep routine.
- **Avoid Caffeine Late in the Day**: Caffeine can interfere with sleep quality. Try to avoid consuming caffeine in the afternoon or evening.
- **Create a Relaxing Bedtime Routine**: Engage in activities that help you wind down before bed, such as reading, meditating, or taking a warm bath.

3. Incorporate Exercise and Physical Activity

Exercise is an excellent technique to alleviate stress and increase cognitive performance. Physical activity boosts blood flow to the brain, which can assist improve focus, memory, and mental clarity. Incorporating regular exercise into your study routine might help you stay refreshed and retain a positive mindset.

How to incorporate exercise:

- **Take Short Walks**: Even a short 15-20 minute walk can help clear your mind and improve focus. Consider taking breaks during your study sessions to stretch your legs and get some fresh air.
- **Engage in Regular Workouts**: Aim to incorporate more structured physical activity into your routine, such as running, yoga, or strength training, at least a few times a week.
- **Stay Active During Breaks**: During your Pomodoro breaks or longer study breaks, do something physical, such as stretching, doing a quick workout, or taking a walk outside.

By organizing your study sessions, utilizing techniques like spaced repetition and active recall, and balancing study time with breaks and exercise, you can improve your retention, reduce stress, and boost your chances of success.

Test-Taking Strategies for the PELT B Exam

When it comes to standardized exams like the PELT B, your success is decided by more than just what you know—it's also about how you take the test. Even with the best preparation, poor test-taking tactics can hinder you from displaying your knowledge successfully. Let's break down the techniques that can help you maximize your performance on exam day.

1. Time Management Tips for Each Section of the Exam

One of the most prevalent issues addressed throughout the PELT B Exam is managing time properly. The exam consists of numerous sections, and each requires a distinct technique to guarantee you pass the test on time without speeding through questions or leaving any unanswered.

How to Manage Time Effectively:

a) Spelling Section: The **spelling section** of the **PELT B Exam** typically includes multiple-choice questions that require you to identify the correct spelling of various words. It's important to approach this section efficiently so that you don't waste time on words you're already familiar with.

- **Time Allocation**: Allocate a specific amount of time to this section, typically around **10 to 15 minutes**, depending on the number of questions. The goal is to answer the questions quickly but accurately.
- **Strategy**: If you encounter a word you're unsure of, skip it and return to it after answering the easier questions. Trust your knowledge of common spelling patterns to quickly eliminate obviously incorrect choices.

b) Vocabulary Section: The **vocabulary section** tests your understanding of word meanings and usage. The key to success in this section is to not only know definitions but also understand how words are used in different contexts.

- **Time Allocation**: Aim to spend about **15 to 20 minutes** on this section, depending on the number of questions. Because vocabulary questions often have multiple-choice options, you can quickly eliminate some choices if you recognize the word or understand its meaning.
- **Strategy**: Focus on **context clues** when answering vocabulary questions. If you don't know the exact definition, look at the surrounding words for hints. Also, if you're stuck, try to choose the option that seems the most contextually appropriate.

c) Reading Comprehension Section: The **reading comprehension section** is one of the most time-consuming parts of the exam, as it involves reading longer passages and answering several questions about them. The ability to efficiently read and analyze the text is essential for completing this section on time.

- **Time Allocation**: Dedicate **30 to 35 minutes** for this section, as it generally involves multiple passages with several questions each. Be mindful of your time while reading and answering.
- **Strategy**: Start by **skimming** the passage to get a general idea of the topic, and then read the questions before diving into the passage itself. This allows you to know what to focus on while reading, saving time when answering the questions.

d) Clarity Section: The **clarity section** typically involves evaluating sentences for their structure and clarity. You may need to identify errors in sentence construction or choose the most clearly written sentence from a set of options.

- **Time Allocation**: Spend about **10 to 15 minutes** on this section, focusing on identifying issues with sentence clarity, such as unnecessary complexity or passive voice.
- **Strategy**: Look for sentences that are **too wordy** or **lack focus**. The clearest sentence is usually the one that gets straight to the point and communicates the idea in the simplest possible way.

2. Approaching Multiple-Choice Questions with Confidence

Multiple-choice questions (MCQs) are a prevalent format on the PELT B Exam, and learning the ability of answering them successfully will substantially increase your score. Multiple-choice questions may appear simple, but they often test your critical thinking and ability to handle information under pressure.

Effective Strategies for Tackling Multiple-Choice Questions:

a) Read the Question Carefully: It's easy to jump into the answer choices without fully understanding the question, but this can lead to mistakes. Take a moment to carefully read the question, paying attention to keywords like **"except," "always," "not,"** and **"most likely."** These words can significantly change the meaning of the question.

b) Eliminate Clearly Incorrect Choices: When faced with multiple choices, you should always start by eliminating the answers that are obviously wrong. This narrows down your options and increases your chances of selecting the correct one. Sometimes, eliminating just one wrong answer can make the correct answer more apparent.

c) Use Contextual Clues: If you encounter a question that you're unsure about, use the information in the passage to guide your choice. Often, **PELT B Exam** passages contain clues that point directly to the correct answer. Don't second-guess yourself too much—go with the answer that best fits the context.

d) Don't Overthink the Answer: It's natural to second-guess yourself during the exam, but overthinking multiple-choice questions can lead to confusion and mistakes. Trust your instincts and go with the answer that seems most logical based on the information provided.

e) Time Management for Multiple-Choice Questions: Multiple-choice questions should not take you too long to answer, so if you're stuck on a question for more than a minute or two, it's okay to move on. Mark the question and return to it if time permits. This will help you maintain momentum throughout the exam.

---

3. Handling Test Anxiety and Staying Calm During the Exam

Test anxiety is something that many test-takers experience, especially when facing high-stakes exams like the **PELT B Exam**. Stress and anxiety can affect your ability to think clearly and perform well, so it's important to have strategies in place to manage these emotions.

Tips for Managing Test Anxiety:

a) Practice Relaxation Techniques: Relaxation techniques, such as deep breathing or meditation, can help calm your nerves before and during the exam. Practice **deep breathing** exercises to slow your heart rate and reduce physical symptoms of anxiety. Inhale slowly for 4 seconds, hold for 4 seconds, and exhale for 4 seconds. Doing this several times can help ground you and reduce anxiety.

b) Focus on the Present Moment: During the exam, it's easy to get overwhelmed by the fear of not finishing or worrying about difficult questions. Instead, focus on the **present moment**. Focus on answering the current question to the best of your ability, without thinking ahead. If you catch yourself worrying, refocus by taking a few deep breaths and concentrating on the task at hand.

c) Stay Positive and Maintain Confidence: A positive mindset can significantly improve your performance. If you've put in the preparation and practice, trust that you have the skills to succeed. Don't let one challenging question or a moment of doubt derail your focus. If you encounter a tough question, move on and return to it later with a clear mind.

d) Get Enough Rest and Sleep: Test anxiety often worsens when you're tired or sleep deprived. A lack of sleep can impair your ability to think clearly and stay focused. Aim for **7-9 hours of sleep** the night before the exam to ensure that you're mentally sharp. Proper rest can also help reduce feelings of anxiety and improve your overall performance.

e) Visualize Success: Visualization is a powerful technique used by athletes and performers to boost confidence and reduce anxiety. Take a few minutes before the exam to close your eyes and visualize yourself walking into the exam room with confidence, tackling each question with ease, and finishing the exam successfully. This positive imagery will help calm your nerves and set you up for a successful test-taking experience.

f) Maintain Perspective: Remember that while the **PELT B Exam** is important, it is not the only factor in your law enforcement journey. Staying relaxed and maintaining perspective will help you perform at your best. If you find yourself feeling overwhelmed, remind yourself that this is just one step in a long career, and doing your best is all you can control.

Common Mistakes to Avoid in All Sections

The PELT B Exam measures your ability to process and apply information fast, which is no simple accomplishment. Whether you're tackling the spelling, vocabulary, reading comprehension, or clarity parts, it's simple to make frequent mistakes if you don't keep watchful and focused. Here are some of the most prevalent mistakes that test-takers make and how you may avoid them:

1. Second-Guessing Your Answers

One of the most typical mistakes students make during tests is second-guessing their answers. This often happens when you feel confused about a choice you made and subsequently doubt your initial judgment. Second-guessing can be problematic since it often leads to choosing an inaccurate response that sounded better in the moment but is actually wrong.

How to avoid second-guessing:

- **Trust Your Instincts**: If you've studied well and prepared, your first instinct is often the correct one. Trust your judgment and don't waste time overthinking questions. If you're unsure about an answer, mark the question and come back to it later instead of changing your answer out of doubt.
- **Practice During Your Prep**: One way to build confidence in your initial responses is to practice under timed conditions. The more you practice, the more confident you'll become in your ability to make decisions quickly and correctly.
- **Don't Dwell on the Past**: If you've made a choice and moved on, let it go. Spending time worrying about a question you've already answered can waste precious time and distract you from the remaining questions.
- **Take a Break If Needed**: If you're feeling overwhelmed or unsure about a particular question, take a few deep breaths. Sometimes stepping away from the question for a moment helps you clear your mind and return to it with fresh eyes.

2. Not Fully Reading the Question

Sometimes, in an attempt to work quickly, test-takers don't fully read the question and instead jump straight to the answer choices. This is a dangerous habit because it often leads to misunderstandings or misinterpretation of what the question is asking.

How to avoid this mistake:

- **Read Carefully**: Always read each question thoroughly before looking at the answer choices. Pay attention to any qualifiers (e.g., "always," "never," "except") that can change the meaning of the question.
- **Look for Keywords**: Focus on keywords in the question that will guide your search for the correct answer. For example, words like "most" or "best" can significantly alter your understanding of the question and the expected answer.

- **Double-Check Your Understanding**: Before you pick an answer, make sure you understand the question fully. If you need to, paraphrase the question in your own words to make sure you're clear on what's being asked.

3. Falling for "Trap" Answers

Trap answers are designed to seem correct but are actually misleading. They may sound like they fit the context, but closer inspection reveals that they don't align with the passage or question's intent. These answers are often designed to trick you into making a decision based on superficial similarities.

How to avoid falling for trap answers:

- **Look for Extreme Language**: Many trap answers contain extreme or exaggerated language such as "always," "never," or "must." These terms are usually a red flag. In most cases, the correct answer will be more moderate and nuanced.
- **Examine All Answer Choices**: Don't rush to select the first answer that seems correct. Review all the available answer choices before making your decision. The first option may sound correct at first, but further options may provide more context or a clearer fit to the question.
- **Beware of Repetition**: Sometimes, trap answers contain repetitive or redundant information that may mislead you. Pay attention to whether the answer choice is simply rephrasing part of the question or passage.
- **Focus on the Passage**: If the answer seems too perfect or seems to align too well with your assumptions, double-check the passage. Sometimes, trap answers are designed to appeal to your preconceived notions, but the passage will provide the true, accurate answer.

4. Skipping Questions Without Thinking It Through

While it's okay to skip questions that are giving you trouble, it's important not to skip too many questions in a row without carefully thinking it through. Skipping without a strategy can result in missed opportunities or incorrect guesses when you return to those questions.

How to avoid this mistake:

- **Don't Skip Without a Strategy**: If you don't know the answer to a question, try to eliminate the obviously incorrect options first. This can help you make a more educated guess if you decide to skip and come back later.
- **Mark and Move On**: If you're unsure about a question, mark it and move on. Don't waste time pondering it. You can return to it later with fresh eyes or after answering easier questions that give you more confidence.

- **Time Management**: If you find yourself skipping a lot of questions, reassess your time management strategy. Spend less time on individual questions so you can cover the whole test and leave yourself enough time to revisit difficult questions.

---

5. Overthinking Answer Choices

Overthinking is a common mistake, especially in exams that require critical thinking, such as the **PELT B Exam**. Test-takers often spend too much time thinking about what the "perfect" answer is, which leads them to lose confidence in their initial choice.

How to avoid overthinking:

- **Trust Your First Choice**: Once you have made a decision, trust it. Second-guessing or overthinking will only introduce more confusion. If you've studied well, your first instinct is usually the right one.
- **Use the Process of Elimination**: When faced with complex answer choices, narrow down your options by eliminating clearly wrong answers. This process helps reduce the number of possibilities and makes it easier to make an educated decision.
- **Be Efficient with Your Time**: Overthinking can result in time wastage. If you find yourself doubting your answer, move on. If you have time at the end, you can revisit the question with a clearer mindset.

6. Misinterpreting the Passage in Reading Comprehension

Reading comprehension sections can present another tricky challenge. It's easy to misinterpret a passage, especially if it contains abstract language or unfamiliar concepts. Misinterpretations can lead to wrong answers, so careful attention to detail is essential.

How to avoid misinterpreting the passage:

- **Understand the Main Idea**: When reading a passage, focus on identifying the **main idea** before delving into specific details. This will help you understand the context and avoid getting bogged down by less important information.
- **Underline Key Points**: As you read, underline or highlight key details, especially facts or phrases that answer specific questions. This will help you focus on the most relevant information and avoid distractions.
- **Summarize in Your Own Words**: After reading a paragraph or passage, briefly summarize it in your own words. This reinforces the information and ensures that you've understood the key points.

7. Underestimating the Difficulty of Some Questions

Many test-takers fall into the trap of underestimating the difficulty of certain questions, especially in sections that seem easy at first glance. Reading comprehension or vocabulary questions, for example, may seem simple, but they can include subtle nuances that are easy to miss.

How to avoid this mistake:

- **Read Carefully**: Even seemingly straightforward questions can contain tricky wording or subtle details. Always read the question and passage carefully, even if you think you know the answer.
- **Don't Rush**: Take your time with each question and avoid rushing through the test. Spending a few extra seconds on each question will improve your accuracy and help you avoid common mistakes.

---

8. Focusing Too Much on One Section

While it's important to do well on each section of the **PELT B Exam**, focusing too much on one section can cause you to lose valuable time and negatively affect your performance on other sections.

How to avoid this mistake:

- **Time Allocation**: Set a time limit for each section before starting. If you find yourself spending too much time on one section, move on. You can always return to unanswered questions during the final moments of the exam.
- **Keep a Steady Pace**: Maintain a consistent pace throughout the exam. If you feel that you're spending too long on any question, make a note to come back to it later and move on with the test.

By focusing on **avoiding second-guessing answers**, recognizing **trap answers**, and applying **effective test-taking strategies**, you'll be well-equipped to tackle the exam confidently.

Final Review Tips for All Sections

By the time the last week before your PELT B Exam arrives, you should have already covered most of the material. Now, it's time to focus on reinforcing that knowledge, fine-tuning your skills, and improving your test-taking tactics. Here are some crucial final review recommendations that can help you maximize your preparation for the PELT B Exam:

1. General Final Review Tips

Before going into the intricacies of each area, let's first explore some general review tactics that will aid you throughout all parts of the exam.

a) Set a Study Schedule for the Last Week

In the last week before the exam, creating and sticking to a structured study schedule is essential. A well-structured schedule helps ensure that you're reviewing all the material without feeling overwhelmed. Your study schedule should prioritize areas where you feel the least confident, while still revisiting topics you've already mastered to keep them fresh in your mind.

How to organize your last week:

- **Day 1-2**: Focus on the sections where you need the most improvement. For example, if you struggle with **spelling** or **vocabulary**, spend extra time reviewing these areas, taking practice tests, and using flashcards.
- **Day 3-4**: Revisit your strongest areas (e.g., **clarity** or **reading comprehension**). This helps reinforce the knowledge you've already built and ensures you are confident going into the exam.
- **Day 5-6**: Take a full-length practice test under timed conditions to simulate the real exam environment. Review your results thoroughly to identify any mistakes or areas for improvement.
- **Day 7**: Spend the last day focusing on light review. Don't cram or overexert yourself. A relaxed review will help keep your mind fresh for the exam.

b) Focus on Active Recall and Spaced Repetition

In the final week, use **active recall** and **spaced repetition** to reinforce your knowledge. Active recall involves retrieving information from memory rather than just passively reviewing notes. Spaced repetition involves reviewing material at increasing intervals to reinforce long-term retention.

How to use active recall and spaced repetition:

- **Active recall**: Quiz yourself regularly on important concepts. This can be done using **flashcards** or by practicing with sample questions. Don't just passively read through your notes; test your memory and comprehension.
- **Spaced repetition**: Revisit topics you've studied throughout the week, spacing out your reviews. Use apps like **Anki** or **Quizlet** to create flashcards with spaced repetition algorithms, helping you retain important information more effectively.

c) Take Care of Your Health

As you enter the final stages of preparation, it's easy to become overwhelmed and neglect your physical and mental health. However, maintaining a balanced lifestyle is crucial for optimal performance. Ensure you are getting **enough sleep**, eating nutritious meals, and taking breaks to rest and recharge. If you are stressed, practice relaxation techniques such as deep breathing or meditation to stay calm and focused.

How to take care of your health:

- **Sleep**: Aim for **7-8 hours** of quality sleep every night, especially in the days leading up to the exam.
- **Nutrition**: Eat a balanced diet rich in **fruits, vegetables**, and **whole grains**, and avoid excessive caffeine or sugar that can lead to energy crashes.
- **Exercise**: Engage in light physical activity, such as walking or stretching, to reduce stress and improve circulation.

Final Review Tips for Each Section

Now that we've covered broad review tactics, let's break down specific review recommendations for each section of the PELT B Exam. Focus on these tactics in the last week before the exam to ensure you're properly prepared for each area of the examination.

2. Spelling Section

The spelling component of the PELT B Exam examines your ability to accurately identify and spell words widely used in law enforcement situations. This section requires considerable attention to detail and familiarity with both normal English spelling norms and specific law enforcement words.

Review Tips for the Spelling Section:

- **Review Commonly Misspelled Words**: Focus on law enforcement-related terms you've encountered in your studies, such as **suspect**, **parole**, **evidence**, and **surveillance**. These terms are frequently tested and may be tricky.
- **Practice with Flashcards**: Use **flashcards** to drill yourself on spelling. Write the word on one side and the correct spelling on the other. This method helps reinforce your recall.
- **Take Practice Quizzes**: There are numerous online spelling quizzes and practice tests available that focus on law enforcement terminology. Take these quizzes to gauge your understanding and identify areas where you need further review.
- **Focus on Difficult Words**: Identify the words you tend to miss and spend extra time practicing them. Sometimes, **repetition** and **association** (e.g., associating the word with a visual or definition) can make a difference in remembering the correct spelling.

3. Vocabulary Section

The vocabulary component of the PELT B Exam examines your understanding of terms and their meanings. This section generally includes terminology that are commonly used in law enforcement contexts, and mastering these terms is vital for speaking effectively in your work.

Review Tips for the Vocabulary Section:

- **Review Word Definitions and Context**: Focus not only on the definitions of words but also how they are used in context. For example, understanding the word **"covert"** might involve knowing that it refers to secret or undercover operations in law enforcement.
- **Use Flashcards for Quick Review**: Flashcards are again a great tool here. Write the word on one side and the definition or an example sentence on the other. Review these regularly throughout the week.
- **Practice with Contextual Questions**: Practice answering **multiple-choice questions** or **sentence completion exercises** where you have to choose the word that fits within a sentence. This helps you understand the word's meaning in context.
- **Group Words by Theme**: Organize words into groups based on themes (e.g., law enforcement procedures, legal terms, etc.). This will help you remember words more easily by associating them with related concepts.

4. Reading Comprehension Section

The **reading comprehension** section tests your ability to read a passage and extract key information, such as the main idea, supporting details, and inferences. This section can be particularly challenging if you are not familiar with the types of texts you may encounter.

Review Tips for the Reading Comprehension Section:

- **Practice Reading Passages**: In the final week, make it a point to complete at least **one full-length reading comprehension practice test**. Time yourself to ensure that you are working within the constraints of the exam.
- **Focus on Identifying the Main Idea**: Often, reading comprehension questions ask you to identify the **main idea** or **central theme** of the passage. Practice identifying this early in the passage to guide your understanding of the entire text.
- **Use Process of Elimination**: For each question, eliminate answer choices that you know are incorrect. This technique will help you focus on the most plausible answers, especially for questions that require inferences.
- **Practice Inference Questions**: Reading comprehension often includes questions that require you to make inferences based on the text. Practice answering these by paying close attention to **context clues** that indicate the author's intent or the underlying message.

5. Clarity Section

The clarity section of the **PELT B Exam** involves evaluating sentence structure and identifying errors in grammar, punctuation, and clarity. This section tests your ability to recognize and correct poorly written sentences, which is an important skill for law enforcement professionals.

Review Tips for the Clarity Section:

- **Review Common Sentence Structure Issues**: Focus on issues such as **run-on sentences, fragments**, and **awkward phrasing**. Practice identifying these issues in sample sentences.
- **Read Sentences Out Loud**: Reading sentences aloud can help you identify unclear or awkward wording. If a sentence doesn't sound right when spoken, it's likely not clear.
- **Practice Sentence Correction**: Work through sentence correction exercises that focus on improving clarity. Take note of common grammar rules and principles that contribute to clear writing.
- **Test Your Knowledge of Grammar Rules**: Refresh your understanding of grammar rules that impact sentence clarity, such as **subject-verb agreement, parallel structure**, and **proper punctuation**.

In the Last Week: Simulating the Exam Experience

One of the finest strategies to prepare for the PELT B Exam in the final week is to imitate the test day experience. Taking full-length practice examinations under timed conditions will help you get used to the pacing of the exam and highlight any areas where you may need further preparation.

How to simulate the exam experience:

- **Take Full-Length Practice Tests**: Set aside several hours to complete a full-length practice exam under timed conditions. This will help you get used to the timing for each section and identify any areas where you need more review.
- **Review Your Performance**: After completing a practice exam, thoroughly review your answers. Take note of any mistakes and make sure you understand why the correct answers are right.
- **Analyze Your Time Management**: Keep track of how long you spend on each section during the practice exam. Use this information to adjust your study schedule and ensure that you can finish each section within the allotted time during the real exam.

The penultimate week coming up to the PELT B Exam is your final opportunity to cement your knowledge and prepare for test day. By following the review tactics provided in this chapter, you may maximize your preparation, focus on your weaker areas, and enter the exam with confidence.

With structured study sessions, active recall, and good self-care, you will be ready to confront the PELT B Exam head-on and succeed in your road toward a law enforcement career.

Remember, success in the PELT B Exam doesn't come from cramming at the last minute; it comes from constant, focused effort throughout your study period. Use the final week to reinforce what you've already learnt and ensure that you are prepared both mentally and physically for the test.

Chapter 7

Full-Length Practice Tests and Detailed Answer Explanations

Congratulations on taking the first step toward your law enforcement career! This practice test is designed to help you prepare for the **PELT B (Police Entry-Level Test Battery)** by providing a simulated experience of the actual exam. The PELLET B is an essential assessment used by law enforcement agencies to evaluate candidates' basic reading, writing, and comprehension abilities.

General Instructions:

1. **Read each question carefully**: Take your time to understand what each question is asking. While time management is important, it's essential that you give each question the attention it deserves.
2. **Answer the questions to the best of your ability**: This practice test is an opportunity for you to gauge your strengths and areas for improvement. Do not worry about perfection—focus on learning and improving.
3. **Manage your time wisely**: Each section has a specific time limit. Make sure to pace yourself so that you have enough time to answer all the questions.
4. **Use the answer sheet**: Write your answers clearly in the spaces provided. You will have multiple-choice options for each question. Select the best possible answer for each.
5. **No assistance**: This is a **self-paced test**, and no external help or resources should be used while you are taking the practice exam. This will give you the most accurate assessment of your current knowledge and skills.
6. **Stay focused and calm**: This is a practice test, not the actual exam. Treat it as a valuable tool for preparation. Relax and do your best.

Test-Taking Tips:

1. **Pace yourself**: Time management is important, but do not rush. You have enough time to complete the test if you keep a steady pace.
2. **Read all the answer choices**: In some cases, two answer choices may seem similar. Be sure to evaluate each option carefully before making your decision.
3. **Don't second-guess**: After answering a question, move on to the next. If you're unsure about an answer, skip it and return to it later if time allows.

4. **Stay calm**: It's natural to feel nervous, but try to stay calm and focused. Clear thinking will help you choose the correct answers.
5. **Review your answers**: If time permits, review your answers at the end of each section. This will help you catch any mistakes you might have missed.

Scoring Guide:

- Each correct answer is worth **1 point**.
- There are **20 questions** in each section, for a total of **80 points**.
- Your score for each section is calculated by counting the number of correct answers you provided.

Interpreting Your Score:

- **70-80 points**: Excellent! You are well-prepared for the PELLET B exam. Focus on maintaining this level of knowledge.
- **50-69 points**: Good. You have a solid foundation, but some areas may need more attention. Review the sections where you scored lower and focus on improving them.
- **30-49 points**: Fair. You need to focus on improving key areas. Review your answers carefully, especially in sections where you struggled the most.
- **Below 30 points**: Needs improvement. Focus on each section individually and allocate time to understand the areas that are challenging.

Final Thoughts:

This **Full-Scale Practice Test** is designed to help you assess your strengths and areas for improvement as you prepare for the **PELT B exam**. Take this test seriously, but also view it as a learning tool. Whether you do exceptionally well or need to spend more time reviewing, this test will give you invaluable insight into what areas you need to focus on to succeed.

Now that you are prepared, proceed to the Practice Question Section. Good luck!

Full-Scale Practice Test 1

Section 1: Spelling (20 Questions)

Time Limit: 15 minutes

Instructions:

- This section tests your ability to accurately spell words that are commonly used in law enforcement scenarios.
- You will be presented with 20 words in the form of multiple-choice questions. For each question, choose the correct spelling of the word.
- **Tip**: Pay close attention to common spelling pitfalls such as double letters, homophones (words that sound the same but are spelled differently), and prefixes/suffixes.
- **Goal**: Accuracy is key. Be sure to focus on details, as a single letter can alter the meaning of a word and its appropriateness in law enforcement communication.

Questions:

1. The officer took the necessary steps to _____ the suspect's alibi during the investigation.

A. confrim
B. confirm
C. comfirm
D. confurm

2. The detective was able to identify the _____ fingerprint found on the stolen goods.

A. printe
B. print
C. prent
D. print

3. The officer asked the witness to _____ the events of the night in detail.

A. recount
B. recount
C. re-count
D. recunte

---

4. The evidence was deemed _____, as it was too damaged to be useful in court.

A. inadmissable
B. inadmissible
C. inadmissable
D. inadmissibl

---

5. The officer was able to _____ the suspect's whereabouts at the time of the crime.

A. determain
B. determin
C. determine
D. determind

---

6. The police used a variety of methods to _____ the suspect's involvement in the robbery.

A. determine
B. determin
C. determan
D. determen

---

7. The detective found the _____ evidence that led to the arrest of the suspect.

A. key
B. kee
C. keye
D. kye

8. The suspect gave a _____ statement, which conflicted with the witness's account.

A. contraditory
B. contradictory
C. contridictory
D. contradictary

---

9. The officer was asked to _____ the report with additional information from the scene.

A. complet
B. complette
C. complete
D. compleat

---

10. The investigation was delayed due to the _____ of crucial evidence.

A. absense
B. absence
C. absense
D. absance

---

11. The officer was tasked with _____ the suspect's criminal history before the interrogation.

A. verifying
B. verifiying
C. verfiying
D. verifiying

---

12. The crime scene was carefully _____ to ensure no evidence was overlooked.

A. examined
B. examened
C. exaimined
D. exmained

136

13. The detective was careful to _____ all relevant facts during the investigation.

A. include
B. inclued
C. inclued
D. inclued

14. The officer made sure the report was _____ to avoid any confusion in court.

A. clear
B. cleer
C. clere
D. cleaer

15. The suspect's actions were deemed _____ to public safety by the authorities.

A. detramental
B. detrimental
C. detrimantal
D. detrimenal

16. The detective couldn't _____ the accuracy of the witness's testimony.

A. veirfy
B. verfiy
C. verify
D. virify

17. The officer had to _____ the suspect's whereabouts during the night of the incident.

A. confirm
B. comfirm
C. confirm
D. confirmed

18. The witness's _____ of the event was consistent with the surveillance footage.

A. account
B. acccount
C. accunt
D. acount

19. The officer was tasked with _____ the situation before making any arrests.

A. assesing
B. assessing
C. asseseing
D. assassing

20. The investigator was able to _____ the suspect's involvement in the crime.

A. confirm
B. confim
C. comfirm
D. confirming

Section 2: Vocabulary (20 Questions)

Time Limit: 20 minutes

Instructions:

- This section evaluates your understanding of vocabulary used in law enforcement contexts.
- You will be presented with 20 sentences, each containing an underlined word. Your task is to choose the synonym that best fits the context of the sentence.
- **Tip**: Pay attention to the context of the sentence. Many law enforcement-related words have specific meanings that might differ from their everyday use. Think about how the word is used in context, not just its dictionary definition.
- **Goal**: This section tests your ability to understand and apply law enforcement terminology effectively. Take your time to ensure the synonym you choose fits the tone and meaning of the sentence.

Questions:

1. The officer was praised for his **astute** observation during the investigation.

A. Quick
B. Clever
C. Timid
D. Weak

2. The suspect's **defiant** behavior during the questioning raised suspicions.

A. Submissive
B. Resistant
C. Polite
D. Supportive

3. The detective was known for his **methodical** approach to solving cases.

A. Random
B. Hasty
C. Systematic
D. Reckless

---

4. The officer's **candid** testimony was crucial in securing a conviction.

A. Honest
B. Shady
C. Biased
D. Misleading

---

5. The officer was able to **dispel** the rumors by providing concrete evidence.

A. Confirm
B. Ignore
C. Clarify
D. Disprove

---

6. The detective presented a **convincing** argument that led to the suspect's arrest.

A. Weak
B. Uncertain
C. Persuasive
D. Unbelievable

---

7. The officer maintained a **stern** expression during the interrogation.

A. Soft
B. Angry
C. Serious
D. Friendly

8. The officer's **perceptive** remarks about the suspect's behavior helped solve the case.

A. Insensitive
B. Insightful
C. Ignorant
D. Misleading

9. The officer's **vigilant** monitoring of the area helped prevent any further incidents.

A. Inattentive
B. Watchful
C. Careless
D. Hasty

10. The officer's **inquisitive** nature helped him uncover hidden details during the investigation.

A. Indifferent
B. Curious
C. Uninterested
D. Hostile

11. The detective used his **keen** intellect to solve the mystery that had puzzled others for months.

A. Dull
B. Sharp
C. Slow
D. Weak

12. The officer made a **subtle** observation that helped link the suspect to the crime.

A. Obvious
B. Indirect
C. Noticeable
D. Delicate

13. The officer's **unwavering** commitment to his duty earned him respect from his colleagues.

A. Steady
B. Hesitant
C. Uncertain
D. Weak

---

14. The detective's **methodical** investigation uncovered vital information that led to the suspect's arrest.

A. Disorganized
B. Systematic
C. Haphazard
D. Impulsive

---

15. The officer's **compassionate** response to the victim's situation demonstrated his commitment to public service.

A. Indifferent
B. Sympathetic
C. Hostile
D. Apathetic

---

16. The suspect's _____ behavior caused alarm among the officers, who were unsure of his next move.

A. Predictable
B. Erratic
C. Calm
D. Subdued

17. The officer was able to **dispel** the myth by providing clear and factual information about the incident.

A. Confirm
B. Reject
C. Disprove
D. Ignore

---

18. The officer's ability to **articulate** the details of the case was critical in presenting the evidence clearly to the jury.

A. Confuse
B. Simplify
C. Express
D. Mumble

---

19. The detective's **astute** observations during the case led to the discovery of crucial evidence.

A. Sharp
B. Blunt
C. Careless
D. Obvious

---

20. The officer worked **tirelessly** to ensure the suspect's identity was accurately determined before the trial.

A. Relentlessly
B. Lazily
C. Slowly
D. Haphazardly

Section 3: Reading Comprehension (20 Questions)

Time Limit: 25 minutes

Instructions:

- In this section, you will read two passages and answer 10 multiple-choice questions for each passage.
- Each passage is designed to assess your ability to comprehend written material related to law enforcement and public service.
- **Tip**: Focus on **key ideas**, **main points**, and **inferences** rather than memorizing every detail. The goal is to assess your ability to extract and understand information quickly and efficiently.
- **Goal**: To test your ability to read and understand complex material, which is a crucial skill for law enforcement officers who regularly work with reports, legal documents, and other written materials.

Questions:

Passage 1: Cybersecurity and the Modern Workforce

In the digital age, cybersecurity has become a critical concern for organizations worldwide. As businesses and governments shift their operations online, the frequency and sophistication of cyberattacks have escalated. Cybersecurity threats, such as ransomware, phishing attacks, and data breaches, have the potential to cripple organizations, causing financial loss, damage to reputation, and the theft of sensitive data. The growing reliance on cloud services and remote work arrangements has expanded the potential attack surface for cybercriminals.

One of the primary challenges facing organizations today is securing their networks and systems against these evolving threats. Cybersecurity professionals are tasked with not only defending against attacks but also educating employees about safe online practices. Training and awareness programs are essential to ensuring that staff members understand the importance of strong passwords, recognizing phishing attempts, and using encryption tools. Additionally, organizations are increasingly investing in advanced cybersecurity tools, such as artificial intelligence and machine learning, to detect and respond to threats in real-time.

Despite the increase in awareness and investment, many companies still struggle with the growing complexity of cybersecurity. Part of the issue lies in the ever-changing landscape of technology. New software and hardware innovations, combined with the increasing integration of Internet of Things (IoT) devices, create more potential vulnerabilities. The rapid development of technologies also creates a gap in skills, as there is a significant shortage of qualified cybersecurity professionals. As the demand for experts continues to rise, companies are faced with the challenge of attracting and retaining top talent.

Moreover, the importance of collaboration in cybersecurity cannot be overstated. Threats often span multiple sectors, and effective defense requires cooperation between private and public entities. Information sharing, joint task forces, and international partnerships are vital for identifying and neutralizing cyber threats that cross borders. Global cyberattacks, like the WannaCry ransomware attack, have demonstrated how interconnected and vulnerable the digital world has become, and how collective efforts are required to combat the growing problem.

In summary, cybersecurity is more than just a technical issue; it is a business imperative. With the rise of cyber threats, organizations must be proactive in developing robust security measures, ensuring staff training, and collaborating with external entities to strengthen defenses. As cyber threats continue to evolve, organizations that prioritize cybersecurity will be better positioned to protect their assets, reputation, and future growth.

---

1. What is the primary concern highlighted in the passage regarding modern organizations?

A. The financial costs associated with cybersecurity
B. The growing reliance on artificial intelligence in cybersecurity
C. The increasing frequency and sophistication of cyberattacks
D. The shortage of skilled professionals in the cybersecurity field

---

2. According to the passage, what is one of the main challenges faced by organizations in cybersecurity?

A. The rapid development of new software and hardware
B. The lack of public support for cybersecurity initiatives
C. The reluctance of employees to engage in cybersecurity training
D. The increasing cost of cybersecurity tools

3. What role do cybersecurity professionals play, as described in the passage?

A. Creating new software to combat cyberattacks
B. Developing policies for data privacy laws
C. Defending against cyberattacks and educating employees
D. Handling customer complaints regarding security breaches

---

4. What does the passage suggest about the shortage of cybersecurity professionals?

A. It is not a major issue, as many companies are finding qualified candidates
B. It has made it difficult for organizations to protect their networks effectively
C. It is solely due to a lack of interest in the cybersecurity field
D. It has been solved through increased automation in cybersecurity tools

---

5. How does the passage suggest cybersecurity collaboration can improve defense against cyber threats?

A. By allowing organizations to keep their cybersecurity measures private
B. By reducing the financial burden on individual organizations
C. Through information sharing and international cooperation
D. By focusing solely on private sector efforts

Passage 2: The Future of Renewable Energy

As the global demand for energy continues to rise, the need for cleaner, more sustainable sources of power has become more pressing. Renewable energy, which includes solar, wind, hydroelectric, and geothermal power, has emerged as a viable solution to the environmental and economic challenges posed by fossil fuels. Countries around the world are investing heavily in renewable energy technologies to reduce carbon emissions, combat climate change, and increase energy security.

Solar power, in particular, has experienced significant growth in recent years. Advances in photovoltaic (PV) technology have made solar panels more efficient and affordable, allowing them to be installed in homes, businesses, and utility-scale solar farms. Additionally, large-scale solar projects in regions with abundant sunlight, such as the Middle East and Southwest United States, are now capable of producing vast amounts of energy. Similarly, wind power has also seen considerable expansion, with offshore wind farms becoming increasingly common along coastlines, generating electricity without taking up valuable land space.

Hydroelectric power, which harnesses the energy of flowing water, has been a cornerstone of renewable energy for decades. However, its growth potential is limited due to environmental concerns and the need for large-scale infrastructure projects. The environmental impact of building dams and diverting water has raised questions about their sustainability, especially in sensitive ecosystems. Despite this, hydroelectric power remains an important part of the renewable energy mix in many countries, particularly in regions with abundant rivers and water resources.

Geothermal energy, which taps into the Earth's internal heat, is another promising renewable source. While geothermal power plants are still relatively few in number, they have the potential to provide continuous, baseload power that is not dependent on weather conditions or time of day, unlike solar and wind power. However, the development of geothermal energy is limited by geographic factors, as it requires specific geological conditions that are only found in certain regions of the world.

Despite the progress made in renewable energy, there are still challenges to overcome. One of the major obstacles is energy storage. Since renewable sources like solar and wind are intermittent, meaning they don't produce energy consistently, it is crucial to develop reliable and cost-effective energy storage systems. Batteries and other storage technologies, such as pumped hydro storage, are key to ensuring that renewable energy can be stored and used when demand exceeds supply.

In conclusion, renewable energy has made significant strides in recent years, and it holds the key to a more sustainable energy future. However, for it to fully replace fossil fuels, continued investment in research, infrastructure, and storage technologies is essential. The transition to renewable energy will not only help reduce environmental harm but also create new economic opportunities, generate jobs, and contribute to a more resilient global energy system.

---

6. According to the passage, what is one of the main reasons renewable energy is gaining importance?

A. To reduce carbon emissions and combat climate change
B. To reduce the financial costs of energy production
C. To improve the efficiency of fossil fuel power plants
D. To provide unlimited energy at a low cost

7. What challenge does the passage mention regarding the expansion of hydroelectric power?

A. The high cost of building hydroelectric plants
B. The limited number of suitable locations for hydroelectric plants
C. The intermittent nature of energy production
D. The impact on wildlife and ecosystems

---

8. How has solar power improved in recent years, according to the passage?

A. By decreasing the cost of installation
B. By becoming more efficient and affordable
C. By becoming less dependent on weather conditions
D. By producing power at night

---

9. Why is geothermal energy not as widely used as other renewable sources, according to the passage?

A. It is too expensive to develop
B. It requires specific geological conditions
C. It is not reliable as a power source
D. It has a limited environmental impact

---

10. According to the passage, what is a major obstacle to the widespread use of renewable energy?

A. The high environmental cost of renewable energy
B. The intermittency of sources like solar and wind
C. The lack of public support for renewable energy initiatives
D. The difficulty of maintaining renewable energy plants

Passage 3: The Evolution of Artificial Intelligence in Healthcare

In recent years, artificial intelligence (AI) has made significant strides in revolutionizing the healthcare industry. Initially, AI was viewed as a tool for automating routine tasks, but its potential has expanded far beyond that. Today, AI is not only helping doctors and medical professionals with diagnostics and treatment decisions but is also enhancing patient care, improving efficiency, and reducing costs across the healthcare system.

One of the key areas where AI has had the greatest impact is in medical imaging. AI-powered systems can now analyze medical images with incredible precision, sometimes outperforming human radiologists in detecting certain conditions, such as tumors, fractures, and other abnormalities. Machine learning algorithms, which allow AI systems to improve over time, have been trained on millions of medical images, enabling them to spot patterns and anomalies that may be missed by the human eye. For example, AI has shown great promise in the early detection of cancers, where timely intervention is crucial for successful treatment.

In addition to diagnostics, AI is also playing an increasingly important role in personalized medicine. By analyzing vast amounts of patient data, including genetic information, lifestyle factors, and medical history, AI algorithms can help tailor treatments to the individual's unique needs. This allows healthcare providers to offer more effective, customized care that is more likely to result in positive outcomes. For instance, AI is used to predict how a patient will respond to a specific drug based on their genetic profile, reducing the trial-and-error approach that has traditionally been used in prescribing medication.

Another area where AI is making a major difference is in drug discovery. Developing new medications can take years, even decades, and requires extensive testing and research. AI systems can analyze vast datasets of chemical compounds, biological information, and clinical trial data much faster than humans, identifying promising drug candidates and speeding up the development process. For example, in the fight against COVID-19, AI algorithms were employed to analyze existing drugs that might be repurposed for the virus, significantly reducing the time it took to find potential treatments.

Despite its many successes, the integration of AI into healthcare is not without challenges. One major hurdle is the issue of data privacy and security. AI systems rely on vast amounts of patient data to function effectively, and this raises concerns about the security of sensitive medical information. Ensuring that AI systems comply with privacy regulations, such as the Health Insurance Portability and Accountability Act (HIPAA), is crucial for gaining public trust and ensuring that AI can be safely used in healthcare settings.

Another challenge is the need for greater transparency in AI decision-making processes. While AI systems can produce highly accurate results, understanding how these systems arrive at their conclusions is often a "black box" for many users.

Healthcare providers and patients need to have confidence in the recommendations made by AI systems, and this requires clear, interpretable reasoning behind AI-generated decisions. Efforts are underway to make AI more transparent and explainable, which will be key to its continued adoption in healthcare.

Looking ahead, the future of AI in healthcare holds enormous potential. As technology continues to evolve, AI is expected to become an even more integral part of healthcare delivery. From improving diagnostics and personalized treatments to accelerating drug development and reducing administrative burdens, AI's impact on healthcare is only beginning to be fully realized.

However, addressing issues such as data security, ethical considerations, and ensuring the proper integration of AI into healthcare systems will be essential to ensure that AI's benefits are maximized while minimizing potential risks.

---

11. According to the passage, what is one of the major impacts AI has had on healthcare?

A. Reducing the cost of healthcare facilities
B. Increasing the number of patients treated by doctors
C. Revolutionizing medical imaging and diagnostics
D. Making medical professionals obsolete

---

12. How has AI contributed to personalized medicine, as described in the passage?

A. By automating surgeries to reduce human error
B. By helping to tailor treatments based on individual patient data
C. By replacing human doctors in treatment planning
D. By reducing the need for patient consultations

---

13. What role did AI play in the response to the COVID-19 pandemic, according to the passage?

A. It was used to create vaccines from scratch
B. It analyzed drugs that might be repurposed for COVID-19
C. It provided mental health support to patients
D. It helped develop new diagnostic tools for COVID-19

14. What challenge regarding AI in healthcare is mentioned in the passage?

A. The need for AI to replace human healthcare workers
B. Data privacy and security concerns
C. The lack of technological advancements in AI
D. The high cost of AI systems for healthcare providers

---

15. What is one of the efforts underway to improve AI in healthcare, according to the passage?

A. Reducing the use of AI in medical decision-making
B. Making AI more transparent and explainable
C. Limiting AI to research and development only
D. Using AI to replace traditional medical procedures

Passage 4: The Importance of PELT B for Law Enforcement Careers

The **PELT B (Police Entry-Level Test Battery)** is an essential assessment used by law enforcement agencies across the United States to evaluate candidates seeking to enter the police force. The test is designed to assess the basic reading and writing skills necessary for law enforcement officers to perform their duties effectively. While police officers undergo extensive training once hired, the PELT B serves as an important indicator of a candidate's ability to succeed in a highly demanding profession that requires quick thinking, clear communication, and the ability to process information under pressure.

The PELT B consists of four key sections: **Spelling, Vocabulary, Clarity,** and **Reading Comprehension**. Each section is tailored to assess a different aspect of cognitive and language proficiency, all of which are critical for the day-to-day responsibilities of a law enforcement officer. The Spelling section tests the candidate's ability to accurately spell words, which is important for completing reports and writing citations. The Vocabulary section evaluates a candidate's knowledge of words commonly used in law enforcement contexts. The Clarity section assesses the candidate's ability to understand and structure clear, concise sentences. Finally, the Reading Comprehension section measures the candidate's ability to read and understand various types of written material, such as incident reports, law manuals, and legal documents.

For law enforcement officers, communication skills are of utmost importance. Officers must be able to write clear and accurate reports, communicate effectively with the public, and understand legal documents that may be pivotal to their work. The PELT B ensures that candidates possess the foundational skills necessary for these tasks. While the test may seem basic, it provides a solid foundation for the complex tasks that officers will encounter in the field. It also serves as a way for law enforcement agencies to ensure that only candidates with the necessary skills and attention to detail are selected for the job.

In addition to testing a candidate's proficiency in reading and writing, the PELT B also plays a role in ensuring fairness and consistency in the hiring process. By administering a standardized test, agencies can assess candidates in a uniform manner, ensuring that all applicants are held to the same criteria. This helps to prevent bias and favoritism in the selection process and ensures that the most qualified candidates are chosen to serve their communities.

One of the most important aspects of the PELT B is its ability to help identify candidates who may struggle with the basic reading and writing tasks required by the job. While the test is not designed to measure intelligence or job performance directly, it acts as an early indicator of a candidate's potential challenges. Candidates who do not pass the PELT B may require additional language or communication training before they can be considered for the role. This early identification of skill gaps is vital in helping law enforcement agencies address deficiencies before they become more significant problems later in an officer's career.

For those who pass the PELT B, the next steps in the hiring process typically include a physical fitness test, a background check, and psychological evaluation. These subsequent assessments are designed to ensure that candidates are physically fit, morally sound, and psychologically capable of handling the stresses of law enforcement work. Together, the PELT B and these additional tests create a comprehensive evaluation process that seeks to select the most qualified individuals for one of the most challenging and important careers in public service.

The growing importance of the PELT B reflects broader trends in law enforcement hiring practices, which have increasingly prioritized academic and cognitive skills. As the profession evolves, law enforcement agencies are placing more emphasis on candidates who can demonstrate strong communication skills, problem-solving abilities, and the capacity to understand and process information quickly and accurately. The PELT B is an essential tool in this process, ensuring that officers are equipped with the foundational skills needed to succeed in their demanding roles.

As we look to the future, it is clear that law enforcement agencies will continue to place a premium on the quality of their recruits. The PELT B, in its various forms, will remain an integral part of the hiring process, helping to ensure that only the best candidates are selected to serve and protect the public.

16. What is the main purpose of the PELT B exam?

A. To assess a candidate's fitness level for law enforcement
B. To evaluate a candidate's basic reading and writing skills
C. To test a candidate's physical strength and endurance
D. To assess a candidate's knowledge of criminal law

---

17. How does the PELT B contribute to fairness in the hiring process?

A. It ensures all candidates are evaluated based on the same set of criteria
B. It eliminates the need for interviews and background checks
C. It determines the candidates' criminal history
D. It offers bonuses for high test scores

---

18. What aspect of law enforcement work does the PELT B primarily assess?

A. A candidate's ability to arrest suspects
B. A candidate's proficiency in reading and writing
C. A candidate's knowledge of law enforcement procedures
D. A candidate's physical fitness

---

19. How does the PELT B help identify potential challenges for law enforcement candidates?

A. By measuring their physical endurance
B. By identifying gaps in language and communication skills
C. By assessing their knowledge of criminal law
D. By determining their leadership capabilities

---

20. According to the passage, what is one of the benefits of the PELT B exam for law enforcement agencies?

A. It guarantees that all candidates will be hired
B. It ensures that candidates can perform their jobs effectively from day one
C. It identifies weaknesses in candidates' cognitive abilities early in the hiring process
D. It eliminates the need for further training

Section 4: Clarity (20 Questions)

Time Limit: 20 minutes

Instructions:

- This section evaluates your ability to identify clear and concise sentences in law enforcement communication.
- You will be given two similar sentences, and you must choose the one that is written more clearly.
- **Tip**: Pay attention to sentence structure. Avoiding excessive use of passive voice and maintaining logical sentence flow will help you recognize the clearer sentence.
- **Goal**: To assess your ability to write and understand clear communication, an essential skill for law enforcement officers who must often write reports and communicate with others under pressure.

Questions:

Question 1

A. The officer's response was timely and he handled the situation calmly.
B. The officer's response was timely, and he handled the situation calmly.

Question 2

A. The suspect was arrested after he was caught fleeing the scene of the crime.
B. The suspect, after being caught fleeing the scene of the crime, was arrested.

Question 3

A. The team had prepared thoroughly and was ready for the operation.
B. The team had prepared thoroughly, and ready for the operation.

Question 4

A. Upon arriving at the scene, the officers quickly assessed the situation and acted.
B. The officers quickly assessed the situation and upon arriving at the scene, acted.

Question 5

A. While responding to the call, the officer noticed a suspicious vehicle parked in the lot.
B. The officer noticed a suspicious vehicle parked in the lot, while responding to the call.

Question 6

A. He was forced to make a difficult decision but acted decisively.
B. He acted decisively, despite the difficult decision he was forced to make.

Question 7

A. The officer explained for the new recruits, the rules clearly and precisely.
B. The officer explained the rules clearly and precisely for the new recruits.

Question 8

A. The suspect's actions were suspicious, causing the officer to intervene immediately.
B. The suspect's suspicious actions, causing the officer to intervene immediately, were alarming.

Question 9

A. After realizing the situation was escalating, the officer requested backup.
B. The officer requested backup after he realized the situation was escalating.

Question 10

A. The suspect fled the scene as the officers approached the area.
B. As the officers approached the area, the suspect fled the scene.

Question 11

A. The investigation revealed that the suspect had a history of violent behavior.
B. The investigation had revealed that the suspect had a violent history of behavior.

Question 12

A. The officer arrested the suspect after receiving a call from a witness.
B. After receiving a call from a witness, the officer arrested the suspect.

Question 13

A. The patrol officer was able to immediately assess the situation and make an informed decision.
B. Immediately assessing the situation, the patrol officer was able to make a decision that was informed.

Question 14

A. The police chief held a press conference to discuss the recent crime wave in the city.
B. To discuss the recent crime wave in the city, the police chief held a press conference.

Question 15

A. The sergeant had reviewed the case files thoroughly, which enabled him to solve the case efficiently.
B. The sergeant solved the case efficiently, after having thoroughly reviewed the case files.

Question 16

A. The detective was able to solve the crime, despite the challenges, piecing together the clues.
B. Despite the challenges, the detective was able to piece together the clues and solve the crime.

Question 17

A. The police department has implemented new strategies to improve community engagement and safety.
B. New strategies to improve community engagement and safety have been implemented by the police department.

Question 18

A. After investigating the crime scene, the officers collected evidence that helped solve the case.
B. The officers collected evidence after investigating the crime scene, which helped solve the case.

Question 19

A. The detective has been working tirelessly on the case, ensuring that no details are overlooked.
B. Ensuring that no details are overlooked, the detective has been working tirelessly on the case.

Question 20

A. After receiving the report, the officer immediately began his investigation into the incident.
B. The officer immediately began his investigation into the incident, after receiving the report.

Practice Test 1: Answer Key.

Section 1: Spelling.

Question Number	Correct Option
1	B
2	B
3	B
4	B
5	C
6	A
7	A
8	B
9	C
10	B
11	A
12	A
13	A
14	A
15	B
16	C
17	A
18	A
19	B
20	A

Section 2: Vocabulary.

Question Number	Correct Option
1	B
2	B
3	C
4	A
5	D
6	C
7	C
8	B
9	B
10	B
11	B
12	D
13	A
14	B
15	B
16	B
17	C
18	C
19	A
20	A

Section 3: Reading Comprehension.

Question Number	Correct Option
1	C
2	A
3	C
4	B
5	C
6	A
7	D
8	B
9	B
10	B
11	C
12	B
13	B
14	B
15	B
16	B
17	A
18	B
19	B
20	C

Section 4: Clarity.

Question Number	Correct Option
1	B
2	A
3	A
4	A
5	A
6	A
7	B
8	A
9	B
10	B
11	A
12	B
13	A
14	A
15	A
16	B
17	A
18	A
19	A
20	A

Practice Test 1: Answer And Explanation.

Section 1: Spelling.

1. **Answer**: B. confirm
   Explanation: "Confirm" is the correct spelling, meaning to verify or establish the truth. The other options are misspellings of the word.
2. **Answer**: B. print
   Explanation: "Print" is the correct word, referring to a mark made by pressing something onto a surface. The other options are incorrect spellings.
3. **Answer**: B. recount
   Explanation: "Recount" is the correct verb meaning to tell a story or account of something. The other options are incorrect variations of the word.
4. **Answer**: B. inadmissible
   Explanation: "Inadmissible" means not accepted or allowed, especially in a legal context. The other options are misspellings.
5. **Answer**: C. determine
   Explanation: "Determine" is the correct verb meaning to establish or find out. The other options are misspellings of the word.
6. **Answer**: A. determine
   Explanation: "Determine" is the correct form of the verb, meaning to decide or establish something after analysis. The other options are incorrect spellings.
7. **Answer**: A. key
   Explanation: "Key" is the correct word meaning something crucial or of great importance. The other options are misspelled versions of the word.
8. **Answer**: B. contradictory
   Explanation: "Contradictory" is the correct spelling, meaning opposing or inconsistent with something. The other options are misspellings.
9. **Answer**: C. complete
   Explanation: "Complete" is the correct spelling, meaning to finish or add the necessary information. The other options are incorrect spellings.
10. **Answer**: B. absence
    Explanation: "Absence" is the correct word, meaning the state of being absent or not present. The other options are incorrect spellings.
11. **Answer**: A. verifying
    Explanation: "Verifying" is the correct spelling, meaning to confirm or establish the truth. The other options are misspellings of the word.

12. **Answer**: A. examined
    Explanation: "Examined" is the correct past tense of "examine," meaning to inspect or look at closely. The other options are incorrect spellings.
13. **Answer**: A. include
    Explanation: "Include" is the correct spelling, meaning to incorporate something as part of a whole. The other options are incorrect variations of the word.
14. **Answer**: A. clear
    Explanation: "Clear" is the correct spelling, meaning easy to understand or free of ambiguity. The other options are incorrect spellings.
15. **Answer**: B. detrimental
    Explanation: "Detrimental" is the correct spelling, meaning harmful or damaging. The other options are misspelled versions of the word.
16. **Answer**: C. verify
    Explanation: "Verify" is the correct word, meaning to confirm the truth or validity of something. The other options are misspellings of the word.
17. **Answer**: A. confirm
    Explanation: "Confirm" is the correct spelling, meaning to verify or validate. The other options are incorrect variations of the word.
18. **Answer**: A. account
    Explanation: "Account" is the correct spelling, meaning a detailed report of something. The other options are misspellings of the word.
19. **Answer**: B. assessing
    Explanation: "Assessing" is the correct spelling, meaning to evaluate or analyze. The other options are incorrect variations of the word.
20. **Answer**: A. confirm
    Explanation: "Confirm" is the correct spelling, meaning to verify or validate. The other options are misspellings.

Section 2: Vocabulary.

1. **Answer**: B. Clever
   Explanation: "Astute" means having the ability to notice and understand things clearly, especially in a practical or clever way. "Clever" is the closest synonym, meaning quick to learn and understand. Option A, "quick," refers to speed, not mental sharpness. Option C, "timid," means lacking confidence, and option D, "weak," refers to a lack of strength, neither of which match "astute."
2. **Answer**: B. Resistant
   Explanation: "Defiant" means showing resistance or opposition to authority or control. "Resistant" is the best synonym, meaning opposing or refusing something. Option A,

"submissive," means yielding or obedient, which is the opposite of "defiant." Option C, "polite," and option D, "supportive," both indicate cooperation or kindness, which do not match the context of defiance.

3. **Answer**: C. Systematic
   Explanation: "Methodical" means doing things in an organized, orderly, and planned way. "Systematic" is the best synonym, meaning following a method or plan. Option A, "random," refers to something happening without a specific pattern. Option B, "hasty," means done too quickly without careful planning. Option D, "reckless," means doing something carelessly or without thinking of the consequences.

4. **Answer**: A. Honest
   Explanation: "Candid" means being open, truthful, and straightforward, especially about sensitive matters. "Honest" is the best synonym, meaning truthful and sincere. Option B, "shady," refers to something suspicious or dishonest. Option C, "biased," means showing unfair preference, and option D, "misleading," refers to giving false information, both of which contradict "candid."

5. **Answer**: D. Disprove
   Explanation: "Dispel" means to drive away or eliminate something, especially a misconception or rumor. "Disprove" is the closest synonym, meaning to prove something false. Option A, "confirm," means to establish the truth of something, which is the opposite of "dispel." Option B, "ignore," means to deliberately avoid, and option C, "clarify," means to make something clear but doesn't fully match the meaning of "dispel."

6. **Answer**: C. Persuasive
   Explanation: "Convincing" means having the power to persuade or make someone believe something. "Persuasive" is the best synonym, meaning having the ability to convince. Option A, "weak," means lacking strength, which is opposite in meaning. Option B, "uncertain," refers to something doubtful or unsure. Option D, "unbelievable," means something difficult to believe, which is the opposite of "convincing."

7. **Answer**: C. Serious
   Explanation: "Stern" means firm or strict in manner, often showing seriousness. "Serious" is the closest synonym, meaning showing concern or gravity. Option A, "soft," refers to something gentle or not harsh. Option B, "angry," implies strong displeasure, which does not match "stern" as much as "serious" does. Option D, "friendly," implies kindness, which is the opposite of "stern."

8. **Answer**: B. Insightful
   Explanation: "Perceptive" means having or showing an understanding of things that are not immediately obvious, often involving insight. "Insightful" is the best synonym, meaning showing deep understanding. Option A, "insensitive," means not showing empathy or understanding. Option C, "ignorant," means lacking knowledge, and option D, "misleading," means providing false or incorrect information, all of which are the opposite of "perceptive."

9. **Answer**: B. Watchful
   Explanation: "Vigilant" means being alert and watchful, especially to detect potential dangers or problems. "Watchful" is the best synonym, meaning being observant and careful. Option A, "inattentive," means not paying attention, the opposite of "vigilant." Option C, "careless," means lacking attention or concern. Option D, "hasty," refers to acting quickly without careful thought, which doesn't match the meaning of "vigilant."

10. **Answer**: B. Curious
    Explanation: "Inquisitive" means eager to learn or ask questions, often out of curiosity. "Curious" is the best synonym, meaning eager to know or learn something. Option A, "indifferent," means having no particular interest or concern, which is the opposite of "inquisitive." Option C, "uninterested," also means lacking interest. Option D, "hostile," refers to being unfriendly or aggressive, which doesn't align with "inquisitive."

11. **Answer**: B. Sharp
    Explanation: "Keen" means having a sharp, perceptive mind, often used to describe someone who is quick to understand or notice things. "Sharp" is the best synonym, as it also implies keen awareness and mental alertness. Option A, "dull," means lacking sharpness or interest, which is the opposite of "keen." Option C, "slow," refers to a lack of speed or mental agility, which contrasts with the idea of a "keen" intellect. Option D, "weak," refers to something lacking strength, which doesn't align with the meaning of "keen."

12. **Answer**: D. Delicate
    Explanation: "Subtle" refers to something delicate, slight, or not immediately obvious, often requiring careful attention. "Delicate" is the best synonym here, as it captures the nuanced and understated nature of the observation. Option A, "obvious," refers to something easy to detect or see, which is the opposite of "subtle." Option B, "indirect," means not straightforward, but doesn't capture the fine or slight quality of a "subtle" observation. Option C, "noticeable," means easy to see or detect, which again contrasts with "subtle."

13. **Answer**: A. Steady
    Explanation: "Unwavering" means firm, resolute, or steady, especially in the face of challenges. "Steady" is the best synonym, implying consistency and reliability. Option B, "hesitant," refers to being unsure or reluctant, which is opposite of the commitment shown in the sentence. Option C, "uncertain," also conveys doubt, which contradicts the concept of "unwavering." Option D, "weak," implies a lack of strength or resolve, which is not consistent with the idea of being "unwavering."

14. **Answer**: B. Systematic
    Explanation: "Methodical" means done according to a fixed or systematic method, implying careful planning and organization. "Systematic" is the closest synonym, meaning organized and methodical. Option A, "disorganized," means lacking order or structure, which directly contrasts with "methodical." Option C, "haphazard," means

lacking a plan or organization, and Option D, "impulsive," refers to actions done without careful thought or planning, which does not match the meaning of "methodical."

15. **Answer**: B. Sympathetic

    Explanation: "Compassionate" refers to showing care and understanding, especially for those suffering or in need. "Sympathetic" is the best synonym, as it refers to showing concern or empathy for others' emotions or difficulties. Option A, "indifferent," means showing no interest or care, which is the opposite of "compassionate." Option C, "hostile," means showing anger or opposition, which contradicts the caring nature of "compassionate." Option D, "apathetic," means showing a lack of emotion or interest, again the opposite of "compassionate."

16. **Answer**: B. Erratic

    Explanation: "Erratic" refers to behavior that is unpredictable or inconsistent, often causing concern or confusion. "Erratic" is the best synonym, as it suggests unpredictability. Option A, "predictable," means behavior that is expected or consistent, which is the opposite of "erratic." Option C, "calm," refers to a state of tranquility, and Option D, "subdued," means quiet or restrained, which doesn't fit the context of alarm caused by unexpected behavior.

17. **Answer**: C. Disprove

    Explanation: "Dispel" means to make something disappear, especially a myth, misconception, or false belief. "Disprove" is the best synonym, meaning to show that something is false. Option A, "confirm," means to verify the truth, which is opposite to dispelling something. Option B, "reject," means to dismiss or refuse something, but doesn't capture the idea of making something disappear. Option D, "ignore," means to overlook, which doesn't relate to disproving or dispelling a myth.

18. **Answer**: C. Express

    Explanation: "Articulate" means to express clearly and effectively, especially when explaining something important. "Express" is the best synonym, as it means to communicate thoughts or feelings clearly. Option A, "confuse," means to make something unclear or hard to understand, the opposite of articulate. Option B, "simplify," refers to making something easier to understand, but doesn't necessarily imply clear expression. Option D, "mumble," means to speak unclearly or quietly, which is the opposite of "articulate."

19. **Answer**: A. Sharp

    Explanation: "Astute" means having or showing sharpness in understanding, often related to intelligence and insight. "Sharp" is the best synonym, as it also refers to being mentally alert and perceptive. Option B, "blunt," means direct and straightforward, but not insightful or sharp. Option C, "careless," refers to a lack of attention or thought, which is the opposite of "astute." Option D, "obvious," refers to something easy to see or understand, which doesn't match the depth of "astute."

20. **Answer**: A. Relentlessly
    Explanation: "Tirelessly" means working without rest, often in a focused or persistent way. "Relentlessly" is the best synonym, as it means continuing without stopping or giving up. Option B, "lazily," means doing something without energy or effort, which is the opposite of "tirelessly." Option C, "slowly," refers to a lack of speed, and Option D, "haphazardly," means in a careless or disorganized manner, neither of which fit the context of working "tirelessly."

Section 3: Reading Comprehension.

1. **Answer**: C. The increasing frequency and sophistication of cyberattacks
   Explanation: The passage emphasizes the **growing frequency and sophistication of cyberattacks** as the primary concern. While other issues, such as financial costs and the shortage of skilled professionals, are mentioned, the main focus is on the escalation of cyber threats. Option A addresses financial costs, but it is not the passage's main concern. Option B discusses AI, but it is part of the solution, not the primary issue. Option D discusses the shortage of professionals, but it is not the central theme.
2. **Answer**: A. The rapid development of new software and hardware
   Explanation: The passage highlights that the **rapid development of new software and hardware** creates more potential vulnerabilities, which is one of the main challenges faced by organizations. Option B, the lack of public support, is not mentioned. Option C, reluctance of employees, is not highlighted as a key challenge. Option D, increasing costs, is not the focus of the passage either.
3. **Answer**: C. Defending against cyberattacks and educating employees
   Explanation: The passage clearly states that **cybersecurity professionals are tasked with defending against attacks and educating employees** about safe online practices. Option A is not mentioned; professionals are not creating new software, but rather using existing tools. Option B focuses on policy development, which is not emphasized. Option D is irrelevant to the passage's focus on defense and education.
4. **Answer**: B. It has made it difficult for organizations to protect their networks effectively
   Explanation: The passage highlights the **shortage of qualified cybersecurity professionals** as a significant challenge, making it difficult for organizations to keep up with the growing demand for skilled workers. Option A is incorrect as the passage explicitly mentions the shortage as an issue. Option C incorrectly suggests that the shortage is due to lack of interest, which is not discussed. Option D is not mentioned in the passage; automation is not offered as a solution to the shortage.
5. **Answer**: C. Through information sharing and international cooperation
   Explanation: The passage stresses that **collaboration between private and public entities, including information sharing and international cooperation**, is key to

167

improving cybersecurity defenses. Option A contradicts the idea of collaboration. Option B focuses on financial burden, which is not the main point of the passage. Option D excludes public sector cooperation, which is crucial for effective defense as mentioned in the text.

6. **Answer**: A. To reduce carbon emissions and combat climate change
   Explanation: The passage clearly mentions that one of the primary reasons for the shift toward renewable energy is to **reduce carbon emissions** and **combat climate change**. Option B is not mentioned as the main driving force. Option C is not correct because the passage focuses on the shift from fossil fuels, not improving their efficiency. Option D is not accurate, as renewable energy, while sustainable, does not guarantee unlimited energy at a low cost.

7. **Answer**: D. The impact on wildlife and ecosystems
   Explanation: The passage discusses the **environmental impact** of hydroelectric power, particularly in relation to building dams and diverting water, which can affect ecosystems. Option A is not mentioned; the passage does not focus on the cost. Option B is incorrect because the passage does not suggest a limited number of locations but highlights environmental concerns. Option C addresses the issue of intermittency, which applies more to solar and wind power, not hydroelectric.

8. **Answer**: B. By becoming more efficient and affordable
   Explanation: The passage notes that **solar power** has improved through advances in **photovoltaic (PV) technology**, making solar panels more **efficient and affordable**. Option A is a valid aspect but doesn't fully capture the advancement in efficiency. Option C is incorrect because solar power is still dependent on sunlight. Option D is not mentioned, as solar power doesn't produce power at night without storage.

9. **Answer**: B. It requires specific geological conditions
   Explanation: The passage mentions that **geothermal energy** is limited by **geographic factors**, specifically that it requires **specific geological conditions**. Option A is not correct as the passage doesn't focus on cost as the primary limitation. Option C is incorrect because geothermal energy is continuous and reliable. Option D is inaccurate as the passage does not claim geothermal energy has limited environmental impact compared to other forms.

10. **Answer**: B. The intermittency of sources like solar and wind
    Explanation: The passage highlights the **intermittent nature** of renewable energy sources like **solar and wind**, meaning they don't produce energy consistently. This is the key challenge mentioned. Option A is incorrect as the passage focuses on the environmental benefits of renewable energy. Option C is not discussed in the context of public support. Option D, the difficulty of maintaining plants, is not the main issue addressed in the passage.

11. **Answer**: C. Revolutionizing medical imaging and diagnostics
    Explanation: The passage clearly states that AI has had a **great impact on medical**

168

imaging, improving the accuracy and efficiency of diagnostics, sometimes even outperforming human radiologists. Option A is not mentioned; the passage doesn't focus on the cost reduction of healthcare facilities. Option B, increasing the number of patients treated, is not mentioned either. Option D is incorrect because the passage highlights how AI assists medical professionals rather than replacing them.

12. **Answer**: B. By helping to tailor treatments based on individual patient data
    Explanation: The passage describes how AI **analyzes patient data**, including genetic information and medical history, to help healthcare providers offer more personalized, effective treatments. Option A, automating surgeries, is not discussed in the passage. Option C, replacing human doctors, is incorrect; the passage emphasizes that AI assists doctors, not replaces them. Option D, reducing consultations, is not mentioned as a benefit of AI.

13. **Answer**: B. It analyzed drugs that might be repurposed for COVID-19
    Explanation: The passage states that AI was used to **analyze existing drugs** to determine which ones might be repurposed for treating COVID-19, helping to speed up the response. Option A is incorrect as the passage does not mention AI creating vaccines. Option C, mental health support, is not mentioned. Option D refers to diagnostics, but the focus in the passage is on drug discovery.

14. **Answer**: B. Data privacy and security concerns
    Explanation: The passage discusses **data privacy and security** as a major challenge when integrating AI into healthcare systems, as AI systems rely on sensitive patient data. Option A is incorrect because the passage does not suggest that AI should replace healthcare workers. Option C, the lack of technological advancements, is also not mentioned; the passage highlights advancements in AI. Option D mentions the cost of AI, but the main concern addressed is privacy and security.

15. **Answer**: B. Making AI more transparent and explainable
    Explanation: The passage highlights the need for **increased transparency** in AI decision-making so that healthcare providers and patients can understand how AI systems reach their conclusions. Option A is incorrect as the passage does not suggest reducing AI's role in medical decision-making. Option C, limiting AI to research, is not mentioned in the passage. Option D, using AI to replace traditional procedures, is not discussed as a goal of AI integration in healthcare.

16. **Answer**: B. To evaluate a candidate's basic reading and writing skills
    Explanation: The passage clearly states that the **PELT B** is designed to assess **basic reading and writing skills**, which are essential for performing law enforcement duties such as report writing and communication. Option A is incorrect because physical fitness is assessed separately. Option C is not relevant, as the PELT B does not focus on physical strength. Option D is also incorrect because the test is focused on language proficiency, not specific legal knowledge.

17. **Answer**: A. It ensures all candidates are evaluated based on the same set of criteria
    Explanation: The passage mentions that the PELT B helps **ensure fairness and consistency** by using a **standardized test** that evaluates all candidates according to the same criteria. Option B is incorrect because the test does not eliminate interviews or background checks. Option C is incorrect because criminal history is not evaluated by the PELT B. Option D is incorrect as the test does not involve bonuses for scores.
18. **Answer**: B. A candidate's proficiency in reading and writing
    Explanation: The passage explains that the PELT B is focused on assessing a candidate's **proficiency in reading and writing**, as these skills are critical for tasks like report writing and communication. Option A is not correct because arresting suspects is not related to the PELT B. Option C is incorrect, as knowledge of procedures is not assessed by this exam. Option D is irrelevant because physical fitness is assessed separately.
19. **Answer**: B. By identifying gaps in language and communication skills
    Explanation: The passage explains that the PELT B helps identify candidates who may struggle with basic **language and communication skills**, allowing agencies to address these deficiencies early. Option A is incorrect because physical endurance is tested separately. Option C is not accurate since the PELT B does not assess criminal law knowledge. Option D is irrelevant as the focus is on language skills, not leadership.
20. **Answer**: C. It identifies weaknesses in candidates' cognitive abilities early in the hiring process
    Explanation: The passage explains that the PELT B is useful for **identifying weaknesses** in a candidate's **cognitive abilities** (such as reading and writing skills) early, so these can be addressed before they become more significant issues. Option A is incorrect because the PELT B is just part of the hiring process and does not guarantee hiring. Option B is not correct because the PELT B assesses foundational skills but does not ensure candidates can perform all job functions from day one. Option D is incorrect, as further training is still required after passing the PELT B.

Section 4: Clarity.

1. **Answer**: B
   Explanation: Sentence **B** is more clearly written because it correctly uses the comma after "timely" to separate two independent clauses. In sentence **A**, the lack of a comma before "and" creates a **comma splice**, which is a grammatical error.
2. **Answer**: A
   Explanation: Sentence **A** is more straightforward and clear. It places the **action of arresting** at the end, making the sentence easier to follow. Sentence **B** is slightly more cumbersome due to the awkward placement of the phrase "after being caught fleeing," which causes a slight disruption in the sentence flow.

3. **Answer**: A

   Explanation: Sentence **A** is grammatically correct and complete, as it properly links two actions with "and" and maintains parallel structure ("had prepared" and "was ready"). In **B**, the phrase "and ready for the operation" is incomplete, as it lacks a verb to properly connect to the first clause.

4. **Answer**: A

   Explanation: Sentence **A** is more clearly written as it follows a logical order: "Upon arriving" starts the sentence and is followed by the officers' actions. In **B**, the phrase "upon arriving at the scene" interrupts the flow and makes the sentence less direct.

5. **Answer**: A

   Explanation: Sentence **A** is clearer because it logically presents the officer's actions in sequence: noticing the vehicle while responding to the call. Sentence **B** is grammatically correct, but the phrase "while responding to the call" at the end feels like an afterthought, which weakens the flow.

6. **Answer**: A

   Explanation: Sentence **A** is more direct and places the **action** at the forefront, which makes the sentence more engaging and impactful. Sentence **B** has a slightly weaker structure by delaying the important point ("acted decisively") until later in the sentence.

7. **Answer**: B

   Explanation: Sentence **A** is more clearly written because the adverbs "clearly" and "precisely" directly modify the verb "explained," making the sentence easy to follow. In **B**, the placement of "for the new recruits" interrupts the flow and makes the sentence harder to understand.

8. **Answer**: A

   Explanation: Sentence **A** is more direct and logically structured. It presents the reason for the officer's intervention at the end, which maintains clarity. In **B**, the phrase "causing the officer to intervene immediately" is inserted awkwardly, disrupting the sentence's natural flow.

9. **Answer**: B

   Explanation: Sentence **B** is clearer because it begins by stating the officer's **action** first ("requested backup"), followed by the reason for that action. Sentence **A** uses a less clear structure, delaying the officer's action and making it less immediate.

10. **Answer**: B

    Explanation: Sentence **B** is clearer because it follows the natural chronological order: "As the officers approached," which leads into the subsequent action of the suspect fleeing. Sentence **A** feels slightly disjointed as it starts with the suspect's action before explaining the officers' approach.

11. **Answer**: A

    Explanation: Sentence **A** is clearer because it uses **simple, direct phrasing**. The focus is on the investigation leading to the discovery of the suspect's violent history. Sentence **B** is somewhat awkward because it unnecessarily uses "had revealed" and places "history of behavior" in a convoluted order, which makes the sentence harder to understand.

12. **Answer**: B

    Explanation: Sentence **B** is more fluid because it follows a **logical cause-and-effect order**: the officer receives a call and then makes the arrest. In sentence **A**, the cause and effect are not presented in the most intuitive order, as it leads with the officer's action before providing the cause (the call from the witness).

13. **Answer**: A

    Explanation: Sentence **A** is more straightforward and clearly communicates the **timeliness** and the **action**. Sentence **B** is unnecessarily complex by placing the descriptive phrase "immediately assessing the situation" at the start, which can confuse the reader and disrupt the flow of the sentence.

14. **Answer**: A

    Explanation: Sentence **A** is simpler and more direct, starting with the main action ("held a press conference") and then providing the reason for it. Sentence **B** uses an **awkward construction** where "To discuss the recent crime wave" is placed at the beginning, which makes the sentence less fluid.

15. **Answer**: A

    Explanation: Sentence **A** is clearer because it logically places the cause (thorough review of the case files) before the effect (solving the case efficiently). Sentence **B** is not incorrect, but the phrasing feels a little convoluted with "after having thoroughly reviewed," which makes it sound unnecessarily complicated.

16. **Answer**: B

    Explanation: Sentence **B** is clearer because it presents the challenge first and then highlights the detective's ability to solve the crime. It maintains a smooth flow by focusing on the detective's success despite the challenges. Sentence **A** places "piecing together the clues" in a position that makes the sentence feel more disjointed and unnecessarily complex.

17. **Answer**: A

    Explanation: Sentence **A** is more direct, as it starts with the subject "The police department" and follows with the action "has implemented new strategies." This makes it easier to understand. Sentence **B** is grammatically correct but awkwardly shifts the sentence structure, which reduces clarity.

18. **Answer**: A

    Explanation: Sentence **A** is clearer because it presents the **order of actions** clearly: first, the officers investigate, then they collect evidence, and the evidence helps solve the case. Sentence **B** is not incorrect, but it causes a slight delay in the clarity of the sequence of events.

19. **Answer**: A

    Explanation: Sentence **A** is more clear because the action is presented in the order it happened: the detective has been working tirelessly and is careful to ensure that no details are overlooked. Sentence **B** starts with an introductory phrase "Ensuring that no details are overlooked," which unnecessarily delays the subject and action.

20. **Answer**: A

    Explanation: Sentence **A** is more clear and direct because it states the cause (receiving the report) first, followed by the effect (beginning the investigation). This structure makes it easier for the reader to follow. Sentence **B** delays the cause and places it at the end, which weakens the clarity of the action.

Full-Scale Practice Test 2

Section 1: Spelling (20 Questions)

Time Limit: 15 minutes

Instructions:

- This section tests your ability to accurately spell words that are commonly used in law enforcement scenarios.
- You will be presented with 20 words in the form of multiple-choice questions. For each question, choose the correct spelling of the word.
- **Tip**: Pay close attention to common spelling pitfalls such as double letters, homophones (words that sound the same but are spelled differently), and prefixes/suffixes.
- **Goal**: Accuracy is key. Be sure to focus on details, as a single letter can alter the meaning of a word and its appropriateness in law enforcement communication.

Questions:

1. The officer _____ the suspect for questioning after receiving a _____ complaint from the victim.

A. arrest, distress
B. arrested, distressed
C. arrested, distress
D. arrest, distressed

2. The police officer _____ the door open and found the suspect _____ in the room.

A. forced, hiding
B. force, hiden
C. forced, hid
D. force, hiding

174

3. The detective asked the witness to _____ all the details of the suspect's _____ at the scene.

A. recall, action
B. recale, actions
C. recall, actions
D. recalled, action

---

4. After a thorough search, the officer _____ the suspect's _____ under the mattress.

A. found, gun
B. founded, guns
C. found, guns
D. find, gun

---

5. The police officer _____ to take a statement from the _____ of the burglary.

A. decide, victim
B. deciding, victims
C. decided, victim
D. decides, victim

---

6. The detective carefully _____ all the evidence found at the scene and _____ the suspect's involvement.

A. collected, verify
B. collected, verified
C. collect, verifies
D. collecting, verify

175

7. The officer had to _____ the situation before calling for _____ backup.

A. assess, further
B. assessed, further
C. assessing, further
D. assess, furthur

---

8. The officer's _____ skills were crucial in the successful _____ of the suspect.

A. negotiation, arrest
B. negotiate, arrest
C. negociation, arrested
D. negotiation, arrested

---

9. After a series of violent incidents, the officers were asked to _____ the situation and _____ their approach.

A. evaluate, adjust
B. evaluated, adjusted
C. evaluation, adjusting
D. evaluate, adjusted

---

10. The officer was able to _____ the criminal's _____, leading to the suspect's capture.

A. identify, location
B. identified, location
C. identify, locations
D. identifying, locations

---

11. The officer was called to _____ the situation and _____ the safety of the officers on the scene.

A. assess, ensure
B. assess, insure
C. assessed, insure
D. assessing, ensure

12. The officer's _____ of the crime scene was crucial to uncovering the _____ of the suspect.

A. investigation, evidence
B. investigatin, evidences
C. investigating, evidense
D. investigation, evidences

13. The officer needed to _____ the suspect's alibi, which was proven to be _____ after further investigation.

A. verify, false
B. veriffy, faulse
C. verfiy, fals
D. verify, faulse

14. The detective was able to _____ the suspect's involvement in the crime after obtaining _____ evidence.

A. confirm, vital
B. confurm, vitle
C. confim, vitale
D. confirmed, vitel

15. The officer's _____ behavior during the incident helped to _____ the situation before it escalated.

A. calm, deescalate
B. calmed, deescalated
C. calming, deescalate
D. calm, de-escalate

16. The officers were able to _____ the suspect after receiving a _____ tip from an anonymous informant.

A. apprehend, reliable
B. apprehand, reliable
C. apprehend, reliabe
D. apprehend, relable

---

17. The officer's _____ skills were demonstrated when he successfully _____ the suspect's story.

A. interogation, discreditted
B. interogation, discredite
C. interrogation, discredit
D. interrogation, discredited

---

18. The officer arrived at the scene to find the suspect _____ the scene in an attempt to _____ the investigation.

A. flee, hindering
B. fleed, hinder
C. fleeing, hinder
D. fleeing, hindered

---

19. The officer was able to _____ the suspect's identity through a thorough _____ of his fingerprints.

A. confirming, analysis
B. confirm, analyzation
C. confirmed, analysys
D. confirm, analysis

---

20. The suspect's _____ alibi was disproven after a _____ investigation by the officers.

A. fals, thru
B. faulse, thorugh
C. false, thorough
D. false, through

Section 2: Vocabulary (20 Questions)

Time Limit: 20 minutes

Instructions:

- This section evaluates your understanding of vocabulary used in law enforcement contexts.
- You will be presented with 20 sentences, each containing an undrlined word. Your task is to choose the synonym that best fits the context of the sentence.
- **Tip**: Pay attention to the context of the sentence. Many law enforcement-related words have specific meanings that might differ from their everyday use. Think about how the word is used in context, not just its dictionary definition.
- **Goal**: This section tests your ability to understand and apply law enforcement terminology effectively. Take your time to ensure the synonym you choose fits the tone and meaning of the sentence.

Questions:

1. The officer's **pragmatic** approach to the case helped streamline the investigation and focus on the most critical leads.

A. Theoretical
B. Sensible
C. Unfocused
D. Rigid

2. The detective's **scrupulous** attention to detail ensured that no piece of evidence was overlooked during the investigation.

A. Careless
B. Precise
C. Casual
D. Disorganized

3. The officer faced **intense** scrutiny from the public regarding the controversial arrest.

A. Mild
B. Harsh
C. Temporary
D. Friendly

4. The officer had to **reconcile** the conflicting statements made by the witnesses before proceeding with the case.

A. Resolve
B. Aggravate
C. Challenge
D. Ignore

5. The detective's **indefatigable** efforts were crucial in solving the case that had remained unsolved for years.

A. Exhausting
B. Relentless
C. Hesitant
D. Sporadic

6. The officer's **diplomatic** approach to the situation helped ease the tension between the conflicting parties.

A. Tactful
B. Direct
C. Abrupt
D. Aggressive

7. The detective found the suspect's **equivocal** answers to be suspicious and in need of further investigation.

A. Unclear
B. Honest
C. Direct
D. Concise

---

8. The detective had to **divulge** sensitive information about the case to the prosecutor to proceed with the trial.

A. Conceal
B. Disclose
C. Withhold
D. Evade

---

9. The officer's **unfaltering** commitment to justice was admired by his colleagues.

A. Unyielding
B. Uncertain
C. Irregular
D. Unpredictable

---

10. The detective used his **astute** knowledge of criminal behavior to anticipate the suspect's next move.

A. Sharp
B. Weak
C. Shallow
D. Dull

11. The officer's **resolute** decision to pursue the suspect despite the risks earned him commendations.

A. Uncertain
B. Decisive
C. Reluctant
D. Hesitant

12. The suspect's **inflammatory** remarks during the interrogation escalated the tension in the room.

A. Neutral
B. Provocative
C. Calm
D. Defensive

13. The officer's **prudent** approach to handling the situation helped prevent further escalation.

A. Reckless
B. Wise
C. Hasty
D. Impulsive

14. The detective's **meticulous** examination of the crime scene led to the discovery of crucial evidence.

A. Careless
B. Thorough
C. Hasty
D. Disorganized

15. The officer's **intrepid** behavior in the face of danger earned him recognition from his peers.

A. Timid
B. Fearless
C. Cautious
D. Anxious

16. The officer's **ardent** commitment to justice was evident in his relentless pursuit of the truth.

A. Indifferent
B. Apathetic
C. Passionate
D. Cold

17. The detective's **candid** statements about the case made him highly respected in the department.

A. Honest
B. Reserved
C. Dishonest
D. Evasive

18. The officer was **meticulous** in his report, ensuring every detail was _____.

A. Overlooked
B. Scrutinized
C. Forgotten
D. Ignored

19. The suspect's behavior was considered **aberrant**, as it deviated from the usual criminal patterns in the area.

A. Typical
B. Unusual
C. Repetitive
D. Predictable

20. The officer's **inquisitive** nature led him to uncover hidden facts that were crucial to the investigation.

A. Curious
B. Uninterested
C. Disengaged
D. Hostile

Section 3: Reading Comprehension (20 Questions)

Time Limit: 25 minutes

Instructions:

- In this section, you will read two passages and answer 10 multiple-choice questions for each passage.
- Each passage is designed to assess your ability to comprehend written material related to law enforcement and public service.
- **Tip**: Focus on **key ideas**, **main points**, and **inferences** rather than memorizing every detail. The goal is to assess your ability to extract and understand information quickly and efficiently.
- **Goal**: To test your ability to read and understand complex material, which is a crucial skill for law enforcement officers who regularly work with reports, legal documents, and other written materials.

Questions:

Passage 1: The Impact of Social Media on Modern Society.

Over the past two decades, social media has transformed from a casual networking tool to a dominant force in communication, business, and culture. With billions of users worldwide, platforms like Facebook, Twitter, Instagram, and LinkedIn have reshaped how individuals interact, access information, and build their personal and professional identities. Social media's influence on society is undeniable, and its role continues to evolve as technology and user behaviors change.

One of the most significant impacts of social media is its ability to connect people across geographical boundaries. With a simple click or swipe, users can communicate with others around the world, engage in discussions, and share experiences. This connectivity has allowed individuals to find like-minded communities, regardless of location. In many cases, it has provided a platform for marginalized groups to raise their voices and advocate for social and political change, enabling grassroots movements to gain momentum. Social media has also allowed for the rapid spread of information, making it a tool for both education and awareness on a global scale.

However, while social media has numerous positive attributes, there are also serious concerns about its impact on mental health. Studies have shown that excessive social media use can lead to feelings of loneliness, depression, and anxiety. The constant comparison to others' curated, idealized lives can create unrealistic expectations and lead to self-esteem issues, particularly among young people. Additionally, the pressure to maintain a perfect online persona can cause stress, as individuals strive to meet societal standards of beauty, success, and happiness.

Another major issue is the proliferation of misinformation and fake news on social media platforms. With the ability to quickly share content, both factual and misleading information can spread widely, often with little verification. This has had serious consequences, particularly in the realms of politics and public health. Misinformation about COVID-19, for example, spread rapidly across social media, leading to confusion and a lack of trust in experts and government officials. The spread of false information undermines public confidence and can lead to widespread confusion and division within society.

Despite these concerns, social media remains an essential tool in modern society. Its ability to influence culture, politics, and even the economy cannot be overstated. For businesses, social media is a vital marketing tool, allowing companies to connect directly with consumers and promote their products in ways that were previously unimaginable. It has given rise to new forms of advertising, influencer marketing, and customer engagement, reshaping the landscape of commerce and commerce-related media. Similarly, social media has had a profound effect on politics, with politicians and public figures using these platforms to engage with voters, share their policies, and mobilize supporters.

The role of social media in shaping public opinion and political discourse has also raised questions about its influence on democracy. While it provides a forum for diverse voices and opinions, it has also been criticized for fostering polarization and the spread of extremist views. Algorithms that prioritize sensational or polarizing content can create echo chambers, where individuals are exposed only to information that aligns with their pre-existing beliefs. This can reinforce biases and deepen divisions within society, making it increasingly difficult to find common ground on important issues.

In conclusion, social media is a double-edged sword. It has brought people closer together, provided new opportunities for business and activism, and transformed communication in unprecedented ways. At the same time, it has contributed to mental health challenges, the spread of misinformation, and political polarization. As we continue to navigate the complexities of social media's role in society, it is essential to find a balance between its benefits and its potential harms. Moving forward, it will be crucial to address the ethical concerns surrounding social media platforms and develop strategies to mitigate its negative effects, while harnessing its power for positive change.

1. According to the passage, what is one of the major benefits of social media?

A. It creates unrealistic expectations about lifestyle
B. It allows people to connect and engage globally
C. It undermines public trust in government
D. It encourages a focus on individualism

---

2. What is a significant negative impact of social media discussed in the passage?

A. Social media leads to better business strategies
B. Social media has improved political engagement
C. Social media can contribute to loneliness and mental health issues
D. Social media helps spread accurate health information

---

3. What is one of the issues related to misinformation on social media mentioned in the passage?

A. It can promote healthy lifestyle choices
B. It is easily verified through fact-checking systems
C. It leads to confusion and a lack of trust in experts
D. It encourages social media users to act more responsibly

---

4. How has social media affected business practices, according to the passage?

A. It has reduced the effectiveness of traditional advertising
B. It has made businesses less reliant on customer feedback
C. It has enabled businesses to market their products in new ways
D. It has decreased the number of companies using online platforms

---

5. According to the passage, what is one of the criticisms of social media's role in political discourse?

A. It has encouraged the spread of fake news
B. It has increased political polarization and extremist views
C. It has reduced voter turnout in elections
D. It has made political campaigns less engaging

Passage 2: The Role of Technology in Modern Education.

In the past few decades, technology has dramatically reshaped the landscape of education. Gone are the days when classrooms were limited to chalkboards, textbooks, and static lessons. Today, technology is an integral part of the educational experience, enhancing learning, engagement, and accessibility for students around the world. From interactive digital tools to virtual classrooms, technology is changing how teachers instruct and how students learn, creating new possibilities for personalized education.

One of the most significant advancements in education has been the rise of online learning platforms. These platforms allow students to access courses and materials at any time, from any location, often at their own pace. This flexibility has made education more accessible to people who may not have the opportunity to attend traditional schools, such as adult learners, working professionals, and individuals in remote areas. Moreover, online learning has opened up access to a vast array of resources, from video lectures and tutorials to interactive quizzes and peer collaboration.

In addition to online learning, technological tools have revolutionized classroom instruction. Teachers now use interactive whiteboards, digital simulations, and educational apps to engage students in new and exciting ways. For example, instead of merely reading about scientific concepts, students can use digital simulations to observe chemical reactions, explore the human body in 3D, or engage in virtual field trips. This hands-on approach to learning has proven to improve student understanding and retention of complex subjects.

However, despite these advancements, technology in education is not without its challenges. One of the main concerns is the digital divide—the gap between students who have access to modern technology and those who do not. While some students have access to high-speed internet, laptops, and tablets, others, particularly in low-income or rural areas, do not have these resources. This lack of access can create disparities in educational outcomes, as students without the necessary technology may struggle to keep up with their peers.

Another concern is the over-reliance on technology. While technology has the potential to enhance education, there is a risk that it could replace traditional teaching methods that have been proven effective over time. Teachers may become dependent on digital tools, neglecting the importance of interpersonal communication and hands-on learning. Furthermore, the increasing use of technology in education raises questions about data privacy and security, as students' personal information and academic records are increasingly stored and processed online.

Despite these concerns, the integration of technology in education is likely to continue expanding. As technology continues to evolve, it has the potential to further revolutionize how we approach learning, making education more interactive, engaging, and accessible. The future of education will likely see even more personalized learning experiences, where students can learn at their own pace, access real-time feedback, and receive tailored instruction that meets their unique needs.

In conclusion, technology has had a profound impact on modern education, creating new opportunities for students and teachers alike. While challenges such as the digital divide and concerns about over-reliance on technology remain, the benefits of educational technology are clear. As we continue to adapt and integrate these tools, the future of education looks increasingly bright, with the potential to transform learning on a global scale.

---

6. What is one of the key benefits of online learning, according to the passage?

A. It allows students to learn at their own pace and from any location
B. It guarantees students a degree or certification upon completion
C. It replaces traditional teaching methods entirely
D. It provides face-to-face interaction between students and teachers

---

7. What is the main challenge associated with technology in education mentioned in the passage?

A. The difficulty of using digital tools in the classroom
B. The gap between students who have access to technology and those who do not
C. The unwillingness of teachers to adopt new tools
D. The inability to develop new educational apps

---

8. According to the passage, how has technology enhanced classroom instruction?

A. By replacing all traditional teaching methods
B. By providing instant feedback to students
C. By allowing students to engage with subjects in new, interactive ways
D. By making textbooks obsolete

9. What concern about technology in education is raised regarding student data?

A. Technology provides too many options for students to choose from
B. Students' personal information and academic records are increasingly stored and processed online
C. Digital tools prevent students from participating in group work
D. Technology causes students to become distracted and disengaged

---

10. According to the passage, what is expected for the future of education with the integration of technology?

A. Education will become completely online
B. Traditional teaching methods will disappear
C. Learning will become more personalized and interactive
D. The digital divide will be eliminated

Passage 3: The Rise of E-commerce and its Impact on Traditional Retail.

The rise of e-commerce has dramatically changed the retail landscape over the past two decades. Once limited to a few specialized online stores, e-commerce has evolved into a global industry that accounts for a significant share of retail sales worldwide. The convenience of shopping from home, the wide selection of products, and the ability to compare prices easily have made e-commerce increasingly popular among consumers. In fact, the growth of online shopping has forced many traditional brick-and-mortar retailers to reconsider their business models in order to remain competitive.

One of the primary drivers of e-commerce's success is the increasing use of mobile devices. Smartphones and tablets allow consumers to shop from virtually anywhere, making it easier than ever to make purchases on the go. Mobile apps and optimized websites offer streamlined shopping experiences, with features such as one-click purchasing and personalized recommendations. Retailers have quickly recognized the importance of having a mobile-friendly presence, as more and more shoppers turn to their phones to make purchases.

Another key factor in the growth of e-commerce is the rise of social media and influencer marketing. Brands are increasingly partnering with social media influencers to promote their products, reaching millions of potential customers through Instagram, YouTube, and other platforms. Social media has become an essential tool for brand awareness, customer engagement, and direct sales. Influencers, with their large and dedicated followings, are able to provide product recommendations that feel more authentic to their audiences, helping to drive consumer purchasing decisions.

While e-commerce offers many advantages, it also comes with its own set of challenges. One significant issue is the environmental impact of online shopping. The increase in packaging waste, the carbon footprint associated with shipping products, and the energy consumption of data centers all contribute to the environmental toll of e-commerce. Additionally, many online retailers rely on rapid shipping services, such as same-day or two-day delivery, which often involves transportation methods that further contribute to pollution and fuel consumption.

Traditional retailers have also faced challenges due to the rise of e-commerce. Many brick-and-mortar stores have seen a decline in foot traffic as more customers choose to shop online. To counteract this trend, many retailers have embraced an omnichannel approach, blending their physical stores with their online presence. This strategy allows customers to shop online and pick up their purchases in-store, or return items bought online to a physical location. Omnichannel retailing offers a more flexible shopping experience and is a way for traditional retailers to stay relevant in an increasingly digital world.

Despite the challenges, e-commerce shows no signs of slowing down. As technology continues to advance, the future of online shopping looks even more promising. Augmented reality (AR) and virtual reality (VR) are beginning to play a role in e-commerce, offering virtual fitting rooms and 3D product visualizations that allow customers to interact with products before making a purchase. The integration of artificial intelligence (AI) and machine learning also promises to enhance the personalization of shopping experiences, with AI algorithms predicting customer preferences and offering tailored recommendations.

In conclusion, e-commerce has revolutionized the retail industry, providing consumers with greater convenience, selection, and accessibility. However, it also presents challenges, particularly related to the environment and its impact on traditional retail models. As technology continues to advance, the e-commerce landscape will undoubtedly evolve, with innovations in mobile shopping, social media marketing, and AI enhancing the online shopping experience. For retailers, adapting to this changing landscape will be key to staying competitive in the future.

---

11. According to the passage, what is one of the key drivers of e-commerce's success?

A. The affordability of products
B. The increasing use of mobile devices
C. The high-quality customer service provided by online stores
D. The decline of brick-and-mortar stores

12. How has social media contributed to the growth of e-commerce?

A. By creating new retail opportunities for offline businesses
B. By enabling brands to engage with consumers through influencers
C. By restricting the ability of consumers to access online stores
D. By promoting physical stores over online shopping

13. What environmental concern is raised about e-commerce in the passage?

A. The excessive use of plastic for packaging
B. The environmental impact of online shopping
C. The creation of too many shopping websites
D. The lack of online shopping regulations

14. According to the passage, what strategy have traditional retailers adopted to adapt to e-commerce?

A. Reducing their physical store presence
B. Creating only online stores
C. Using an omnichannel approach that blends physical and online stores
D. Focusing on in-store marketing rather than online marketing

15. What role do augmented reality (AR) and virtual reality (VR) play in the future of e-commerce?

A. They will replace all traditional shopping methods
B. They will enhance the online shopping experience by allowing virtual interactions with products
C. They will make physical stores obsolete
D. They will reduce the need for online advertising

Passage 4: The Legacy of the Civil Rights Movement in America.

The Civil Rights Movement in the United States was a pivotal moment in the nation's history, as it sought to end racial segregation and discrimination against African Americans, particularly in the South.

The movement, which spanned from the mid-20th century to the 1960s, was fueled by a series of events that sparked public outcry, including the murder of Emmett Till in 1955 and the arrest of Rosa Parks in 1955 for refusing to give up her seat on a segregated bus in Montgomery, Alabama. These events galvanized activists and sparked a nationwide movement that would change the legal and social landscape of the country.

One of the most significant achievements of the Civil Rights Movement was the passage of the **Civil Rights Act of 1964**, which outlawed discrimination based on race, color, religion, sex, or national origin. This legislation had a profound impact on various sectors of American society, including education, employment, and public accommodations.

For example, it led to the desegregation of public schools and public places, such as restaurants, theaters, and hotels. The act also prohibited discrimination in the workplace, which allowed for greater economic opportunities for African Americans and other minorities.

In addition to the Civil Rights Act, the **Voting Rights Act of 1965** was another landmark piece of legislation that aimed to eliminate barriers to voting for African Americans, particularly in the South, where literacy tests and poll taxes were used to disenfranchise black voters.

The Voting Rights Act banned these discriminatory practices and ensured that African Americans could exercise their right to vote. This legislation played a critical role in increasing African American political participation and representation in government.

The Civil Rights Movement also led to significant cultural shifts in America. Through nonviolent protests, marches, and sit-ins, activists brought national attention to the injustices faced by African Americans.

Leaders such as **Dr. Martin Luther King Jr.**, **Malcolm X**, and **Rosa Parks** became symbols of resistance and change, and their work helped inspire future generations of activists fighting for equality. The movement also paved the way for other social justice movements, including those advocating for women's rights, and the rights of people with disabilities.

Despite the significant progress made during the Civil Rights Movement, many challenges remain. Racial inequality, while less overt, continues to persist in areas such as criminal justice, education, and housing.

Disparities in wealth, health, and education still disproportionately affect African American communities, and racial profiling by law enforcement continues to be a significant issue. Movements such as **Black Lives Matter** have emerged in response to these ongoing challenges, highlighting the need for continued efforts to address racial inequality and social justice in the United States.

In recent years, there has been growing recognition of the importance of diversity and inclusion in all aspects of American life.

Many institutions, from businesses to schools, have implemented diversity initiatives aimed at increasing representation and providing equal opportunities for marginalized groups. However, the road to full equality remains long, and the legacy of the Civil Rights Movement continues to inspire efforts toward justice and equality.

In conclusion, the Civil Rights Movement was a transformative period in American history, marked by the struggle for racial equality and justice. Its achievements, including the Civil Rights Act and the Voting Rights Act, helped dismantle the institutional structures of segregation and discrimination.

While much progress has been made, the movement's legacy reminds us that the fight for equality is ongoing, and the pursuit of a just and inclusive society remains a work in progress.

---

16. What was one of the main achievements of the Civil Rights Movement?

A. The establishment of a new political party for African Americans
B. The passage of the Civil Rights Act of 1964
C. The end of the Vietnam War
D. The founding of the United Nations

---

17. What was the purpose of the Voting Rights Act of 1965?

A. To promote African American participation in the military
B. To eliminate voting barriers for African Americans
C. To establish equal voting rights for women and men
D. To outlaw literacy tests in schools

18. According to the passage, how did the Civil Rights Movement impact American culture?

A. It led to the complete integration of all schools and universities
B. It inspired future generations of activists fighting for equality
C. It led to the abolition of political parties
D. It reduced the number of protests and civil demonstrations

---

19. What ongoing challenge related to racial inequality is mentioned in the passage?

A. Increased opportunities for African Americans in the military
B. The rise in African American political representation
C. The end of racial segregation in the South
D. Disparities in wealth, health, and education

---

20. How did the Civil Rights Movement inspire other social justice movements?

A. It led to the complete integration of all public schools
B. It reduced activism related to minority rights
C. It caused the establishment of a national holiday for civil rights leaders
D. It encouraged the development of other movements advocating for equality

---

Section 4: Clarity (20 Questions)

Time Limit: 20 minutes

Instructions:

- This section evaluates your ability to identify clear and concise sentences in law enforcement communication.
- You will be given two similar sentences, and you must choose the one that is written more clearly.
- **Tip**: Pay attention to sentence structure. Avoiding excessive use of passive voice and maintaining logical sentence flow will help you recognize the clearer sentence.
- **Goal**: To assess your ability to write and understand clear communication, an essential skill for law enforcement officers who must often write reports and communicate with others under pressure.

Questions:

Question 1

A. She agreed to help the officer with the investigation, despite her reluctance to get involved.
B. Despite her reluctance to get involved, she agreed to help the officer with the investigation.

Question 2

A. The sergeant reviewed the report carefully, identifying the discrepancies that could impact the investigation.
B. Identifying the discrepancies that could impact the investigation, the sergeant carefully reviewed the report.

Question 3

A. The officer's decision to withhold evidence was based on legal advice and his understanding of the case.
B. Based on legal advice and his understanding of the case, the officer's decision to withhold evidence was made.

195

Question 4

A. She meticulously gathered all the evidence, organizing it in a way that would make the investigation more efficient.
B. Organizing it in a way that would make the investigation more efficient, she meticulously gathered all the evidence.

Question 5

A. The detective reviewed all the leads, knowing that solving the case would require more than just a superficial examination.
B. Knowing that solving the case would require more than just a superficial examination, the detective reviewed all the leads.

Question 6

A. The officer calmly approached the suspect, fully aware that his actions could escalate the situation.
B. Fully aware that his actions could escalate the situation, the officer calmly approached the suspect.

Question 7

A. The law enforcement officer demonstrated remarkable restraint during the tense standoff.
B. During the tense standoff, the law enforcement officer demonstrated remarkable restraint.

Question 8

A. The team carefully analyzed the evidence, which led them to a breakthrough in the investigation.
B. A breakthrough in the investigation was made after the team carefully analyzed the evidence.

Question 9

A. She filed the report with great attention to detail, knowing that it would be scrutinized by her superiors.
B. Knowing that it would be scrutinized by her superiors, she filed the report with great attention to detail.

Question 10

A. The officer had to make a split-second decision, knowing that hesitation could have deadly consequences.
B. Knowing that hesitation could have deadly consequences, the officer had to make a split-second decision.

Question 11

A. The detective worked diligently, cross-referencing all pieces of evidence to ensure accuracy.
B. Cross-referencing all pieces of evidence to ensure accuracy, the detective worked diligently.

Question 12

A. The officer approached the suspect cautiously, knowing the situation could turn violent at any moment.
B. The officer, knowing the situation could turn violent at any moment, approached the suspect cautiously.

Question 13

A. After being briefed on the situation, the officer was ready to take immediate action.
B. The officer was ready to take immediate action after being briefed on the situation.

Question 14

A. Despite the difficulties, the officer remained calm and handled the situation with composure.
B. The officer remained calm, handling the situation with composure despite the difficulties.

Question 15

A. The suspect fled the scene immediately after realizing the officer had spotted him.
B. After realizing the officer had spotted him, the suspect fled the scene immediately.

Question 16

A. The officer was able to calm the crowd quickly, despite the tense atmosphere.
B. Despite the tense atmosphere, the officer was able to calm the crowd quickly.

Question 17

A. The officer's expertise in conflict resolution played a pivotal role in defusing the situation.
B. Playing a pivotal role in defusing the situation, the officer's expertise in conflict resolution was invaluable.

Question 18

A. The sergeant made sure to gather all necessary information before making a final decision.
B. Before making a final decision, the sergeant made sure to gather all necessary information.

Question 19

A. The officers worked tirelessly to investigate the incident and ensure justice was served.
B. To investigate the incident and ensure justice was served, the officers worked tirelessly.

Question 20

A. The officer swiftly secured the perimeter, ensuring no one could enter or exit the area undetected.
B. Ensuring no one could enter or exit the area undetected, the officer swiftly secured the perimeter.

Practice Test 2: Answer Key.

Section 1: Spelling.

Question Number	Correct Option
1	B
2	A
3	C
4	A
5	C
6	B
7	A
8	A
9	A
10	A
11	A
12	A
13	A
14	A
15	A
16	A
17	D
18	C
19	D
20	C

Section 2: Vocabulary.

Question Number	Correct Option
1	B
2	B
3	B
4	A
5	B
6	A
7	A
8	B
9	A
10	A
11	B
12	B
13	B
14	B
15	B
16	C
17	A
18	B
19	B
20	A

Section 3: Reading Comprehension.

Question Number	Correct Option
1	B
2	C
3	C
4	C
5	B
6	A
7	B
8	C
9	B
10	C
11	B
12	B
13	B
14	C
15	B
16	B
17	B
18	B
19	D
20	D

Section 4: Clarity.

Question Number	Correct Option
1	B
2	A
3	A
4	A
5	B
6	B
7	A
8	A
9	A
10	B
11	A
12	B
13	A
14	A
15	A
16	B
17	A
18	A
19	A
20	A

Practice Test 2: Answer And Explanation.

Section 1: Spelling.

1. **Answer**: B. arrested, distressed
   Explanation: The correct phrase is "arrested" (past tense of arrest) and "distressed" (adjective describing the victim's state of emotion). The verb "arrested" must be used in its past form to match the tense of the sentence, while "distressed" describes the state of the victim after an incident. Option A uses the verb "arrest" incorrectly in present tense, while Option C and D incorrectly use "distress" (noun) instead of the correct adjective "distressed."

2. **Answer**: A. forced, hiding
   Explanation: The correct answer is "forced" (past tense of the verb "force") and "hiding" (present participle) in this context. "Forced" implies the action the officer took, and "hiding" is the correct verb form describing the suspect's action. Option B uses "force" in present tense and "hiden," which is an incorrect form. Option C uses "hid," which is also past tense and doesn't match the progressive action intended in the sentence. Option D uses the wrong form of the verb "force" and makes the sentence grammatically incorrect.

3. **Answer**: C. recall, actions
   Explanation: The correct answer is "recall" (verb, base form) and "actions" (plural noun). "Recall" is used in its correct form as the verb that means to remember or bring to mind, while "actions" is plural, referring to multiple things the suspect did. Option A uses "action" (singular), which does not fit the plural noun form needed here. Option B has a spelling error with "recale" instead of "recall," and also uses "actions" correctly. Option D uses "recalled" (past tense), which doesn't work with the rest of the sentence as well as "recall."

4. **Answer**: A. found, gun
   Explanation: "Found" is the correct past tense of the verb "find," which matches the action completed in the past. "Gun" is singular because it refers to only one weapon. Option B uses "founded" incorrectly, which refers to starting something (e.g., a business or organization) and is not a synonym for "find." Option C uses "guns" incorrectly because the context suggests a singular item. Option D uses "find," which is in the wrong tense.

5. **Answer**: C. decided, victim
   Explanation: The correct phrasing is "decided" (past tense of the verb "decide") and "victim" (singular noun). The action of deciding to take the statement happened in the past, and "victim" refers to one individual. Option A uses "decide" in the present tense,

which is not correct in this context. Option B uses the incorrect present participle "deciding," and the plural form "victims" is unnecessary. Option D uses the present tense "decides," which doesn't fit the context of the sentence.

6. **Answer**: B. collected, verified

    Explanation: "Collected" is the correct past tense of the verb "collect," and "verified" is the correct past tense of "verify." The actions described here are both completed actions, so the past tense of both verbs is required. Option A uses "verify" in the present tense, which doesn't match the context. Option C uses "collect" and "verifies" in the present tense, which is incorrect. Option D uses "collecting," a present participle, which doesn't fit the sentence structure.

7. **Answer**: A. assess, further

    Explanation: "Assess" is the correct verb form (base form) to indicate an action that is happening at the moment. "Further" is the correct word, meaning additional or more, used in this context. Option B uses "assessed," which is past tense, but the sentence context suggests an ongoing action. Option C uses "assessing," which would be correct in some cases, but here the base form is more appropriate. Option D uses "furthur," which is a misspelling of "further."

8. **Answer**: A. negotiation, arrest

    Explanation: "Negotiation" is the correct noun form, referring to the process of discussing or mediating between parties. "Arrest" is the correct noun that refers to the act of apprehending someone. Option B uses the verb "negotiate," which does not fit in this context. Option C uses "negociation," which is a misspelling of "negotiation," and "arrested" is the wrong form for the context. Option D uses "arrested" in the wrong form as well.

9. **Answer**: A. evaluate, adjust

    Explanation: "Evaluate" is the correct verb form in the present tense, while "adjust" is the correct verb form to match. The sentence describes actions being taken during an ongoing situation. Option B uses past tense ("evaluated" and "adjusted"), which doesn't fit the present context. Option C uses incorrect forms ("evaluation" and "adjusting"). Option D uses "adjusted," which is incorrect in this context.

10. **Answer**: A. identify, location

    Explanation: "Identify" is the correct base form of the verb, indicating the officer is in the process of identifying. "Location" is the correct noun (singular) referring to the place of the crime. Option B uses "identified," which is past tense and doesn't match the sentence structure. Option C uses "locations," which is incorrect in this context as only one location is being referenced. Option D uses the present participle "identifying," which doesn't fit the sentence structure.

11. **Answer**: A. assess, ensure

    Explanation: "Assess" is the correct verb form (present tense), meaning to evaluate the situation. "Ensure" is the correct verb for making sure something happens. Option B uses "insure," which is related to insurance, not guaranteeing safety. Option C incorrectly uses "assessed," which is past tense and doesn't fit with the sentence structure. Option D uses "assessing," which is the wrong tense for the sentence.

12. **Answer**: A. investigation, evidence

    Explanation: "Investigation" is the correct noun form, and "evidence" is the correct singular noun referring to proof or material related to the crime. Option B uses "investigatin," which is a misspelling, and "evidences" should not be plural in this context. Option C uses "evidense," which is a misspelling. Option D incorrectly uses the plural form "evidences."

13. **Answer**: A. verify, false

    Explanation: "Verify" is the correct verb meaning to confirm, and "false" is the correct adjective to describe something untrue. Option B uses incorrect spelling of "verify" ("veriffy") and "false" is misspelled as "faulse." Option C makes similar mistakes, using "verfiy" and "fals." Option D also contains the misspelling of "false."

14. **Answer**: A. confirm, vital

    Explanation: "Confirm" is the correct verb meaning to verify, and "vital" is the correct adjective meaning essential or necessary. Option B uses "confurm," which is an incorrect form of "confirm." Option C uses "confim" and "vitale," both of which are misspellings. Option D uses "confirmed" incorrectly as the past tense in a sentence that needs the base form "confirm."

15. **Answer**: A. calm, deescalate

    Explanation: "Calm" is the correct adjective, meaning peaceful and composed, and "deescalate" is the correct verb to describe reducing the intensity of a situation. Option B uses the past tense "calmed" and "deescalated," which does not fit the intended meaning. Option C incorrectly uses the present participle "calming." Option D uses a hyphenated form of "de-escalate," which is an acceptable alternative but isn't as common in American English.

16. **Answer**: A. apprehend, reliable

    Explanation: "Apprehend" is the correct verb, meaning to arrest or take into custody, and "reliable" is the correct adjective to describe the trustworthy nature of the tip. Option B uses "apprehand," which is a misspelling. Option C uses "reliabe," and Option D uses "relable," both incorrect spellings.

17. **Answer**: D. interrogation, discredited

    Explanation: "Interrogation" is the correct noun form referring to the questioning process, and "discredited" is the correct past tense of the verb meaning to prove something untrue. Option B uses the incorrect spelling "interogation," and Option C uses the wrong tense "discredit." Option A uses "discreditted," which is a misspelling of the past tense.

18. **Answer**: C. fleeing, hinder

    Explanation: "Fleeing" is the correct present participle form, meaning running away, and

205

"hinder" is the correct verb meaning to impede or obstruct. Option B uses "fleed," which is incorrect, as the correct past tense of "flee" is "fled." Option A uses "hindering" in the wrong form and tense. Option D uses "hindered," which is past tense and doesn't match the context of the sentence.

19. **Answer**: D. confirm, analysis

    Explanation: "Confirm" is the correct verb in its base form, and "analysis" is the correct noun form meaning a detailed examination. Option B uses "analyzation," which is an uncommon and incorrect form of the word. Option C uses "analysys," which is a misspelling. Option A uses "confirming," the incorrect present participle, in this context.

20. **Answer**: C. false, thorough

    Explanation: "False" is the correct adjective, meaning not true or incorrect, and "thorough" is the correct adjective meaning complete or detailed. Option B uses "faulse," which is a misspelling of "false," and "thorugh," which is a misspelling of "thorough." Option A uses "fals" and "thru," both incorrect forms. Option D is the correct spelling but is included here as the correct answer.

Section 2: Vocabulary.

1. **Answer**: B. Sensible

   Explanation: "Pragmatic" means dealing with things in a sensible, practical, and realistic way. "Sensible" is the best synonym, as it also refers to being wise or practical in approach. Option A, "theoretical," refers to ideas or concepts rather than practical application. Option C, "unfocused," implies a lack of attention or concentration, which contradicts the meaning of "pragmatic." Option D, "rigid," means inflexible or stiff, which doesn't align with "pragmatic."

2. **Answer**: B. Precise

   Explanation: "Scrupulous" means paying great attention to detail, being thorough and careful. "Precise" is the best synonym, as it also refers to accuracy and attention to detail. Option A, "careless," means showing a lack of concern or attention, which is the opposite of "scrupulous." Option C, "casual," means relaxed or not focused, which doesn't match "scrupulous." Option D, "disorganized," refers to being messy or unstructured, which contradicts the attention to detail implied by "scrupulous."

3. **Answer**: B. Harsh

   Explanation: "Intense" refers to something strong or extreme in force or feeling. "Harsh" is the best synonym, as it also implies something severe or strong. Option A, "mild," means gentle or not strong, which is the opposite of "intense." Option C, "temporary," means lasting for only a short period, and Option D, "friendly," refers to a warm or kind approach, which does not fit the context of scrutiny.

4. **Answer**: A. Resolve

   Explanation: "Reconcile" means to find a way to bring things into agreement or harmony, especially when there are conflicts. "Resolve" is the best synonym, as it means to settle or fix a disagreement or issue. Option B, "aggravate," means to make a situation worse, which is the opposite of reconciling. Option C, "challenge," means to confront or dispute, but does not mean bringing conflicting things together. Option D, "ignore," means to overlook, which contradicts the meaning of "reconcile."

5. **Answer**: B. Relentless

   Explanation: "Indefatigable" means not tired or weary, showing relentless persistence and effort. "Relentless" is the best synonym, as it means unyielding or persistent in effort. Option A, "exhausting," means causing fatigue, which is the opposite of "indefatigable." Option C, "hesitant," means unsure or doubtful, and Option D, "sporadic," refers to something occurring at irregular intervals, which doesn't fit the persistent nature of "indefatigable."

6. **Answer**: A. Tactful

   Explanation: "Diplomatic" refers to being sensitive in dealing with others and maintaining good relations. "Tactful" is the best synonym, meaning showing diplomacy or skill in avoiding offense. Option B, "direct," refers to being straightforward or blunt, which may not always be diplomatic. Option C, "abrupt," means sudden and curt, which does not convey the sensitivity implied by "diplomatic." Option D, "aggressive," means forceful or confrontational, which is the opposite of a diplomatic approach.

7. **Answer**: A. Unclear

   Explanation: "Equivocal" means ambiguous or having more than one possible meaning, often used to describe statements that are unclear or evasive. "Unclear" is the best synonym, meaning something not easily understood or lacking clarity. Option B, "honest," means truthful, which is opposite to "equivocal." Option C, "direct," means straightforward and clear, contradicting the meaning of "equivocal." Option D, "concise," refers to being brief but clear, which doesn't match the idea of being "equivocal."

8. **Answer**: B. Disclose

   Explanation: "Divulge" means to reveal or make known, especially something that was previously secret or private. "Disclose" is the best synonym, as it means to reveal or share information. Option A, "conceal," means to hide or keep something secret, which is the opposite of "divulge." Option C, "withhold," means to hold back, which also contradicts the meaning of "divulge." Option D, "evade," means to avoid, which does not align with the idea of revealing information.

9. **Answer**: A. Unyielding

   Explanation: "Unfaltering" means not wavering or weakening, especially in commitment or belief. "Unyielding" is the best synonym, meaning firm or resolute in purpose. Option B, "uncertain," means unsure or lacking confidence, which contradicts "unfaltering." Option C, "irregular," refers to something occurring without pattern or consistency, and

Option D, "unpredictable," means not able to be foreseen, which does not fit the idea of unwavering commitment.

10. **Answer**: A. Sharp

    Explanation: "Astute" means having keen insight or intelligence, often used to describe someone who can quickly and accurately assess situations. "Sharp" is the best synonym, as it implies mental sharpness and quick understanding. Option B, "weak," means lacking strength or power, which contradicts "astute." Option C, "shallow," refers to something lacking depth or thought, and Option D, "dull," means lacking sharpness or interest, which is the opposite of "astute."

11. **Answer**: B. Decisive

    Explanation: "Resolute" means being determined and firm in making decisions, and "decisive" is the best synonym as it implies the ability to make decisions with determination. Option A, "uncertain," means unsure or doubtful, which is the opposite of resolute. Option C, "reluctant," means unwilling to take action, which contradicts the idea of being resolute. Option D, "hesitant," suggests indecision, which also conflicts with the definition of "resolute."

12. **Answer**: B. Provocative

    Explanation: "Inflammatory" refers to something that provokes strong emotions, particularly anger or aggression. "Provocative" is the best synonym, as it describes something that causes strong reactions. Option A, "neutral," means impartial or uncontroversial, which does not provoke a reaction. Option C, "calm," implies a lack of emotional intensity, which contradicts "inflammatory." Option D, "defensive," means protecting oneself, which does not match the idea of provocation.

13. **Answer**: B. Wise

    Explanation: "Prudent" means showing careful judgment and caution, especially when making decisions. "Wise" is the best synonym, as it implies having good judgment and making thoughtful decisions. Option A, "reckless," means acting without regard for consequences, which is the opposite of "prudent." Option C, "hasty," means doing something too quickly without thought, and Option D, "impulsive," refers to acting without careful consideration, both of which contrast with "prudent."

14. **Answer**: B. Thorough

    Explanation: "Meticulous" means showing great attention to detail and precision, often with a focus on accuracy. "Thorough" is the best synonym, as it refers to being complete and exhaustive in an investigation. Option A, "careless," means lacking attention or concern, which is the opposite of "meticulous." Option C, "hasty," means doing something quickly without full attention, and Option D, "disorganized," means lacking structure, which contrasts with being meticulous.

15. **Answer**: B. Fearless

    Explanation: "Intrepid" means showing courage and determination in the face of danger or adversity. "Fearless" is the best synonym, as it conveys a lack of fear in challenging situations. Option A, "timid," means lacking confidence or courage, which is the opposite of "intrepid." Option C, "cautious," means careful or avoiding risk, which contradicts the idea of being intrepid. Option D, "anxious," refers to being nervous or worried, which also contrasts with "intrepid."

16. **Answer**: C. Passionate

    Explanation: "Ardent" means showing strong enthusiasm or passion for something. "Passionate" is the best synonym, as it conveys intense feelings and dedication. Option A, "indifferent," means lacking interest or enthusiasm, which is the opposite of "ardent." Option B, "apathetic," means showing little emotion or interest, and Option D, "cold," suggests a lack of warmth or feeling, which also contradicts "ardent."

17. **Answer**: A. Honest

    Explanation: "Candid" means being straightforward, honest, and open, especially about difficult matters. "Honest" is the best synonym, as it implies being truthful and sincere. Option B, "reserved," means holding back or being quiet, which doesn't fit the openness implied by "candid." Option C, "dishonest," means being untruthful, which is the opposite of "candid." Option D, "evasive," means avoiding or dodging questions, which also contradicts being "candid."

18. **Answer**: B. Scrutinized

    Explanation: "Meticulous" refers to being very detailed and precise. "Scrutinized" is the best synonym, as it means examined closely and thoroughly. Option A, "overlooked," means missed or not noticed, which is the opposite of being meticulous. Option C, "forgotten," refers to not remembering something, and Option D, "ignored," means deliberately not paying attention, neither of which fits the meaning of "meticulous."

19. **Answer**: B. Unusual

    Explanation: "Aberrant" means deviating from the normal or expected course. "Unusual" is the best synonym, as it refers to something not commonly seen or occurring. Option A, "typical," means regular or usual, which is the opposite of "aberrant." Option C, "repetitive," refers to something occurring again and again, which doesn't match the idea of being out of the ordinary. Option D, "predictable," means something that can be foreseen, which contrasts with the unpredictability of "aberrant."

20. **Answer**: A. Curious

    Explanation: "Inquisitive" means eager to learn or ask questions, often out of curiosity. "Curious" is the best synonym, as it means wanting to learn or explore something. Option B, "uninterested," means not caring or lacking interest, which is the opposite of "inquisitive." Option C, "disengaged," means detached or not involved, which doesn't fit the context of an inquisitive nature. Option D, "hostile," means unfriendly or aggressive, which contrasts with the inquisitive desire for knowledge.

Section 3: Reading Comprehension.

1. **Answer**: B. It allows people to connect and engage globally
   Explanation: The passage clearly highlights that **social media enables global connectivity**, allowing people to interact with others worldwide and form communities regardless of geographical boundaries. Option A refers to a negative aspect of social media, not a benefit. Option C, undermining trust, is a concern but not a benefit. Option D, focusing on individualism, is not mentioned as a primary benefit.

2. **Answer**: C. Social media can contribute to loneliness and mental health issues
   Explanation: The passage discusses the negative effects of social media on **mental health**, including loneliness, depression, and anxiety, particularly due to the pressure of comparing one's life to others'. Option A is incorrect as the passage does not discuss improved business strategies as a negative. Option B is also incorrect because political engagement is discussed in a neutral context, not as a negative. Option D is wrong because the passage emphasizes the spread of misinformation rather than accurate health information.

3. **Answer**: C. It leads to confusion and a lack of trust in experts
   Explanation: The passage specifically mentions that the **spread of misinformation** on social media, especially regarding topics like COVID-19, **leads to confusion and a lack of trust in experts and government officials**. Option A is incorrect because misinformation does not promote healthy choices. Option B is incorrect as the passage highlights that misinformation spreads with little verification. Option D does not align with the passage's focus on the negative effects of misinformation.

4. **Answer**: C. It has enabled businesses to market their products in new ways
   Explanation: The passage mentions that social media has allowed businesses to **connect directly with consumers** and promote their products in innovative ways, such as through influencer marketing. Option A is incorrect because the passage does not state that traditional advertising is less effective. Option B is incorrect because businesses still rely on customer feedback, which is not discussed negatively. Option D is also incorrect; businesses are increasingly utilizing online platforms.

5. **Answer**: B. It has increased political polarization and extremist views
   Explanation: The passage discusses how **social media has been criticized for fostering political polarization** and the spread of extremist views due to algorithms that prioritize sensational or polarizing content. Option A is mentioned but is not the main criticism in this context. Option C is not addressed in the passage. Option D does not reflect the criticism mentioned in the passage.

6. **Answer**: A. It allows students to learn at their own pace and from any location
   Explanation: The passage emphasizes that **online learning platforms offer flexibility**, allowing students to learn at their own pace and from any location, which is a major

benefit. Option B is incorrect as the passage does not claim that online learning guarantees a degree or certification. Option C is incorrect because the passage does not suggest replacing traditional methods entirely. Option D is also incorrect, as online learning typically lacks face-to-face interaction.

7. **Answer**: B. The gap between students who have access to technology and those who do not

   Explanation: The passage highlights the **digital divide** as a primary concern, with some students lacking access to the necessary technology, which affects educational equity. Option A, the difficulty of using digital tools, is not mentioned as a primary challenge. Option C, teachers' unwillingness to adopt new tools, is not discussed in the passage. Option D, the inability to develop educational apps, is not addressed either.

8. **Answer**: C. By allowing students to engage with subjects in new, interactive ways

   Explanation: The passage notes that **teachers now use interactive whiteboards, simulations, and apps** to engage students in new and exciting ways, making subjects more hands-on and interactive. Option A is incorrect because technology does not replace all traditional methods; it supplements them. Option B, providing instant feedback, is not discussed in the passage as a direct benefit of technology. Option D is incorrect because the passage does not mention making textbooks obsolete.

9. **Answer**: B. Students' personal information and academic records are increasingly stored and processed online

   Explanation: The passage mentions that the **increased use of technology raises concerns about data privacy** and security, particularly regarding the storage and processing of student information. Option A, having too many options, is not mentioned as a concern. Option C, preventing group work, is not discussed. Option D, distraction and disengagement, is not addressed as a primary concern in the passage.

10. **Answer**: C. Learning will become more personalized and interactive

    Explanation: The passage discusses how **the future of education will see more personalized learning experiences**, with students able to learn at their own pace and receive tailored instruction. Option A is incorrect as the passage does not suggest that education will be entirely online. Option B is incorrect because traditional methods will not disappear but will evolve with technology. Option D is hopeful but not explicitly stated in the passage as something that will be entirely eliminated.

11. **Answer**: B. The increasing use of mobile devices

    Explanation: The passage clearly highlights that **mobile devices** such as smartphones and tablets have contributed significantly to the success of e-commerce by allowing consumers to shop anywhere and anytime. Option A, affordability, is not mentioned as a key driver. Option C, customer service, is not emphasized in the passage. Option D, the decline of brick-and-mortar stores, is mentioned but as a consequence of e-commerce, not a key driver.

12. **Answer**: B. By enabling brands to engage with consumers through influencers
    Explanation: The passage explains that **social media**, especially through **influencers**, has played a key role in promoting products and driving consumer purchases. Option A is incorrect because social media has primarily affected online retail, not offline. Option C is not correct because social media enables access to online stores. Option D is also incorrect as the passage emphasizes social media's role in promoting online shopping, not physical stores.

13. **Answer**: B. The environmental impact of online shopping
    Explanation: The passage discusses the **environmental toll of e-commerce**, including **packaging waste, carbon footprint from shipping, and energy consumption by data centers**. Option A, the excessive use of plastic, is not specifically mentioned. Option C, the creation of too many websites, is not a focus in the passage. Option D is incorrect because the passage does not discuss online shopping regulations as a concern.

14. **Answer**: C. Using an omnichannel approach that blends physical and online stores
    Explanation: The passage explains that traditional retailers have adopted an **omnichannel strategy**, combining physical stores with online shopping options, such as offering **in-store pick-up and returns for online orders**. Option A is not correct because the passage doesn't suggest reducing physical stores but adapting them. Option B is incorrect; retailers have not shifted entirely to online stores but are integrating both approaches. Option D does not align with the focus on omnichannel strategies.

15. **Answer**: B. They will enhance the online shopping experience by allowing virtual interactions with products
    Explanation: The passage discusses how **AR and VR** are being used to enhance online shopping by providing **virtual fitting rooms** and 3D product visualizations, allowing customers to interact with products before purchasing. Option A is incorrect because AR and VR are enhancing, not replacing, traditional shopping methods. Option C is incorrect because physical stores are still relevant in the omnichannel approach. Option D is incorrect; the passage doesn't suggest AR and VR will reduce online advertising.

16. **Answer**: B. The passage of the Civil Rights Act of 1964
    Explanation: The passage clearly highlights the **Civil Rights Act of 1964** as a key achievement of the movement, outlawing discrimination based on race, color, religion, sex, or national origin. Option A is incorrect because the passage does not mention the establishment of a new political party. Option C is irrelevant as the Vietnam War is not the focus of the passage. Option D is incorrect because the United Nations was not related to the Civil Rights Movement.

17. **Answer**: B. To eliminate voting barriers for African Americans
    Explanation: The passage explains that the **Voting Rights Act of 1965** aimed to eliminate voting barriers, such as literacy tests and poll taxes, that were used to disenfranchise African American voters. Option A is incorrect because the act was focused on voting, not military participation. Option C is incorrect because the Voting

Rights Act addressed racial discrimination, not gender. Option D, while related to literacy, does not fully address the purpose of the Voting Rights Act.

18. **Answer**: B. It inspired future generations of activists fighting for equality
    Explanation: The passage notes that the **Civil Rights Movement** not only brought attention to racial injustice but also **inspired future generations of activists** fighting for broader social justice issues. Option A is incorrect because the passage does not suggest complete integration of schools. Option C is not discussed in the passage. Option D is inaccurate because the movement sparked protests, not reduced them.

19. **Answer**: D. Disparities in wealth, health, and education
    Explanation: The passage mentions that, despite the Civil Rights Movement's progress, **disparities in wealth, health, and education** still disproportionately affect African American communities. Option A is incorrect because the passage does not mention the military. Option C is outdated as racial segregation has been largely addressed, but inequality remains. Option B, while political representation has increased, does not directly address ongoing challenges.

20. **Answer**: D. It encouraged the development of other movements advocating for equality
    Explanation: The passage explains that the Civil Rights Movement served as an **inspiration for other social justice movements**, such as those advocating for women's rights, and disability rights. Option A is incorrect as the passage does not claim that all schools were completely integrated. Option C, the establishment of a national holiday, is not discussed. Option B is incorrect because the Civil Rights Movement encouraged, rather than reduced, activism.

Section 4: Clarity.

1. **Answer**: B
   Explanation: Sentence **B** is clearer because it presents the cause (her reluctance) first, which helps highlight the significance of her decision to agree to help. It draws attention to her reluctance and contrasts it with her decision, giving the sentence more impact. Sentence **A** is not incorrect, but placing the cause at the end weakens the sentence's emotional weight and logical flow.

2. **Answer**: A
   Explanation: Sentence **A** is clearer because it follows a straightforward order of actions: **reviewing the report carefully** and then **identifying discrepancies**. It maintains a logical progression. Sentence **B** places the action of identifying discrepancies at the start, which causes unnecessary disruption to the flow of the sentence.

3. **Answer**: A
   Explanation: Sentence **A** is more direct and focuses on the cause (legal advice and understanding) followed by the effect (the officer's decision). It maintains clarity and

immediacy. In **B**, placing the reason at the beginning ("Based on legal advice...") introduces an awkward phrasing that weakens the sentence and makes it less natural to read.

4. **Answer**: A

    Explanation: Sentence **A** is clearer because it presents the action of gathering evidence first, followed by the explanation of how it was organized. This structure keeps the sentence focused and direct. In **B**, the introductory clause disrupts the flow and makes the main action (gathering evidence) feel like an afterthought.

5. **Answer**: B

    Explanation: Sentence **B** is preferred because it sets the **context** first ("knowing that solving the case would require more"), which prepares the reader for the detective's subsequent action. It creates a sense of anticipation and makes the action of reviewing the leads more impactful. Sentence **A** also works but places the context after the action, which slightly lessens the sentence's emphasis on the detective's critical thinking.

6. **Answer**: B

    Explanation: Sentence **B** is more effective because it presents the **awareness** first, providing context for why the officer is calm. The phrasing emphasizes the officer's **level of caution** before revealing the action. In **A**, the main action (approaching the suspect) comes first, and while it's correct, it lacks the same emphasis on the officer's awareness of the potential consequences.

7. **Answer**: A

    Explanation: Sentence **A** is more direct and impactful. It places the **action** of demonstrating restraint before introducing the context of the standoff, which emphasizes the officer's behavior first. Sentence **B** feels more like an afterthought by placing the context of the standoff at the beginning, weakening the focus on the restraint.

8. **Answer**: A

    Explanation: Sentence **A** is clearer because it logically connects the **analysis of evidence** with the result (breakthrough). It presents the cause before the effect. Sentence **B** reverses the order and starts with the result, which makes the connection between the evidence analysis and the breakthrough less immediate and clear.

9. **Answer**: A

    Explanation: Sentence **A** is more natural and effective, as it starts with the **action** of filing the report and then provides the context (the scrutiny). This keeps the sentence direct and focused. Sentence **B** begins with the context ("Knowing that it would be scrutinized"), which somewhat weakens the sentence by delaying the action and making it feel less immediate.

10. **Answer**: B

    Explanation: Sentence **B** is more powerful because it emphasizes the **consequence** first, which draws attention to the gravity of the situation and why the officer's quick decision is crucial. Sentence **A**, while clear, presents the decision first, which makes the impact of hesitation feel secondary.

11. **Answer**: A

    Explanation: Sentence **A** is clearer because it presents the action of the detective working diligently first, followed by the method of ensuring accuracy (cross-referencing). This structure keeps the sentence direct and impactful. Sentence **B** disrupts the flow by placing the method at the start, which makes the sentence feel awkward and less fluid.

12. **Answer**: B

    Explanation: Sentence **B** works better because it begins with the reason for the officer's cautious approach, which sets the context and builds anticipation. It emphasizes the officer's awareness of the potential danger first. Sentence **A** is also correct but feels more rushed by placing the reason after the action, which reduces its emphasis on the potential threat.

13. **Answer**: A

    Explanation: Sentence **A** is more effective because it places the action (being briefed) before the readiness to act, creating a natural and logical flow of events. Sentence **B** is grammatically correct but starts with the officer's readiness, which feels slightly disjointed and makes the action less immediate.

14. **Answer**: A

    Explanation: Sentence **A** is preferred because it first presents the **challenge** (difficulties) and then emphasizes the officer's **calmness and composure**. This structure gives the sentence more emphasis on the officer's response to the difficulties. Sentence **B** places the difficulty at the end, making it feel like an afterthought and weakening the sentence's focus on the officer's actions.

15. **Answer**: A

    Explanation: Sentence **A** is clearer and follows a **logical sequence of actions**: the suspect first realizes he's been spotted, then flees. Sentence **B** feels slightly clunky by starting with the realization, which delays the action of fleeing.

16. **Answer**: B

    Explanation: Sentence **B** is better because it presents the **challenge** (tense atmosphere) first, which builds tension and gives context to the officer's ability to remain calm and act effectively. Sentence **A** is still correct but feels less impactful as it starts with the result of the officer calming the crowd before addressing the difficult environment.

17. **Answer**: A

    Explanation: Sentence **A** is more direct and clearly emphasizes the officer's **expertise** and its impact on the situation. Sentence **B** is unnecessarily convoluted by starting with the role the officer's expertise played, making the sentence feel awkward and hard to follow.

18. **Answer**: A

    Explanation: Sentence **A** is clearer because it keeps the **action** of gathering information in the forefront, with the decision-making as a natural consequence. Sentence **B** is still correct, but it places the decision-making first, which weakens the emphasis on the preparation and makes the sentence feel more detached.

19. **Answer**: A

    Explanation: Sentence **A** is more direct and concise, as it clearly links the officers' effort with the outcome. Sentence **B**, though correct, feels slightly more convoluted by beginning with the purpose ("To investigate"), which makes it more difficult to follow.

20. **Answer**: A

    Explanation: Sentence **A** is clearer because it presents the **action** of securing the perimeter first, followed by the result (ensuring security). This maintains the logical flow of the sentence. Sentence **B** starts with the result, making it feel slightly awkward as the cause (securing the perimeter) is delayed.

Full-Scale Practice Test 3

Section 1: Spelling (20 Questions)

Time Limit: 15 minutes

Instructions:

- This section tests your ability to accurately spell words that are commonly used in law enforcement scenarios.
- You will be presented with 20 words in the form of multiple-choice questions. For each question, choose the correct spelling of the word.
- **Tip**: Pay close attention to common spelling pitfalls such as double letters, homophones (words that sound the same but are spelled differently), and prefixes/suffixes.
- **Goal**: Accuracy is key. Be sure to focus on details, as a single letter can alter the meaning of a word and its appropriateness in law enforcement communication.

Questions:

1. The detective had to _____ the validity of the evidence before proceeding with the case.

A. evaluate
B. evalute
C. evaluat
D. evaluatte

2. The officer was able to _____ the suspect's criminal history after reviewing the _____ records.

A. examine, criminal
B. exmine, criminel
C. examane, crimminal
D. examine, crimminal

3. The officer gave a _____ description of the suspect's appearance to the police artists, ensuring that the sketch was _____.

A. detailed, accurate
B. detaile, accuratte
C. detalied, accurat
D. detailed, accuratte

---

4. The officer was asked to _____ the report on the incident with the _____ facts obtained during the investigation.

A. complet, facual
B. complite, factuel
C. complete, factual
D. complete, factuall

---

5. The detective needed to _____ the suspect's alibi with the _____ evidence available to verify the truth.

A. corroborated, sufficent
B. corroborate, sufficent
C. coroborate, suffeicient
D. corroborate, sufficient

---

6. The police had to _____ the premises to ensure no one was _____ before making an arrest.

A. securr, presnt
B. secur, presant
C. secure, present
D. secure, presense

7. The officer was called to _____ the situation in a _____ manner, ensuring that the suspect was treated fairly.

A. handle, professional
B. handel, profesinal
C. handle, profeional
D. handle, professional

---

8. After a lengthy _____, the officers were able to _____ the suspect's actions during the robbery.

A. investigation, reconstruct
B. investegation, reconstruate
C. investigation, reconsturct
D. invistigation, reconstract

---

9. The officer was asked to _____ the suspect's _____ after the witness gave conflicting statements.

A. clarify, statement
B. clarrify, statemant
C. clarifie, statment
D. clarify, statment

---

10. The detective's _____ approach helped solve the case by gathering _____ evidence from multiple sources.

A. methodical, relevant
B. methodical, relevnt
C. methodical, relavant
D. methoical, relevant

11. The officer's actions were deemed to be _____, as they directly _____ the outcome of the investigation.

A. influencial, affect
B. influential, affected
C. influentual, effected
D. influential, affect

---

12. The suspect's alibi was thoroughly _____ and ultimately proven to be _____ by the detectives.

A. examined, false
B. examin, falce
C. examine, fals
D. examend, fauls

---

13. The officer's testimony was deemed _____ by the court, as it _____ with the physical evidence presented.

A. credible, mathed
B. creditable, mathed
C. credable, matche
D. credible, matched

---

14. The detective was careful to _____ the facts of the case and avoid any _____ statements that could mislead the investigation.

A. verify, misleading
B. verifie, mislead
C. verifiy, misleade
D. verify, mislead

---

15. The suspect was apprehended after the officers _____ a _____ to his whereabouts using surveillance footage.

A. tracked, lead
B. track, lead
C. tracked, leaded
D. tracking, lead

16. The investigator could not _____ the evidence that would have _____ the suspect's innocence.

A. ignore, proven
B. ignored, proven
C. ignore, prove
D. ignores, proved

17. The law enforcement agency's actions were later deemed _____ after a thorough _____ of the incident by internal affairs.

A. justified, review
B. justifiably, reveiw
C. justify, reveiw
D. justified, reveiw

18. The officer was able to _____ the threat when the suspect became _____ and aggressive during the encounter.

A. neutralize, hostile
B. nuetralize, hostile
C. neutralize, hostil
D. neutralize, hostiled

19. The officer's _____ decision was instrumental in preventing further _____ during the confrontation.

A. split-second, escalation
B. split-sec, escallation
C. split-second, escalation
D. splitted-second, escalated

20. After analyzing the suspect's _____, the investigator found the _____ indicating a possible motive for the crime.

A. behavior, clue
B. behavious, clew
C. behavior, clew
D. behavior, clue

221

Section 2: Vocabulary (20 Questions)

Time Limit: 20 minutes

Instructions:

- This section evaluates your understanding of vocabulary used in law enforcement contexts.
- You will be presented with 20 sentences, each containing an underlined word. Your task is to choose the synonym that best fits the context of the sentence.
- **Tip**: Pay attention to the context of the sentence. Many law enforcement-related words have specific meanings that might differ from their everyday use. Think about how the word is used in context, not just its dictionary definition.
- **Goal**: This section tests your ability to understand and apply law enforcement terminology effectively. Take your time to ensure the synonym you choose fits the tone and meaning of the sentence.

Questions:

1. The officer's **dispassionate** approach to the case allowed him to evaluate the evidence without any emotional influence.

A. Biased
B. Detached
C. Sensitive
D. Compassionate

2. The suspect's **obfuscation** of the facts during questioning made it difficult to discern the truth.

A. Clarification
B. Evasion
C. Explanation
D. Illumination

3. The detective's **discernment** allowed him to recognize the subtle discrepancies in the suspect's statements.

A. Confusion
B. Understanding
C. Inability
D. Ignorance

---

4. The officer was praised for his **empathy** towards the victim during the investigation.

A. Indifference
B. Compassion
C. Disdain
D. Hostility

---

5. The officer was able to **mitigate** the situation by speaking calmly and diffusing the tension.

A. Aggravate
B. Reduce
C. Exacerbate
D. Heighten

---

6. The detective's **subtle** questioning revealed the inconsistencies in the suspect's testimony.

A. Obvious
B. Harsh
C. Delicate
D. Blunt

---

7. The officer's **lucid** explanation of the complex law made it easy for the jury to understand.

A. Clear
B. Confusing
C. Obscure
D. Complex

8. The detective's **methodical** approach allowed him to thoroughly investigate every lead.

A. Disorganized, neglect
B. Organized, analyze
C. Random, clarify
D. Hasty, ignore

9. The officer's **obstinate** refusal to back down in the face of opposition was a testament to his dedication to the case.

A. Determined
B. Flexible
C. Timid
D. Indifferent

10. The officer had to **intervene** in the heated dispute to prevent it from escalating into violence.

A. Participate
B. Ignore
C. Mediate
D. Watch

11. The detective's **impeccable** reputation for integrity made him the ideal candidate to lead the investigation.

A. Flawless
B. Faulty
C. Inconsistent
D. Unreliable

12. The officer's **forthright** manner in addressing the situation helped establish trust with the community.

A. Evasive
B. Honest
C. Deceptive
D. Suspicious

---

13. The officer's **exemplary** conduct in the face of adversity set a standard for others to follow.

A. Mediocre
B. Outstanding
C. Faulty
D. Average

---

14. The officer's **discretion** in handling the delicate situation showed his ability to assess it with care.

A. Indiscretion
B. Judgment
C. Foolishness
D. Recklessness

---

15. The officer's **cursory** glance at the scene was not enough to detect the key piece of evidence.

A. Thorough
B. Superficial
C. Exhaustive
D. Detailed

---

16. The officer was **perturbed** by the suspect's sudden outburst during the interview.

A. Unconcerned
B. Calm
C. Disturbed
D. Delighted

17. The officer was **resilient** in the face of criticism, continuing his work without letting it affect his performance.

A. Fragile
B. Weak
C. Tenacious
D. Overwhelmed

18. The officer's **conscientious** approach to his duties earned him the respect of his colleagues.

A. Careless
B. Thoughtful
C. Lazy
D. Indifferent

19. The officer's **unflappable** demeanor during the chaotic situation helped keep the crowd calm.

A. Nervous
B. Calm
C. Agitated
D. Anxious

20. The officer used his **erudite** knowledge of criminal law to successfully argue his case in court.

A. Shallow
B. Educated
C. Confused
D. Illiterate

Section 3: Reading Comprehension (20 Questions)

Time Limit: 25 minutes

Instructions:

- In this section, you will read two passages and answer 10 multiple-choice questions for each passage.
- Each passage is designed to assess your ability to comprehend written material related to law enforcement and public service.
- **Tip**: Focus on **key ideas**, **main points**, and **inferences** rather than memorizing every detail. The goal is to assess your ability to extract and understand information quickly and efficiently.
- **Goal**: To test your ability to read and understand complex material, which is a crucial skill for law enforcement officers who regularly work with reports, legal documents, and other written materials.

Questions:

Passage 1: The Importance of Early Childhood Education.

The first few years of a child's life are crucial in shaping their future success, both academically and socially. Early childhood education (ECE) refers to the period of learning that occurs from birth to age eight, a time when the brain is developing rapidly. Research consistently shows that high-quality early education can have long-lasting positive effects on a child's cognitive, emotional, and social development. As such, early childhood education has become a key focus for policymakers, educators, and parents alike.

One of the most significant benefits of early childhood education is its ability to close the achievement gap. Children from disadvantaged backgrounds often enter school with fewer resources and less exposure to early learning experiences. ECE programs can level the playing field by providing children with a strong foundation in literacy, numeracy, and critical thinking skills. These early experiences help children develop the cognitive abilities needed for success in school, reducing the chances of falling behind in later years.

Moreover, early childhood education programs provide children with important social skills that will serve them throughout their lives. In addition to learning academic content, children in ECE programs learn how to interact with peers, follow directions, and develop self-control. These skills are essential for success in school and later in life, as they help children navigate social situations, work in teams, and build positive relationships.

Another key aspect of early childhood education is the role it plays in promoting emotional well-being. High-quality early education programs provide a safe and nurturing environment where children can develop a sense of security and confidence.

Teachers in these programs are trained to recognize and respond to the emotional needs of young children, helping them regulate their emotions and develop resilience. This emotional support is critical for children as they face the challenges of growing up, as it lays the foundation for healthy mental health and emotional development.

Despite the numerous benefits of early childhood education, access to quality programs is still a major issue in many parts of the world. Many children, particularly those from low-income families, do not have access to high-quality early education due to financial, logistical, or geographical barriers.

Additionally, the demand for early childhood educators often outstrips the supply, leading to overcrowded classrooms and overworked teachers. As a result, the quality of early childhood education can vary greatly from one location to another.

To address these challenges, governments and organizations around the world are working to expand access to early childhood education. This includes increasing funding for public ECE programs, providing subsidies for low-income families, and investing in the training and professional development of early childhood educators. Many countries have recognized the importance of ECE and have made it a priority to ensure that all children, regardless of their background, have access to high-quality early learning experiences.

In conclusion, early childhood education is a critical investment in a child's future. The benefits of ECE go beyond academic achievement, providing children with the social, emotional, and cognitive skills they need to succeed in school and life. While challenges remain in providing equitable access to high-quality programs, the growing recognition of the importance of ECE provides hope for a more inclusive and successful future for all children.

1. According to the passage, what is one of the most significant benefits of early childhood education?

A. It reduces the need for parental involvement
B. It helps children develop cognitive, emotional, and social skills
C. It eliminates the achievement gap in later years
D. It focuses primarily on preparing children for standardized tests

2. How does early childhood education help reduce the achievement gap, according to the passage?

A. By teaching children how to excel in standardized tests
B. By providing children with a strong foundation in basic subjects
C. By increasing the number of hours spent in school
D. By preparing children for life after graduation

3. What social skills does early childhood education help children develop?

A. The ability to manage personal finances
B. The ability to navigate social situations and build relationships
C. The ability to lead large groups of people
D. The ability to write formal reports

4. According to the passage, how does early childhood education support emotional well-being?

A. By providing children with academic counseling
B. By teaching children advanced emotional regulation techniques
C. By offering a nurturing and secure environment for children
D. By helping children avoid negative emotions

5. What challenge regarding early childhood education is discussed in the passage?

A. The increasing quality of early education in all regions
B. The reluctance of families to participate in education
C. The oversupply of qualified early childhood educators
D. The financial, logistical, and geographical barriers to access

---

Passage 2: The Impact of Urbanization on the Environment.

Urbanization, the process by which rural areas become cities, has dramatically increased over the last century. As more people move into urban areas in search of better job opportunities, education, and healthcare, cities have grown at an unprecedented rate. This expansion has brought about numerous economic benefits, but it has also had significant environmental consequences that cannot be ignored. The transformation of the landscape, the rise of industrial activity, and the intensification of transportation networks all contribute to the growing environmental challenges facing urban areas.

One of the most prominent issues associated with urbanization is air pollution. As cities grow, so too does the number of vehicles on the road, factories producing goods, and buildings generating waste. These activities release harmful pollutants into the atmosphere, including particulate matter, nitrogen oxides, and carbon dioxide. The buildup of these pollutants contributes to poor air quality, which in turn affects human health and the climate. Chronic exposure to polluted air can lead to respiratory diseases, cardiovascular issues, and premature deaths, particularly in densely populated urban centers.

In addition to air pollution, urbanization has a profound impact on local ecosystems. The expansion of cities often leads to the destruction of natural habitats, such as forests, wetlands, and grasslands, which are vital for biodiversity. The construction of buildings, roads, and other infrastructure fragments these habitats, making it difficult for wildlife to survive and thrive. The loss of green spaces also affects human well-being, as natural areas play a crucial role in improving mental health, providing recreational opportunities, and reducing the urban heat island effect.

Urbanization also places immense pressure on water resources. As populations in cities grow, the demand for water increases. This often leads to over-extraction of water from rivers, lakes, and underground aquifers, which can result in water shortages and the degradation of water quality. Furthermore, urban areas are more prone to flooding due to the prevalence of impervious surfaces such as concrete and asphalt. These surfaces prevent rainwater from being absorbed into the ground, leading to increased runoff and higher risks of flooding, particularly during heavy rains.

The environmental challenges posed by urbanization have prompted governments and organizations to adopt more sustainable practices. Many cities are investing in green infrastructure, such as parks, green roofs, and urban forests, to mitigate the effects of urbanization on the environment.

These initiatives not only help to improve air and water quality but also provide much-needed green spaces for residents. Additionally, cities are exploring alternative transportation options, such as electric buses and bike-sharing programs, to reduce their reliance on fossil fuels and decrease air pollution.

Another important strategy is the promotion of energy efficiency and renewable energy sources. Many urban areas are transitioning to solar, wind, and other renewable energy sources to power buildings, transportation systems, and industries.

By reducing reliance on fossil fuels, these efforts aim to cut down on greenhouse gas emissions and combat climate change. The use of energy-efficient technologies, such as LED lighting, smart grids, and energy-efficient appliances, is also helping to reduce the carbon footprint of cities.

Despite these efforts, urbanization continues to be a major driver of environmental degradation. As cities expand, they consume more resources, produce more waste, and generate more pollution. It is clear that urbanization must be managed carefully to minimize its environmental impact. To achieve this, policymakers, urban planners, and citizens must work together to create cities that are not only economically vibrant but also environmentally sustainable.

In conclusion, while urbanization has brought many benefits, it has also presented significant environmental challenges. Air pollution, loss of biodiversity, water shortages, and the urban heat island effect are just a few of the issues that need to be addressed.

By embracing sustainable practices and making smart decisions about urban growth, cities can mitigate the negative effects of urbanization and create a more sustainable future for all.

---

6. What is one of the major environmental challenges caused by urbanization, according to the passage?

A. The destruction of natural habitats
B. The depletion of natural resources
C. The growth of renewable energy sources
D. The increase in rural populations

7. How does air pollution in urban areas impact human health, according to the passage?

A. It causes respiratory diseases and cardiovascular issues
B. It promotes the growth of healthy bacteria
C. It improves the quality of the environment
D. It leads to longer life expectancy

---

8. What is one strategy mentioned in the passage to reduce the environmental impact of urbanization?

A. Decreasing urban populations
B. Increasing the number of vehicles on the road
C. Investing in green infrastructure such as parks and green roofs
D. Encouraging the use of fossil fuels for energy

---

9. What problem related to water resources is exacerbated by urbanization?

A. Over-extraction of water from natural sources
B. The disappearance of water-based wildlife
C. The rapid cooling of water sources
D. The increased use of clean drinking water in rural areas

---

10. According to the passage, what is a future direction for sustainable urban growth?

A. Reducing the number of residents in urban areas
B. Promoting energy efficiency and renewable energy sources
C. Increasing the use of fossil fuels in transportation
D. Expanding urban areas without considering environmental impact

---

Passage 3: The Role of Civil Service in American Governance.

In the United States, the civil service plays a critical role in the effective functioning of the government. Civil servants, who are non-elected government employees, are responsible for implementing the policies and programs created by elected officials. They work in various government agencies at the federal, state, and local levels, ensuring that the day-to-day operations of government run smoothly. Civil service positions span a wide range of fields, from law enforcement and healthcare to education and public administration.

The origins of the American civil service system date back to the 19th century. Before then, government positions were often filled through patronage, where elected officials appointed friends, allies, or supporters to various roles, regardless of their qualifications. This system, known as the "spoils system," led to inefficiency, corruption, and political favoritism. In response, reformers called for a merit-based system, in which government employees would be selected based on their qualifications and abilities, rather than political connections.

The **Pendleton Civil Service Reform Act of 1883** was a landmark piece of legislation that established the foundation of the modern civil service system in the United States. The law created a merit-based selection process for federal employees, ensuring that candidates were hired based on their qualifications rather than political loyalty. It also established the **Civil Service Commission**, which oversaw the hiring process and ensured that employees were protected from political pressures once hired. This reform helped professionalize the federal workforce and set a precedent for state and local governments to follow suit. Today, civil service employees are hired through a competitive examination process, and their careers are governed by a set of rules and regulations designed to ensure fairness, transparency, and accountability. The goal of this system is to create an efficient, skilled, and non-partisan workforce that can implement policies effectively, regardless of political changes or administration shifts.

One of the key aspects of the modern civil service system is its commitment to diversity and equal opportunity. Over the years, the U.S. government has made efforts to ensure that civil service positions are accessible to people from all backgrounds, regardless of race, gender, or socioeconomic status. Laws such as the **Civil Rights Act of 1964** and the **Equal Employment Opportunity Act of 1972** have been instrumental in preventing discrimination and promoting a more inclusive workforce. These laws have also established affirmative action programs to ensure that underrepresented groups have a fair opportunity to compete for government jobs.

Another important function of civil service employees is their role in providing essential public services. Civil servants work in fields such as healthcare, education, law enforcement, and emergency services, ensuring that citizens have access to necessary services. For example, public health workers monitor disease outbreaks, law enforcement officers uphold public safety, and teachers provide education to the next generation. These services are essential for maintaining the well-being of society and ensuring that citizens have access to the resources they need.

However, the civil service system is not without its challenges. One of the most significant issues facing the civil service today is the growing concern about government bureaucracy. Critics argue that the system is too complex and that the proliferation of rules and regulations can lead to inefficiency and delays. Additionally, there are concerns about government employees becoming too entrenched in their positions, making it difficult for new ideas and innovations to take hold.

Despite these challenges, the civil service system remains a cornerstone of American governance. It is essential for ensuring that government policies are carried out effectively and that public services are provided to those in need. The continued professionalization and diversification of the civil service workforce will be crucial for addressing the challenges of the 21st century and ensuring that the government can meet the needs of a changing society.

---

11. What was one of the main problems with the "spoils system" in American government?

A. Government positions were awarded based on political loyalty, not qualifications
B. It promoted equal opportunity for all citizens
C. It created a highly skilled and efficient workforce
D. It was designed to create a merit-based selection process

---

12. Which of the following was a key result of the Pendleton Civil Service Reform Act of 1883?

A. The introduction of political patronage for government hiring
B. The establishment of a merit-based system for hiring federal employees
C. The elimination of government job opportunities for minorities
D. The creation of a unified political party for government appointments

---

13. What is one of the goals of the modern civil service system in the U.S.?

A. To create a skilled and non-partisan workforce
B. To ensure all government positions are filled by elected officials
C. To eliminate federal agencies in charge of public services
D. To reduce the size of the federal government

---

14. How have laws like the Civil Rights Act of 1964 and the Equal Employment Opportunity Act of 1972 impacted the civil service?

A. By promoting discrimination in hiring processes
B. By preventing discrimination and promoting diversity in hiring
C. By eliminating merit-based hiring practices
D. By reducing the number of civil service jobs available

15. According to the passage, what is one of the challenges facing the civil service system today?

A. The growing efficiency of government operations
B. Government bureaucracy and inefficiency
C. The increasing number of public services available
D. The lack of training for government employees

Passage 4: The Evolution of Public Health Policy in the United States.

Public health policy in the United States has evolved significantly over the past century, responding to both emerging health threats and shifts in societal values. From the early days of the 20th century, when infectious diseases like tuberculosis and smallpox were the primary concern, to the modern focus on chronic diseases, mental health, and environmental factors, public health policy has continually adapted to meet the changing needs of the population. The evolution of public health policy reflects broader trends in science, technology, and social movements, and it plays a crucial role in determining how the country addresses health challenges and promotes well-being.

One of the key milestones in the development of public health policy was the establishment of the **Centers for Disease Control and Prevention (CDC)** in 1946. The CDC was created to combat the spread of infectious diseases and to coordinate national efforts to respond to public health crises. Over the years, the CDC's role expanded beyond infectious disease control to include chronic disease prevention, environmental health, and health promotion. The agency became the cornerstone of the U.S. public health system, conducting research, providing data, and shaping health policy.

Another important milestone came with the passage of the **Social Security Act of 1935**, which established the framework for the United States' social safety net. While the Act primarily focused on providing financial assistance to older adults, it laid the foundation for future public health programs, including Medicare and Medicaid, which provide health insurance for the elderly, low-income individuals, and people with disabilities. These programs have been instrumental in expanding access to healthcare, particularly for underserved populations.

In the 1960s and 1970s, public health policy began to shift its focus from infectious diseases to the growing burden of chronic diseases, such as heart disease, cancer, and diabetes. Advances in medical research and technology had allowed for the treatment and control of infectious diseases, and public health experts began to turn their attention to the rising prevalence of lifestyle-related diseases. Policies were introduced to address risk factors such as smoking, poor diet, and physical inactivity, with a focus on prevention and health promotion. The **National Cancer Act**

of 1971 and the creation of the **National Institutes of Health (NIH)** Cancer Institute helped direct significant funding and research into cancer prevention and treatment.

In recent decades, there has been a growing recognition of the importance of mental health in public health policy. Historically, mental health was often neglected or stigmatized, but over time, the understanding of mental health has shifted, and it is now seen as an integral component of overall well-being. The **Mental Health Parity and Addiction Equity Act of 2008** required that insurance companies provide equal coverage for mental health and substance use disorders, marking a significant step toward the integration of mental health care into mainstream healthcare systems. This law aimed to reduce disparities in access to care for individuals struggling with mental health and addiction issues.

More recently, public health policy has had to respond to emerging global health threats, such as the COVID-19 pandemic. The pandemic exposed significant gaps in the U.S. healthcare system, including disparities in access to care and health outcomes. It also underscored the importance of public health infrastructure and the need for timely, coordinated responses to health emergencies. In response, public health policy has increasingly emphasized the importance of **pandemic preparedness**, **global health collaboration**, and addressing health inequities, particularly in vulnerable communities.

As we look to the future, the focus of public health policy in the United States will likely continue to evolve. Climate change, for example, is emerging as a critical issue that intersects with public health, as rising temperatures, air quality issues, and changing weather patterns have the potential to increase the spread of infectious diseases and exacerbate chronic conditions like asthma and heart disease. Addressing the health impacts of climate change will require new strategies, policies, and international cooperation.

Public health policy also faces the challenge of addressing the growing burden of health disparities. While access to healthcare has improved for many Americans, significant gaps remain, particularly for racial and ethnic minorities, rural populations, and low-income communities. Reducing health disparities will require systemic changes in healthcare delivery, education, and social policies.

In conclusion, the evolution of public health policy in the United States has been shaped by a wide range of factors, from advances in medical research to shifts in societal priorities. While significant progress has been made in improving health outcomes and expanding access to care, challenges remain. Moving forward, public health policy will need to continue adapting to emerging threats, such as climate change and health inequities, while building on the successes of past public health efforts.

16. According to the passage, what was a key development in public health policy in 1946?

A. The passage of the Social Security Act
B. The creation of the Centers for Disease Control and Prevention (CDC)
C. The establishment of the National Cancer Institute
D. The introduction of Medicare and Medicaid

17. What was a major shift in public health policy in the 1960s and 1970s?

A. A focus on mental health and addiction services
B. A focus on the prevention of chronic diseases
C. A focus on expanding access to healthcare for the elderly
D. A focus on improving hospital infrastructure

18. How has mental health been addressed in recent public health policy?

A. By reducing insurance coverage for mental health services
B. By reducing the number of mental health professionals
C. By integrating mental health care into mainstream healthcare
D. By excluding mental health services from the insurance market

19. What challenge has emerged in recent public health policy, according to the passage?

A. The need for more hospitals
B. The lack of focus on mental health
C. Disparities in access to care and health outcomes
D. The overfunding of public health programs

20. What future challenge for public health policy is mentioned in the passage?

A. The rising cost of healthcare
B. The increasing number of healthcare professionals
C. Addressing the health impacts of climate change
D. The decline in chronic diseases

Section 4: Clarity (20 Questions)

Time Limit: 20 minutes

Instructions:

- This section evaluates your ability to identify clear and concise sentences in law enforcement communication.
- You will be given two similar sentences, and you must choose the one that is written more clearly.
- **Tip**: Pay attention to sentence structure. Avoiding excessive use of passive voice and maintaining logical sentence flow will help you recognize the clearer sentence.
- **Goal**: To assess your ability to write and understand clear communication, an essential skill for law enforcement officers who must often write reports and communicate with others under pressure.

Questions:

Question 1

A. Having gathered all the evidence from the scene, the detective began analyzing the data in hopes of uncovering new leads.
B. The detective, hoping to uncover new leads, began analyzing the data after gathering all the evidence from the scene.

Question 2

A. The suspect was apprehended by the officers, who acted quickly to prevent further harm to the victim.
B. The officers, acting quickly to prevent further harm to the victim, apprehended the suspect.

Question 3

A. The officer was reluctant to use force, but under the circumstances, it was deemed necessary to subdue the suspect.
B. Despite being reluctant to use force, the officer deemed it necessary to subdue the suspect under the circumstances.

Question 4

A. The officer's report was thoroughly examined, revealing discrepancies that could potentially delay the case's progress.
B. Revealing discrepancies that could potentially delay the case's progress, the officer's report was thoroughly examined.

Question 5

A. The officer's calm demeanor was a result of his extensive training, which allowed him to remain composed in high-pressure situations.
B. As a result of his extensive training, the officer's calm demeanor allowed him to remain composed in high-pressure situations.

Question 6

A. Quickly surrounding the area, the officers prevented the suspect's escape after he attempted to flee.
B. The suspect attempted to flee, but the officers quickly surrounded the area, preventing his escape.

Question 7

A. The officer's decision to call for backup was prompted by the escalating danger of the situation.
B. Prompted by the escalating danger of the situation, the officer's decision to call for backup was made.

Question 8

A. The detective carefully reviewed the witness statements and the physical evidence to build a case against the suspect.
B. To build a case against the suspect, the detective carefully reviewed the witness statements and the physical evidence.

Question 9

A. The officer issued a warning to the suspect, but his actions suggested he was unlikely to comply with the law.
B. His actions suggested that he was unlikely to comply with the law, but the officer issued a warning to the suspect.

Question 10

A. Ensuring the safety of the public and bringing the situation to a peaceful resolution, the officers acted decisively.
B. The officers acted decisively, ensuring the safety of the public and bringing the situation to a peaceful resolution.

Question 11

A. The officer quickly assessed the situation, recognizing the potential dangers involved in the standoff.
B. Recognizing the potential dangers involved in the standoff, the officer quickly assessed the situation.

Question 12

A. Despite the complex nature of the case, the detective was able to uncover crucial evidence that led to a breakthrough.
B. The detective uncovered crucial evidence that led to a breakthrough, despite the complex nature of the case.

Question 13

A. The officers pursued the suspect through the alleyway, knowing they needed to act fast to prevent his escape.
B. Knowing they needed to act fast to prevent his escape, the officers pursued the suspect through the alleyway.

Question 14

A. After reviewing the security footage, the officers identified the suspect and began drafting a report.
B. The officers, after reviewing the security footage, began drafting a report and identified the suspect.

Question 15

A. The detective was able to connect the evidence to the suspect, finally leading to an arrest after a prolonged investigation.
B. After a prolonged investigation, the detective finally connected the evidence to the suspect, leading to an arrest.

Question 16

A. The officer made the decision to call for backup quickly, understanding the growing risk of the situation.
B. Understanding the growing risk of the situation, the officer quickly made the decision to call for backup.

Question 17

A. The suspect, having been cornered, was arrested without further incident.
B. Having been cornered, the suspect was arrested without further incident.

Question 18

A. The officers were determined to finish the investigation quickly, understanding the urgency of resolving the case.
B. Understanding the urgency of resolving the case, the officers were determined to finish the investigation quickly.

Question 19

A. The officer was certain that the suspect had committed the crime, based on the overwhelming evidence that had been gathered.
B. Based on the overwhelming evidence that had been gathered, the officer was certain that the suspect had committed the crime.

Question 20

A. The officer immediately began searching for clues, knowing that every second counted in solving the case.
B. Knowing that every second counted in solving the case, the officer immediately began searching for clues.

Practice Test 3: Answer Key.

Section 1: Spelling.

Question Number	Correct Option
1	A
2	A
3	A
4	C
5	D
6	C
7	D
8	A
9	A
10	A
11	B
12	A
13	D
14	D
15	A
16	C
17	A
18	A
19	A
20	D

Section 2: Vocabulary.

Question Number	Correct Option
1	B
2	B
3	B
4	B
5	B
6	C
7	A
8	B
9	A
10	C
11	A
12	B
13	B
14	B
15	B
16	C
17	C
18	B
19	B
20	B

Section 3: Reading Comprehension.

Question Number	Correct Option
1	B
2	B
3	B
4	C
5	D
6	A
7	A
8	C
9	A
10	B
11	A
12	B
13	A
14	B
15	B
16	B
17	B
18	C
19	C
20	C

Section 4: Clarity.

Question Number	Correct Option
1	A
2	B
3	A
4	A
5	A
6	B
7	A
8	A
9	A
10	B
11	A
12	A
13	B
14	A
15	A
16	B
17	A
18	B
19	A
20	B

Practice Test 3: Answer And Explanation.

Section 1: Spelling.

1. **Answer**: A. evaluate
   Explanation: "Evaluate" is the correct spelling, meaning to assess or judge the validity of something. The other options are incorrect spellings of the word. Option B uses "evalute," which is a common misspelling. Option C and D are incorrect due to missing or extra letters.

2. **Answer**: A. examine, criminal
   Explanation: "Examine" is the correct verb meaning to inspect or review, and "criminal" is the correct adjective describing someone involved in crime. Option B uses "exmine," which is a common misspelling. Option C uses "examane," which is incorrect, and "crimminal" in the plural form is incorrect as well.

3. **Answer**: A. detailed, accurate
   Explanation: "Detailed" and "accurate" are both correct forms. "Detailed" refers to a description that includes all relevant aspects, and "accurate" means correct in all details. Option B uses "detaile," which is incorrect, and "accuratte" is a misspelling. Option C uses "detalied" and "accurat," both incorrect spellings.

4. **Answer**: C. complete, factual
   Explanation: "Complete" is the correct verb form meaning to finish or finalize something, and "factual" is the correct adjective describing information based on facts. The other options have incorrect spellings like "complite" and "factuel," which do not exist in this context.

5. **Answer**: D. corroborate, sufficient
   Explanation: "Corroborate" is the correct verb, meaning to support or confirm with evidence, and "sufficient" means enough or adequate. Option B uses "suffcent," which is a misspelling of "sufficient." Option C contains multiple errors: "coroborate" is incorrect, and "suffeicient" is a misspelling. Option A uses "corroborated," which is past tense and doesn't fit the sentence.

6. **Answer**: C. secure, present
   Explanation: "Secure" is the correct verb, meaning to make something safe or locked, and "present" is the correct adjective, meaning being at the location. Option B uses "secur" and "presant," both of which are incorrect spellings. Option A uses "securr" and "presnt," both misspelled. Option D uses "presese," which is a misspelling of "presence."

7. **Answer**: D. handle, professional
   Explanation: "Handle" is the correct verb meaning to deal with, and "professional" is the correct adjective meaning acting with competence and respect. Option A is correct.

Option B uses "handel" and "profesinal," both incorrect. Option C uses "profeional," which is misspelled.

8. **Answer**: A. investigation, reconstruct
   Explanation: "Investigation" is the correct noun for a detailed inquiry, and "reconstruct" is the correct verb for piecing together events. Option B uses "investegation" and "reconstruate," which are incorrect. Option C uses "reconsturct," which is a misspelling. Option D uses "invistigation," which is also a misspelling.

9. **Answer**: A. clarify, statement
   Explanation: "Clarify" is the correct verb, meaning to make something clear or easier to understand, and "statement" is the correct noun referring to a formal declaration. Option B uses "clarrify" and "statemant," both misspelled. Option C uses "clarifie" and "statment," both incorrect. Option D uses "statment," which is also a misspelling.

10. **Answer**: A. methodical, relevant
    Explanation: "Methodical" is the correct adjective, meaning done in an orderly and systematic way, and "relevant" is the correct adjective meaning pertinent or related to the matter at hand. Option B uses "relevnt," which is a misspelling of "relevant." Option C uses "relavant," which is also incorrect. Option D uses "methoical," which is a misspelling of "methodical."

11. **Answer**: B. influential, affected
    Explanation: "Influential" is the correct spelling of the adjective meaning having the power to affect something, while "affected" is the correct verb (past tense) indicating something was impacted. Option A uses the incorrect form "influencial," which is not standard English. Option C incorrectly spells "influential" as "influentual" and uses "effected" incorrectly; "effected" refers to causing something to happen, but "affected" is more appropriate in this context. Option D uses "affect," which is incorrect as "affected" should be used here to match the verb tense.

12. **Answer**: A. examined, false
    Explanation: "Examined" is the correct past-tense verb meaning to investigate or inspect something closely, and "false" is the correct adjective describing something untrue. Option B uses "examin" instead of "examined," and "falce" is a misspelling of "false." Option C uses "fals," which is an incorrect form of "false," and "examine" is not the right tense for this context. Option D uses "examend" and "fauls," both incorrect spellings.

13. **Answer**: D. credible, matched
    Explanation: "Credible" is the correct adjective meaning trustworthy or believable, and "matched" is the correct past-tense verb meaning to be in agreement with. Option B uses "creditable," which means praiseworthy but not necessarily believable in this context, and "mathed" is a misspelling. Option C uses "credable" and "matche," which are both incorrect spellings. Option A uses "mathed," which is also misspelled.

14. **Answer**: D. verify, mislead
    Explanation: "Verify" is the correct verb meaning to check or confirm the facts, and

"mislead" is the correct verb meaning to cause someone to believe something untrue. Option A uses "verify" correctly, but "misleading" should not be used here because it is an adjective, not a verb. Option B uses "verifie," which is a misspelling. Option C uses "verifiy" and "misleade," both incorrect.

15. **Answer**: A. tracked, lead

    Explanation: "Tracked" is the correct past-tense verb meaning to follow or monitor, and "lead" is the correct noun meaning a piece of information that helps guide an investigation. Option B uses "track," which is the wrong tense. Option C uses "leaded," which is not a word in this context. Option D uses "tracking," which is present participle and doesn't fit the past-tense structure of the sentence.

16. **Answer**: C. ignore, prove

    Explanation: "Ignore" is the correct verb form (present tense), meaning to disregard, and "prove" is the correct verb (base form) to demonstrate the truth of something. Option A uses "proven," which is the past participle and is not needed here. Option B uses "ignored," which is past tense and doesn't fit with the rest of the sentence. Option D uses "ignores," which is incorrect in this context.

17. **Answer**: A. justified, review

    Explanation: "Justified" is the correct past-tense adjective meaning reasonable or warranted, and "review" is the correct noun meaning a careful examination. Option B uses "justifiably," which is an adverb and does not fit grammatically in the sentence. Option C uses "justify," which is the verb form and doesn't match the context, and "reveiw" is a misspelling of "review." Option D uses "reveiw," which is also incorrect.

18. **Answer**: A. neutralize, hostile

    Explanation: "Neutralize" is the correct verb meaning to make something ineffective, and "hostile" is the correct adjective meaning unfriendly or aggressive. Option B uses "nuetralize," which is a misspelling. Option C uses "hostil," which is incorrect, and Option D uses "hostiled," which is not a word in this context.

19. **Answer**: A. split-second, escalation

    Explanation: "Split-second" is the correct term referring to an extremely brief moment, and "escalation" is the correct noun for an increase in intensity. Option B uses "split-sec," which is incorrect, and "escallation" is a misspelling of "escalation." Option C is correct. Option D uses "splitted-second" and "escalated," both incorrect for this context.

20. **Answer**: D. behavior, clue

    Explanation: "Behavior" is the correct spelling, referring to the actions or conduct of the suspect, and "clue" is the correct noun referring to a piece of evidence that helps solve a mystery. Option B uses "behavious" and "clew," both of which are misspellings. Option C uses "clew," which is a rare or archaic spelling of "clue," but "clue" is the correct, more commonly used term here.

Section 2: Vocabulary.

1. **Answer**: B. Detached
   Explanation: "Dispassionate" means not influenced by strong feelings, making decisions based on logic and reason. "Detached" is the best synonym, as it refers to being emotionally uninvolved or impartial. Option A, "biased," means having an unfair preference, which contradicts "dispassionate." Option C, "sensitive," refers to being emotionally responsive, which is the opposite. Option D, "compassionate," means feeling sympathy or concern, which is the opposite of being emotionally detached.

2. **Answer**: B. Evasion
   Explanation: "Obfuscation" refers to the act of deliberately making something unclear or confusing. "Evasion" is the best synonym, as it means avoiding the truth or making it difficult to understand. Option A, "clarification," means making something clear, which is the opposite of "obfuscation." Option C, "explanation," refers to providing clarity, which again contradicts the meaning of "obfuscation." Option D, "illumination," means shedding light on something, which also contradicts the act of making something obscure.

3. **Answer**: B. Understanding
   Explanation: "Discernment" means the ability to perceive or recognize something with insight or clarity. "Understanding" is the best synonym, as it refers to the ability to grasp the meaning or significance of something. Option A, "confusion," refers to a lack of clarity or understanding, the opposite of "discernment." Option C, "inability," suggests an incapacity to understand, which contradicts "discernment." Option D, "ignorance," refers to a lack of knowledge, which is opposite to being discerning.

4. **Answer**: B. Compassion
   Explanation: "Empathy" refers to the ability to understand and share another person's feelings, particularly in times of suffering. "Compassion" is the best synonym, as it means deep sympathy and concern for others' suffering. Option A, "indifference," means lack of concern or interest, which is the opposite of "empathy." Option C, "disdain," refers to a feeling of contempt or scorn, which contradicts the caring nature of "empathy." Option D, "hostility," means aggressive or unfriendly behavior, which also contrasts with "empathy."

5. **Answer**: B. Reduce
   Explanation: "Mitigate" means to make a situation less severe or intense. "Reduce" is the best synonym, as it means to decrease or lessen something. Option A, "aggravate," means to make something worse, the opposite of "mitigate." Option C, "exacerbate," means to intensify or make something worse, which contradicts the meaning of "mitigate." Option D, "heighten," means to increase or intensify, also opposite of "mitigate."

6. **Answer**: C. Delicate

   Explanation: "Subtle" means delicate or nuanced, often requiring careful attention to understand. "Delicate" is the best synonym, meaning sensitive or careful in approach. Option A, "obvious," means easy to perceive or understand, which is the opposite of "subtle." Option B, "harsh," means severe or unkind, and Option D, "blunt," means straightforward or rude, both of which are not subtle in nature.

7. **Answer**: A. Clear

   Explanation: "Lucid" means clear, easily understood, or expressed in a way that makes sense. "Clear" is the best synonym, as it directly refers to something easily understood. Option B, "confusing," means causing difficulty in understanding, which is the opposite of "lucid." Option C, "obscure," means unclear or difficult to understand. Option D, "complex," means intricate or complicated, which is the opposite of being "lucid."

8. **Answer**: B. Organized, analyze

   Explanation: "Methodical" means working in a structured and organized way. "Organized" fits as the synonym, and "analyze" is the correct verb meaning to examine carefully. Option A, "disorganized, neglect," suggests a lack of order and not paying attention to details, which is opposite to "methodical." Option C, "random, clarify," doesn't align with the careful and structured approach of a methodical investigation. Option D, "hasty, ignore," implies rushing and neglecting important details, which is contradictory to being "methodical."

9. **Answer**: A. Determined

   Explanation: "Obstinate" means stubbornly refusing to change one's position or opinion, especially in the face of pressure. "Determined" is the best synonym, meaning resolute or having a firm purpose. Option B, "flexible," means willing to adapt or change, which is the opposite of being "obstinate." Option C, "timid," means lacking courage or confidence, which contrasts with the firmness implied by "obstinate." Option D, "indifferent," means having no particular interest or concern, which also contradicts "obstinate."

10. **Answer**: C. Mediate

    Explanation: "Intervene" means to get involved in a situation in order to change or stop its course. "Mediate" is the best synonym, as it refers to helping to resolve a dispute between two parties. Option A, "participate," means to take part in something, but it doesn't imply resolving or changing the course of the dispute. Option B, "ignore," means to avoid paying attention, which contradicts the idea of intervening. Option D, "watch," means to observe without acting, which does not match the proactive nature of "intervene."

11. **Answer**: A. Flawless

    Explanation: "Impeccable" means flawless or without fault, especially in terms of character or behavior. "Flawless" is the best synonym, meaning perfect and without errors. Option B, "faulty," means having defects, the opposite of "impeccable." Option C, "inconsistent," refers to something that varies, which contradicts the idea of being impeccable. Option D, "unreliable," means not dependable, which is also the opposite of "impeccable."

12. **Answer**: B. Honest
    Explanation: "Forthright" means being direct and honest in expressing thoughts, especially in a transparent and open manner. "Honest" is the best synonym, meaning truthful and straightforward. Option A, "evasive," means avoiding or escaping a question or issue, which is the opposite of being forthright. Option C, "deceptive," means misleading or dishonest, which contrasts with the openness of being forthright. Option D, "suspicious," means having doubts or concerns, which is not the same as being forthright.

13. **Answer**: B. Outstanding
    Explanation: "Exemplary" means serving as a model or a perfect example. "Outstanding" is the best synonym, as it means exceptionally good or excellent. Option A, "mediocre," means average or ordinary, which is the opposite of "exemplary." Option C, "faulty," means having defects or flaws, which contradicts the idea of being exemplary. Option D, "average," refers to something typical or not exceptional, and doesn't fit the context of being exemplary.

14. **Answer**: B. Judgment
    Explanation: "Discretion" means the ability to make decisions based on careful judgment, especially when dealing with sensitive issues. "Judgment" is the best synonym, as it refers to the ability to make decisions wisely and thoughtfully. Option A, "indiscretion," means lack of careful judgment, the opposite of "discretion." Option C, "foolishness," means lack of wisdom or good sense, and Option D, "recklessness," implies a lack of caution, which contrasts with discretion.

15. **Answer**: B. Superficial
    Explanation: "Cursory" means done quickly and without attention to detail, often in a superficial manner. "Superficial" is the best synonym, meaning shallow or lacking depth. Option A, "thorough," means comprehensive and careful, which is the opposite of "cursory." Option C, "exhaustive," means covering every possible aspect, which contrasts with a cursory glance. Option D, "detailed," means providing many specifics, again the opposite of "cursory."

16. **Answer**: C. Disturbed
    Explanation: "Perturbed" means disturbed or upset, especially by something unexpected. "Disturbed" is the best synonym, meaning troubled or unsettled. Option A, "unconcerned," means showing no concern, which is the opposite of being perturbed. Option B, "calm," means not disturbed or agitated, and Option D, "delighted," means pleased or happy, which contradicts the meaning of "perturbed."

17. **Answer**: C. Tenacious
    Explanation: "Resilient" means being able to recover quickly from difficulties or setbacks. "Tenacious" is the best synonym, meaning persistent or determined. Option A,

"fragile," means easily broken or delicate, which is the opposite of resilient. Option B, "weak," means lacking strength or ability to resist, contradicting the idea of being resilient. Option D, "overwhelmed," means overcome by stress or emotion, which also contradicts resilience.

18. **Answer**: B. Thoughtful

    Explanation: "Conscientious" means showing great care and attention to detail, especially when performing a task. "Thoughtful" is the best synonym, as it implies careful consideration and mindfulness. Option A, "careless," means lacking attention or concern, which is the opposite of being conscientious. Option C, "lazy," refers to unwillingness to put in effort, and Option D, "indifferent," means lacking interest or concern, which also contradicts being conscientious.

19. **Answer**: B. Calm

    Explanation: "Unflappable" means not easily upset or disturbed, especially in stressful situations. "Calm" is the best synonym, meaning not showing excitement or agitation. Option A, "nervous," means uneasy or anxious, which contradicts "unflappable." Option C, "agitated," means disturbed or upset, and Option D, "anxious," means worried or fearful, both of which are opposite of being unflappable.

20. **Answer**: B. Educated

    Explanation: "Erudite" means having or showing great knowledge or learning, especially in a particular subject. "Educated" is the best synonym, meaning having knowledge or learning from schooling or study. Option A, "shallow," means lacking depth or thoroughness, the opposite of erudition. Option C, "confused," means unclear or uncertain, and Option D, "illiterate," means lacking the ability to read or write, both of which contradict the meaning of "erudite."

Section 3: Reading Comprehension.

1. **Answer**: B. It helps children develop cognitive, emotional, and social skills

    Explanation: The passage emphasizes that **early childhood education (ECE)** helps children develop **cognitive, emotional, and social skills**, which are crucial for their future success. Option A is incorrect as the passage does not suggest that ECE reduces the need for parental involvement. Option C is not fully accurate; while ECE helps reduce the achievement gap, it doesn't eliminate it entirely. Option D is incorrect because the focus of ECE is on broader development, not just preparing for tests.

2. **Answer**: B. By providing children with a strong foundation in basic subjects

    Explanation: The passage explains that **early childhood education helps close the achievement gap** by providing children with a **strong foundation in literacy, numeracy, and critical thinking skills**, which are essential for success in school. Option A is incorrect because the passage does not focus on standardized testing. Option C is not mentioned in the passage as a factor. Option D, preparing for life after graduation, is not the main focus in this context.

3. **Answer**: B. The ability to navigate social situations and build relationships
   Explanation: The passage highlights that in addition to academic skills, **early childhood education helps children learn social skills**, such as how to interact with peers, follow directions, and develop self-control. Option A, personal finances, is not discussed. Option C, leadership of large groups, is not mentioned. Option D, writing formal reports, is not a focus of early childhood education.

4. **Answer**: C. By offering a nurturing and secure environment for children
   Explanation: The passage explains that **high-quality early education programs** offer a **safe and nurturing environment**, where children can develop emotional security and confidence. Option A is incorrect because academic counseling is not a focus of early childhood education. Option B, teaching advanced techniques, is not mentioned. Option D is also incorrect because the goal is not to avoid emotions, but to help children manage them.

5. **Answer**: D. The financial, logistical, and geographical barriers to access
   Explanation: The passage discusses how **financial, logistical, and geographical barriers** prevent many children, especially from low-income families, from accessing high-quality early childhood education. Option A is incorrect because the passage addresses challenges, not increasing quality. Option C, the oversupply of educators, is the opposite of what is mentioned; there is a **shortage** of qualified professionals. Option B is incorrect because the passage doesn't focus on family reluctance but rather access issues.

6. **Answer**: A. The destruction of natural habitats
   Explanation: The passage emphasizes the **destruction of natural habitats**, such as forests and wetlands, as one of the major environmental consequences of urbanization. Option B, the depletion of resources, is not specifically mentioned as the primary challenge. Option C, the growth of renewable energy sources, is not a problem caused by urbanization but rather a solution. Option D, the increase in rural populations, is not addressed in the passage.

7. **Answer**: A. It causes respiratory diseases and cardiovascular issues
   Explanation: The passage states that **exposure to air pollution** in urban areas can lead to **respiratory diseases, cardiovascular issues, and premature deaths**, especially in densely populated cities. Option B is incorrect because the passage does not mention air pollution promoting healthy bacteria. Option C is incorrect because air pollution deteriorates the quality of the environment. Option D is incorrect as the passage notes that air pollution has negative health effects.

8. **Answer**: C. Investing in green infrastructure such as parks and green roofs
   Explanation: The passage suggests **investing in green infrastructure**, such as **parks, green roofs, and urban forests**, as a way to mitigate the environmental impact of urbanization. Option A is incorrect because reducing urban populations is not suggested.

Option A is the opposite of what is recommended in the passage. Option D is incorrect as the passage advocates for reducing reliance on fossil fuels.

9. **Answer**: A. Over-extraction of water from natural sources
   Explanation: The passage states that **urbanization increases the demand for water**, leading to the **over-extraction of water** from rivers, lakes, and aquifers. Option B, the disappearance of wildlife, is not discussed in relation to water resources specifically. Option C is incorrect because the passage does not discuss cooling of water sources. Option D is unrelated to the topic of urbanization.

10. **Answer**: B. Promoting energy efficiency and renewable energy sources
    Explanation: The passage explains that many cities are **transitioning to renewable energy sources** and improving **energy efficiency** as part of efforts to make urban growth more sustainable. Option A is incorrect because the passage doesn't suggest reducing urban populations as a solution. Option C is incorrect because the passage advocates for reducing reliance on fossil fuels. Option D is contrary to the goal of sustainable urban development.

11. **Answer**: A. Government positions were awarded based on political loyalty, not qualifications
    Explanation: The passage explains that under the **spoils system**, government positions were filled based on **political loyalty**, leading to inefficiency and corruption. Option B is incorrect as equal opportunity was not a feature of the spoils system. Option C is incorrect because the system created inefficiencies. Option D is inaccurate since the spoils system did not create a merit-based selection process.

12. **Answer**: B. The establishment of a merit-based system for hiring federal employees
    Explanation: The passage discusses how the **Pendleton Civil Service Reform Act of 1883** established a **merit-based system** for hiring federal employees, ensuring that people were hired based on their qualifications, not political loyalty. Option A is incorrect as the Pendleton Act sought to eliminate patronage. Option C is incorrect because the reform promoted equal opportunity, not the elimination of job opportunities for minorities. Option D is incorrect because the act did not create a political party.

13. **Answer**: A. To create a skilled and non-partisan workforce
    Explanation: The passage highlights that one of the goals of the civil service system is to create a **skilled, non-partisan workforce** that can implement policies effectively, regardless of political shifts. Option B is incorrect as the system aims to hire career professionals, not elected officials. Option C is not mentioned, as the civil service supports the work of public services. Option D is not discussed; the focus is on professionalization, not reducing the government size.

14. **Answer**: B. By preventing discrimination and promoting diversity in hiring
    Explanation: The passage explains that laws such as the **Civil Rights Act of 1964** and the **Equal Employment Opportunity Act of 1972** have been instrumental in **preventing discrimination** and promoting diversity within the civil service workforce. Option A is

incorrect because these laws were aimed at preventing discrimination. Option C is not accurate as the laws supported, not eliminated, merit-based hiring practices. Option D is incorrect because the laws did not reduce jobs but promoted fair opportunities.

15. **Answer**: B. Government bureaucracy and inefficiency

    Explanation: The passage mentions that one of the significant challenges facing the civil service is the concern about **government bureaucracy** and how the proliferation of rules and regulations can lead to **inefficiency** and delays. Option A is incorrect because inefficiency, not efficiency, is the challenge. Option C, the increasing number of public services, is not mentioned as a challenge. Option D is not discussed in the passage.

16. **Answer**: B. The creation of the Centers for Disease Control and Prevention (CDC)

    Explanation: The passage clearly states that the **CDC was created in 1946** to combat infectious diseases and coordinate national public health efforts. Option A refers to the Social Security Act, which was passed earlier, in 1935. Option C mentions the National Cancer Institute, which was later, in the 1970s. Option D refers to Medicare and Medicaid, which were established through the Social Security Act, but not in 1946.

17. **Answer**: B. A focus on the prevention of chronic diseases

    Explanation: The passage notes that in the **1960s and 1970s**, public health policy shifted its focus to address the growing burden of **chronic diseases** like heart disease, cancer, and diabetes, with an emphasis on **prevention and health promotion**. Option A is incorrect because mental health focus came later. Option C refers to the Social Security Act, which was earlier than the 1960s-1970s shift. Option D is not mentioned in the passage.

18. **Answer**: C. By integrating mental health care into mainstream healthcare

    Explanation: The passage explains that recent public health policy has made significant strides in **integrating mental health care** into the broader healthcare system, with laws like the **Mental Health Parity and Addiction Equity Act of 2008** ensuring equal coverage for mental health and substance use disorders. Option A is incorrect because the law provided equal coverage. Option B and D are incorrect as they are not discussed in the passage.

19. **Answer**: C. Disparities in access to care and health outcomes

    Explanation: The passage discusses how the **COVID-19 pandemic exposed significant gaps** in the U.S. healthcare system, particularly **health disparities** in vulnerable communities. Option A, the need for more hospitals, is not mentioned as a specific challenge. Option B, the lack of focus on mental health, is incorrect because mental health has gained attention in recent policy. Option D, overfunding, is not a concern raised in the passage.

20. **Answer**: C. Addressing the health impacts of climate change

    Explanation: The passage mentions that **climate change** is emerging as a significant **public health issue** due to its impact on infectious diseases and chronic conditions. Option A, rising healthcare costs, is not mentioned in this context. Option B, the increasing number of healthcare professionals, is not addressed. Option D, the decline in chronic diseases, is incorrect; chronic diseases remain a major focus.

Section 4: Clarity.

1. **Answer**: A
   Explanation: Sentence **A** is more straightforward and clear because it follows a logical sequence of events: **gathering evidence** first, then **analyzing the data**. The sentence flows smoothly and is easier to follow. In **B**, the phrase "hoping to uncover new leads" interrupts the natural progression of the action, making the sentence more convoluted and harder to read.
2. **Answer**: B
   Explanation: Sentence **B** is more professional and clear because it begins by emphasizing the officers' quick actions to **prevent harm** and then follows with the result: the **apprehension of the suspect**. Sentence **A** places the action of apprehending the suspect at the beginning, which slightly diminishes the focus on the critical immediate action taken by the officers.
3. **Answer**: A
   Explanation: Sentence **A** is clearer because it places the officer's reluctance at the forefront, followed by the necessity of using force, which creates a more natural and dramatic buildup. **B** reverses the order and presents the decision to use force before emphasizing the officer's reluctance, which makes it feel less immediate and impactful.
4. **Answer**: A
   Explanation: Sentence **A** follows a logical and professional sequence: the report is **examined thoroughly**, and **discrepancies** are revealed as a result. It is more natural and clear. In **B**, the phrase "revealing discrepancies" is placed at the beginning, which makes the sentence feel more like an afterthought and disrupts the flow of the information.
5. **Answer**: A
   Explanation: Sentence **A** is clearer because it logically presents the **cause (training)** followed by the **effect (remaining calm)**. This structure makes the sentence easy to follow and understand. Sentence **B** is slightly less clear because it begins with the result (calm demeanor), which delays the introduction of the cause and weakens the sentence's clarity.
6. **Answer**: B
   Explanation: Sentence **B** is more effective because it presents the **sequence of events** clearly: the suspect attempts to flee first, and the officers respond by surrounding the area to prevent his escape. Sentence **A** is grammatically correct, but the inversion of the sentence structure (starting with "quickly surrounding") makes it more difficult to follow and less immediate.

7. **Answer**: A
   Explanation: Sentence **A** is clearer because it places the **cause (escalating danger)** before the **effect (calling for backup)**, which maintains the natural flow of the sentence. In **B**, starting with "Prompted by the escalating danger" creates unnecessary complexity and weakens the clarity of the action.

8. **Answer**: A
   Explanation: Sentence **A** is clearer because it places the action of **reviewing witness statements** and **physical evidence** first, followed by the purpose (building a case). This makes the sentence easier to follow. Sentence **B** starts with the goal (building the case), which weakens the sentence and disrupts the flow of the information.

9. **Answer**: A
   Explanation: Sentence **A** is clearer because it emphasizes the officer's **warning first**, which makes the sequence of events easier to follow. The **cause (suspect's actions)** is presented afterward. In **B**, starting with the suspect's actions detracts from the officer's proactive role in issuing a warning and reduces the natural flow of the sentence.

10. **Answer**: B
    Explanation: Sentence **B** is clearer because it places the **action (acting decisively)** at the forefront, followed by the results (ensuring safety and peaceful resolution). This makes the sentence easier to follow and more engaging. Sentence **A** is grammatically correct but less effective because it starts with the results, which makes the officers' actions feel secondary.

11. **Answer**: A
    Explanation: Sentence **A** is clearer because it starts with the officer's action (assessing the situation), which provides immediate context to the sentence. It flows naturally, with the reason (recognizing potential dangers) following the action. In **B**, starting with "Recognizing the potential dangers" puts the reason before the action, which weakens the immediacy of the officer's response.

12. **Answer**: A
    Explanation: Sentence **A** is clearer because it presents the **challenge** (the complexity of the case) first, followed by the result (the breakthrough). This makes the detective's success more impactful. In **B**, the result is mentioned first, which takes away from the focus on the initial challenge and makes the sentence less effective.

13. **Answer**: B
    Explanation: Sentence **B** is more professional and effective because it starts with the **reason for action** (acting fast) before detailing the officers' pursuit. This approach places the urgency of the situation at the forefront. Sentence **A** is correct, but it begins with the action, which makes the urgency feel secondary.

14. **Answer**: A
    Explanation: Sentence **A** is clearer because it presents the **action of reviewing** the footage first, followed by the identification of the suspect, maintaining a clear

cause-and-effect structure. Sentence **B** places the identification of the suspect after the report drafting, making it feel less organized and confusing.

15. **Answer**: A

    Explanation: Sentence **A** is more effective because it starts with the detective's action (connecting the evidence), which is the focal point of the sentence, and then reveals the result (leading to an arrest). Sentence **B** starts with the context of the investigation, making the sentence feel less direct and somewhat less impactful.

16. **Answer**: B

    Explanation: Sentence **B** is more professional and effective because it starts by emphasizing the **officer's awareness of the risk**, which highlights the importance of the decision to call for backup. Sentence **A**, while grammatically correct, places the awareness at the end, making the sentence less impactful.

17. **Answer**: A

    Explanation: Sentence **A** is more clear because it introduces the **suspect's situation** (being cornered) first, followed by the result (the arrest). This emphasizes the **suspect's vulnerability** and makes the action of arresting more meaningful. Sentence **B** places the phrase "having been cornered" too early, which makes it feel less focused on the arrest.

18. **Answer**: B

    Explanation: Sentence **B** is more effective because it starts with the **officers' awareness of the urgency**, which creates an emphasis on the critical need to resolve the case. The result (their determination to finish the investigation) follows naturally. Sentence **A** is correct but places the urgency after the determination, making the sentence feel less immediate.

19. **Answer**: A

    Explanation: Sentence **A** is clearer because it begins with the officer's **certainty** about the suspect's guilt, and the evidence is introduced as supporting this certainty. In **B**, the emphasis is placed on the evidence, making it feel like the focus is shifted from the officer's decision-making process.

20. **Answer**: B

    Explanation: Sentence **B** is more effective because it places the reason ("knowing that every second counted") before the action, which builds anticipation and emphasizes the urgency of the situation. Sentence **A** is grammatically correct but starts with the action, which feels slightly less impactful in emphasizing the urgency.

How to Analyze Your Practice Test Results

Analyzing your practice test results is not just about analyzing the answers to the questions you got wrong. It's about acquiring a deeper understanding of why you missed particular questions, detecting patterns in your performance, and using that information to direct your future study efforts. Here's how you can efficiently examine your practice tests:

1. Review Incorrect Answers Thoroughly

When reviewing your practice test, don't only look at whether you got the question right or wrong. Focus on why you got it wrong. This can help you uncover the root cause of the mistake and establish a strategy to avoid it in the future.

Questions to ask yourself when reviewing incorrect answers:

- Was this an **issue with understanding** the concept, or was it a matter of **misreading the question**?
- Did I fall for a **trap answer** or did I second-guess my initial choice?
- Was I able to **recall the information** correctly, but I misapplied it, or was I simply unsure about the material?
- If it was a **spelling or vocabulary mistake**, was it due to lack of familiarity with the term, or did I confuse similar words?

By identifying the **specific reason** for each mistake, you can better address the underlying issue in your study plan.

2. Look for Patterns in Your Mistakes

Once you've reviewed individual incorrect answers, take a step back and look for **patterns** in your performance. Are there particular sections or types of questions where you consistently struggle? Recognizing these patterns will help you know where to focus your review.

Types of patterns to look for:

- **Consistent Difficulty with Certain Topics**: Are you consistently missing questions related to certain subjects or types of questions? For example, do you struggle more with **reading comprehension** than with **spelling** or **vocabulary**? This will help you know where to spend more time.
- **Specific Question Formats**: Do you have difficulty with **multiple-choice questions** that require **inferences**? Are there certain types of **vocabulary questions** (such as synonyms or antonyms) that trip you up more often?

- **Timing Issues**: If you found yourself running out of time on certain sections, note which sections took you the longest. This could indicate that you need to work on **time management** in those areas.

Identifying patterns will give you a clear roadmap for focusing your study efforts and refining your approach.

3. Track Your Progress Over Time

As you continue to take practice tests, it's crucial to track your progress. Over time, you should see improvements in your performance, particularly in areas where you previously failed. Keep a diary of your practice test results, noting your score in each part and any patterns you see in your performance.

How to track progress:

- **Record Scores**: Keep a record of your scores on each practice test and compare your results over time. You should aim to see gradual improvement in your performance, particularly in the areas where you initially struggled.
- **Review Specific Question Types**: Track how well you are doing on different types of questions (e.g., multiple-choice, fill-in-the-blank). Are you improving in certain areas? This can indicate that you're effectively addressing your weak spots.
- **Set Goals for Improvement**: Based on your progress, set specific goals for the upcoming week of study. For example, if you are still struggling with **vocabulary**, set a goal to review 20 new vocabulary words each day and take a practice test focused on that area.

Tracking progress is a great motivator and provides you with the data you need to adjust your study plan accordingly.

Identifying Weak Areas and Focusing on Improvements

Once you've examined your practice test results and recognized your weak areas, it's time to focus on improving those areas. This tailored method to studying will help you build your skills and improve your performance in the final phases of preparation.

1. Focusing on the Most Challenging Sections

Not all areas of the PELT B Exam are created equal, and some may be more tough than others dependent on your specific skills and weaknesses. Use the information from your practice exams to pinpoint the most challenging sections for you, and spend more study time to those areas.

For example:

- If you're struggling with **reading comprehension**, spend more time reading passages and practicing questions that test your ability to identify the main idea, supporting details, and inferences.
- If **spelling** is a weak area, focus on reviewing commonly misspelled words and practicing with flashcards. Take timed spelling tests to help you speed up your ability to recall correct spellings.
- If you're having trouble with **vocabulary**, spend more time reviewing vocabulary words and their meanings, using context clues to figure out unfamiliar words.

By giving more time and focus to the areas where you're struggling, you can make the most progress in the shortest amount of time.

2. Practicing Specific Question Types

Another method to narrow your review efforts is by practicing specific question types. If you discover that you tend to get specific sorts of questions wrong (for example, questions that ask you to choose the most clearly written language in the clarity section), spend extra time practicing such question types.

How to practice specific question types:

- **Target Problematic Areas**: If you struggle with multiple-choice questions that require inferences, focus on passages that require you to draw conclusions from implicit information. Practice these types of questions so that you can become more comfortable with them.
- **Work Through Practice Problems**: Look for practice problems that are specifically designed to target areas you need to improve. For example, if you're struggling with identifying the main idea in reading comprehension, practice with passages that focus specifically on this skill.

The more you practice specific question types, the better prepared you will be to tackle those questions on the exam.

3. Reviewing Mistakes and Learning from Them

The key to improving after each practice test is learning from your mistakes. Simply reviewing what you got wrong is not enough—you need to **actively learn** from those mistakes.

How to learn from your mistakes:

- **Understand Why You Missed the Question**: Take the time to analyze why you missed a question. Did you misunderstand the wording of the question? Did you confuse two similar answer choices? Did you fail to read the passage carefully enough? By understanding why you missed the question, you can avoid making the same mistake again.
- **Look for Common Themes in Mistakes**: Are there certain types of questions or topics where you consistently struggle? If so, focus on improving those areas in your study plan.
- **Adjust Your Approach**: Once you understand why you missed a question, adjust your approach for similar questions in the future. For example, if you often second-guess your answers, work on building your confidence and trusting your instincts.

By actively learning from your mistakes, you can improve your performance and avoid repeating the same errors.

Building a Study Plan Around Practice Test Performance

After analyzing your practice test results and identifying areas for improvement, it's time to build a study plan that targets those weaknesses. Here's how to build an effective study plan based on your practice test performance:

1. Prioritize Weak Areas

Your study plan should prioritize the areas where you need the most improvement. If you constantly struggle with **vocabulary**, make sure to devote more time to learning and reviewing new words. If you have difficulty with **reading comprehension**, allocate more time to reading passages and answering questions that test your understanding of the material.

2. Set Clear Goals

Set specific, measurable goals for each area of your study plan. For example:

- **Vocabulary**: Learn 20 new words each day and review previous words using flashcards.
- **Spelling**: Take a timed spelling test every day and track your accuracy.
- **Reading Comprehension**: Complete at least three practice passages each day and track your accuracy and timing.

3. Incorporate Active Learning

Use **active learning** strategies to reinforce your knowledge. This could include self-quizzing, discussing the material with a study partner, or teaching what you've learned to someone else. Active learning is essential for solidifying your understanding and retaining information.

4. Monitor Your Progress

As you implement your study plan, track your progress and adjust as needed. If you find that you're making significant improvements in one area but still struggling with another, reallocate your time to focus more on the challenging areas.

Using practice tests efficiently is one of the greatest strategies to prepare for the PELT B Exam. By assessing your practice test results, identifying weak areas, and constructing a study plan around those results, you can fine-tune your preparation and focus on the areas that will make the largest difference on your performance.

Remember, the key to success is not simply taking practice tests but also learning from them. Use them to find trends in your blunders, better your grasp of the content, and adapt your study strategy to ensure you are well-prepared on test day.

By following these procedures and keeping consistent with your review and practice, you'll boost your chances of success on the PELT B Exam and be one step closer to reaching your law enforcement career goals.

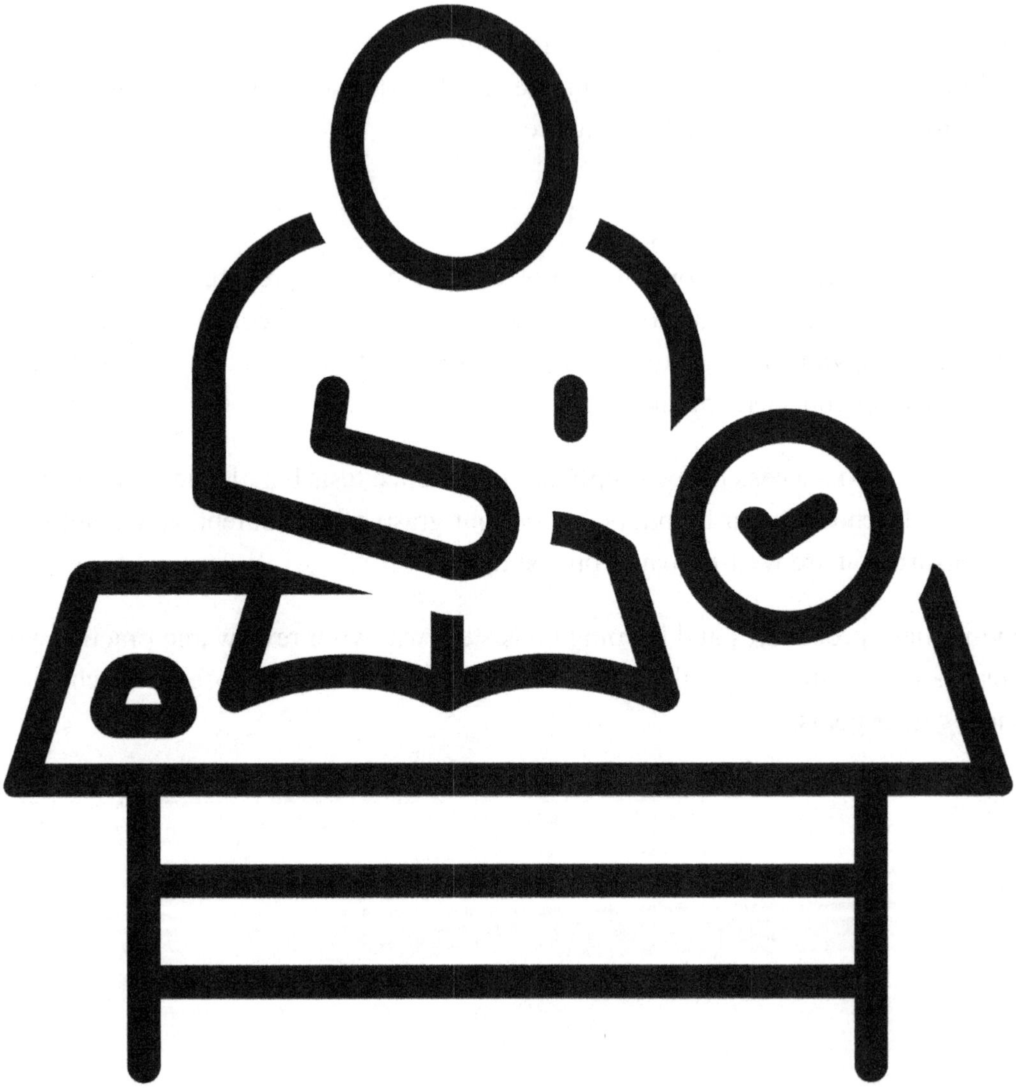

Chapter 8

Preparing for Test Day

As the day of the PELT B Exam approaches, the excitement and nervousness can build up. The hard work and preparation you've put in over the past weeks and months are about to be put to the test, and it's natural to experience a variety of emotions. However, knowing exactly what to expect on test day, understanding the logistics, and having techniques in place to handle the pressure will considerably lessen any anxiety and help you do your best.

In this chapter, we will take you through the exam logistics, explain what to expect during the check-in procedure and the test setting, and suggest tips for handling the strain of test day. The goal is to assist you enter the exam room confident, prepared, and ready to succeed.

What to Expect on Test Day

On the day of the PELT B Exam, preparation goes beyond only the information you've studied. It's also about knowing the logistics of the test, being familiar with the check-in process, and having a strategy for handling the strain of the test setting. Understanding these characteristics will offer you a sense of control and confidence, ensuring that you can focus on what actually matters—performing your best.

1. Exam Logistics: What to Bring, What Not to Bring

The first step in preparing for exam day is knowing what you need to bring with you and, equally essential, what you should leave at home. This guarantees that you are fully prepared, without the stress of searching for paperwork or realizing you've forgotten something vital.

What to Bring to the Test:

- **Valid ID**: You will need a valid, government-issued identification, such as a driver's license or passport. Ensure that the ID you bring matches the name on your registration, as discrepancies may delay or prevent your entry into the exam room.
- **Confirmation of Registration**: If applicable, bring a printout or digital copy of your test registration confirmation. This document verifies that you have registered for the **PELT B Exam** and serves as proof of your appointment.

- **Pencil and Eraser**: For any sections that require written answers or marking, you will need to bring a **pencil** (usually a number 2 pencil) and a **good eraser**. Some testing centers may provide these, but it's always safer to bring your own.
- **Water Bottle and Snacks**: Staying hydrated and having a small snack can help you maintain focus and energy levels during the test. However, make sure to check if food and drinks are allowed in the testing area. It's best to have something light and non-distracting, like granola bars or fruit.
- **Comfortable Clothing**: Dress in layers, as some exam rooms can be cold, while others may be warmer. Comfortable clothing ensures that you're not distracted by physical discomfort during the exam.

What Not to Bring to the Test:

- **Electronic Devices**: Most test centers prohibit the use of electronic devices such as **cell phones**, **smartwatches**, **tablets**, or **laptops**. Make sure to leave them in your car or at home. If you bring a device, you may be asked to leave the test center.
- **Study Materials**: Bring only what's necessary for the exam. Do not bring any books, notes, or reference materials. The exam is meant to test your knowledge and skills, and bringing study materials will not only be distracting but may be considered a violation of test rules.
- **Large Bags or Backpacks**: Typically, you will not be allowed to bring large bags or backpacks into the exam room. If you bring them, you may need to store them in a designated area outside the testing room.
- **Unnecessary Personal Items**: Avoid bringing any personal items that may distract you or others, such as excessive jewelry or unnecessary paperwork.

---

2. The Check-In Process and Test Environment

Arriving early on test day and understanding the check-in process helps guarantee that you start the exam day with a sense of serenity and organization. Most test centers have certain protocols to guarantee that everything goes well and that the testing environment is fair and secure.

Check-In Process:

- **Arrival Time**: Arrive **at least 30 minutes** before your scheduled test time. This gives you plenty of time to check in, get settled, and go over any last-minute details without feeling rushed. It also allows you to find parking and complete any necessary paperwork.
- **ID Verification**: When you check in, you will need to show your **valid ID** for verification. The testing staff will likely take a photo of you for identification purposes and verify that your ID matches your registration details.

- **Security Measures**: Expect to undergo some basic security procedures, including a check to ensure that you are not carrying any prohibited items. Be prepared to leave your belongings in a designated area and follow the security guidelines of the test center.
- **Assigned Seating**: After check-in, you will be directed to your assigned seat in the testing room. Be sure to sit in your designated seat to avoid confusion or delays. Once seated, you'll likely be asked to store your personal items in a secure location, such as a locker or a designated area outside the room.

Test Environment:

The environment in which you take the **PELT B Exam** plays a significant role in your test-taking experience. Most exam centers strive to create a quiet, comfortable, and distraction-free environment to help you focus.

- **Quiet and Controlled Environment**: You will be placed in a quiet room with other candidates. The room is typically equipped with individual desks or cubicles, and you'll be given a specific amount of space to work.
- **Time Management**: You'll be given a clock or will be able to track time throughout the exam. Make sure to manage your time efficiently to complete each section within the allotted time.
- **Clear Instructions**: Test administrators will provide you with clear instructions on how to complete the exam, how to mark your answers, and what to do if you encounter technical issues or have questions during the test.
- **Breaks**: Depending on the test format, you may be allowed a break during the exam. Check the guidelines in advance to know when you can take breaks and how long they will last.

---

3. How to Handle the Pressure of Test Day

Test day can be stressful, especially with the weight of the exam on your shoulders. However, learning how to handle the pressure and stay calm throughout the exam is just as crucial as preparing the subject. Here are some helpful ways for reducing test-day anxiety and ensuring that you perform at your best:

a) Mental Preparation

- **Positive Visualization**: Before the exam, take a few moments to **visualize** yourself succeeding. Imagine yourself sitting confidently in the test room, answering questions with ease, and finishing the exam successfully. Visualization techniques have been shown to reduce anxiety and boost confidence.

- **Affirmations**: Use **positive affirmations** to remind yourself that you are prepared and capable. Repeating phrases like "I am ready," "I can do this," and "I will stay calm" can help calm your nerves and boost your mindset.
- **Keep Perspective**: Remind yourself that while the **PELT B Exam** is important, it is just one step in your journey toward a career in law enforcement. If you've prepared well and done your best, that's all you can control. Keep a positive perspective and focus on the task at hand rather than stressing about the outcome.

b) Physical Preparation

- **Get Enough Sleep**: The night before the exam, make sure you get **7-9 hours of quality sleep**. Sleep is essential for mental clarity, focus, and overall performance. Avoid staying up late cramming; rest is key for optimal performance on test day.
- **Eat a Healthy Breakfast**: Start the day with a **balanced breakfast** that includes protein, whole grains, and fruits. Avoid sugary or greasy foods that could lead to an energy crash during the exam.
- **Hydrate**: Drink enough water before and during the exam to stay hydrated. Dehydration can lead to fatigue and affect your concentration. However, don't overdo it, as too much water can lead to frequent bathroom breaks, which could interrupt your focus.

c) Test-Taking Mindset

- **Stay Calm During the Exam**: Once you start the exam, stay calm and focused. If you come across a difficult question, don't panic. Take a deep breath, pause for a moment, and approach the question logically. If you're unsure, mark it and come back to it later.
- **Pace Yourself**: Be mindful of the time, but don't rush through the questions. Focus on answering each question to the best of your ability. If you find yourself spending too much time on one section, move on to the next and return to it later if time permits.
- **Stay Positive**: Even if you encounter challenging questions, maintain a positive attitude. Don't let difficult questions derail your confidence. Keep going, and remember that you've prepared for this.

Last-Minute Tips for Reviewing Key Concepts

With the exam right around the corner, the focus of your studies should change to revisiting essential ideas and ensuring that your knowledge is fresh and robust. While you should avoid cramming enormous amounts of new knowledge at this time, a systematic evaluation of the material is vital. Here's how you properly use the last week before the exam:

1. Review Your Practice Test Results

One of the most efficient methods to spend the final week of preparation is by reviewing the results of your practice tests. Reviewing these will help you identify areas that need more focus, as well as reinforce your strengths. Here's how to do it:

- **Identify Mistakes**: Go through the mistakes you made during your practice tests. What kinds of errors are you making? Are they related to misreading the questions, forgetting key concepts, or second-guessing your answers? Knowing your weaknesses is the first step in improving them.
- **Target Weak Areas**: After reviewing your mistakes, create a focused study plan that addresses these areas. For example, if you constantly struggle with vocabulary or spelling, dedicate more time to those sections.
- **Revisit Key Concepts**: For questions you got right but felt unsure about, review the underlying concepts that made the answer correct. Reinforce these ideas through additional practice or by explaining them in your own words.

2. Focus on Core Sections

With limited time left, you should focus on the sections that carry the most weight and have the highest likelihood of affecting your overall score. Here's how to approach the major sections of the **PELT B Exam**:

- **Spelling**: This section can trip you up if you're not careful. Make sure to review commonly misspelled words and words related to law enforcement terminology. Use flashcards to test your recall and keep practicing under timed conditions. If you have a list of words you've struggled with in previous practice tests, focus on these during your final review.
- **Vocabulary**: Vocabulary is an area where consistent practice pays off. Review any vocabulary lists you've created, focusing on words that seem more challenging. Pay particular attention to law enforcement terms that you are likely to encounter, such as "parole," "suspect," and "warrant." Additionally, practice using these words in sentences to reinforce your understanding of their meanings in context.
- **Reading Comprehension**: During your final week, don't skip reading comprehension practice. Focus on passages that challenge your ability to identify the main idea and key details. Make sure you can recognize the tone and purpose of the passage, as these elements can often inform the correct answers. Use practice questions to hone your ability to skim and read efficiently without missing crucial details.
- **Clarity**: The clarity section requires you to evaluate sentence structure and grammar. Make sure to review common grammar mistakes such as run-on sentences, fragments, and unclear phrasing. Practice choosing the most concise, clear, and grammatically

correct sentence. If you can, review your own writing and try to identify areas where clarity could be improved.

3. Use Active Recall and Spaced Repetition

In the final week, it's essential to consolidate what you've learned using **active recall** and **spaced repetition**. These techniques are proven to enhance long-term retention and ensure that information stays fresh in your mind.

- **Active Recall**: Instead of passively rereading notes or textbooks, quiz yourself on key concepts. For instance, use flashcards to test your vocabulary knowledge or take practice tests to assess your comprehension skills. Active recall forces your brain to retrieve information, making it easier to recall on test day.
- **Spaced Repetition**: Review the material at increasing intervals, which helps strengthen your memory. Start by reviewing important topics multiple times a day, then space out the repetitions over the week. For instance, review a topic in the morning, then again in the evening, and the following day. This will ensure you don't forget important details.

4. Avoid New Information

The last week is not the time to introduce new material or try to learn entirely new concepts. Stick to **reviewing what you already know**. Cramming in new information can lead to confusion and unnecessary stress. Focus on solidifying your understanding and boosting your confidence in the material you've already studied.

How to Stay Mentally and Physically Prepared in the Week Leading Up to the Test

Maintaining a strong and healthy mindset is just as important as reviewing the material. The final week before the exam should focus on **mental clarity**, **physical well-being**, and **stress management**. Here's how to stay prepared and calm as you approach test day:

1. Manage Stress Effectively

Test anxiety is common, especially as the day of the exam draws near. However, stress can cloud your judgment and affect your performance. Here's how to manage it effectively:

- **Practice Deep Breathing**: Slow, deep breathing can help calm your mind and reduce physical symptoms of stress. Try inhaling for four counts, holding for four counts, and exhaling for four counts. Repeat this several times throughout the day, especially before your practice tests or any review sessions.

- **Take Breaks**: It's important to avoid burnout during the final week. Schedule regular breaks in your study routine to allow your mind to relax and recharge. Step away from your desk and take short walks, stretch, or engage in a hobby that helps you unwind.
- **Stay Positive**: Negative thoughts and self-doubt can undermine your confidence. Practice **positive self-talk** and remind yourself of all the hard work you've put in. Remember that you've been preparing for this moment for a long time, and you have the skills to succeed.
- **Visualize Success**: Visualization is a powerful tool used by athletes, performers, and successful test-takers alike. Spend a few minutes each day visualizing yourself walking into the exam room feeling calm and confident. See yourself answering questions easily and completing the test without anxiety.

2. Get Enough Sleep

Sleep is a vital component of memory consolidation. Your brain absorbs and organizes the knowledge you've acquired while you sleep, making it easier to recall on exam day. During the last week, ensure that you're receiving **7-9 hours** of sleep each night. Lack of sleep might hinder your capacity to focus and retain knowledge.

- **Sleep Hygiene**: Practice good sleep hygiene by maintaining a consistent sleep schedule. Avoid using electronics right before bed, as the blue light from screens can interfere with your ability to fall asleep. Instead, try reading a book or engaging in relaxation techniques before bed.

3. Fuel Your Body and Mind

The food you eat plays a significant role in how you feel and perform. In the week leading up to the test, focus on maintaining a balanced diet that fuels your brain and keeps your energy levels stable.

- **Eat Balanced Meals**: Avoid heavy or greasy foods that might make you sluggish. Focus on eating meals that include a good balance of **protein**, **whole grains**, and **healthy fats**. Foods like **salmon**, **avocados**, and **nuts** are great brain-boosting options.
- **Avoid Caffeine Overload**: While a moderate amount of caffeine can enhance alertness, consuming excessive amounts can increase anxiety and interfere with sleep. Limit your caffeine intake in the days leading up to the exam.
- **Hydrate**: Dehydration can lead to fatigue and difficulty concentrating. Make sure to drink plenty of water throughout the day, but avoid drinking too much right before the exam to prevent unnecessary bathroom breaks.

Relaxation Techniques for a Calm Test Day

The morning of the exam can be a stressful time, but using the right relaxation techniques can help you stay calm and focused. Here are some techniques that will help you prepare mentally for test day:

1. Morning Routine: Start your test day with a **calming routine**. Don't rush through your morning or let the pressure of the exam consume you. A peaceful morning sets the tone for a calm and focused day.

- **Wake Up Early**: Aim to wake up with plenty of time to spare. This will allow you to prepare calmly and avoid any rushed feelings.
- **Eat a Nutritious Breakfast**: Have a healthy breakfast that includes protein, whole grains, and fruits. Foods like **eggs**, **oatmeal**, and **fruit smoothies** will provide sustained energy for the exam.
- **Stretch or Exercise**: Light physical activity can help reduce stress and wake you up. Consider doing some gentle stretches or a quick walk to get your blood flowing and calm your nerves.

2. During the Exam: Stay Calm and Focused: Once you enter the test center, the real challenge is staying **calm and focused** throughout the exam. The best way to do this is by staying in the moment and not letting anxiety about the test cloud your thinking.

- **Breathe Deeply**: If you start to feel anxious during the exam, take a few deep breaths to calm your mind. This can help clear your thoughts and bring your focus back to the task at hand.
- **Take Breaks if Allowed**: If the exam allows for breaks, use this time wisely. Step away from the test materials, close your eyes, stretch, or simply relax for a few minutes to reset.
- **Stay Positive**: Even if you encounter challenging questions, don't get discouraged. Remind yourself that you're prepared and capable. Focus on one question at a time and stay positive throughout the test.

The final week leading up to the PELT B Exam is all about fine-tuning your information, regulating your stress, and ensuring that you are psychologically and physically prepared for the test day. By following these last week preparation tips—reviewing essential subjects, minimizing stress, getting appropriate sleep, and practicing relaxation techniques—you can approach the exam room with confidence and composure.

Chapter 9

Post-Test Analysis and Next Steps

After weeks of preparation, several practice tests, and endless hours of studying, you've finally completed the PELT B Exam. While it's tempting to give out a sigh of relief and think that the hard work is over, there's still one critical step left: reviewing your test findings. Whether you've aced the exam or didn't perform as well as you had planned, understanding your T-score and how to interpret the findings can guide your future actions.

In this chapter, we will discuss how to evaluate your test results and comprehend your T-score and its relevance. We will also cover how to use these findings to aid you with your future applications, whether that's retaking the exam or applying to law enforcement positions. By having a clear picture of your performance and how it fits into your professional path, you can make educated decisions and continue working toward your goals.

Interpreting Your Test Results: Understanding Your T-Score and Its Significance

The PELT B Exam employs a T-score to represent your performance. The T-score is a standardized score that enables test administrators and law enforcement agencies to measure your performance in relation to other candidates who took the exam. Understanding how this score works and how to interpret it is vital for establishing your status and making educated decisions about your next moves.

What is a T-Score?

A T-score is a statistical measurement that standardizes your score on the exam. It takes into account the difficulty level of the exam and compares your performance to that of other test-takers. The T-score places your performance on a bell-shaped curve, where the average score is 50, and the standard deviation is 10.

Here's how to interpret your T-score:

- **T-Score of 50**: A score of 50 represents the **average performance**. This means that your performance is roughly in line with that of other test-takers.
- **T-Score Above 50**: A T-score above 50 indicates that you performed **better than average**. The higher the score, the more above average your performance is compared to other test-takers.

- **T-Score Below 50**: A T-score below 50 means that your performance was **below average** compared to others. The further below 50, the more improvement is needed to reach the average level of performance.

How to Understand the T-Score

The **T-score** is calculated based on the number of correct answers you provide, as well as the overall performance of other candidates. It reflects how well you did relative to the overall test-taker population. The **PELT B Exam** is designed to assess not just basic knowledge but also your ability to apply that knowledge under timed conditions. Here's how the score affects your future:

- **Scores of 60 and Above**: Generally, a score of **60 or higher** is considered to be **above average** and demonstrates strong preparedness. Candidates with T-scores in this range are often highly competitive for law enforcement positions.
- **Scores Between 50-59**: If you score between **50-59**, you are likely in the **average** range. This means you have sufficient knowledge and skills, but there may be areas of improvement that you can work on for future tests or applications.
- **Scores Below 50**: A score below 50 indicates that you may need to **improve in certain areas**. You may need to retake the exam after dedicating more time to studying specific sections or developing a stronger test-taking strategy.

While a T-score above 50 is generally positive, it's crucial to know that many law enforcement agencies have their own cut-off scores or criteria for PELT B Exam results. These agencies may use your T-score when considering your eligibility for their employment processes. However, a high T-score doesn't ensure immediate admittance into a position—it's simply one aspect of the selection process.

How to Interpret Specific Section Scores

The **PELT B Exam** is divided into four main sections: **Spelling, Vocabulary, Reading Comprehension**, and **Clarity**. Each of these sections is scored individually, and your overall T-score is an aggregate of your performance in these areas.

- **Spelling**: A strong score in the spelling section indicates your attention to detail and ability to recall key law enforcement terms correctly. If your score in this section is low, focus on improving your ability to memorize and recognize commonly misspelled words.
- **Vocabulary**: A solid vocabulary score reflects your understanding of law enforcement terminology and your ability to use words correctly in context. If you scored lower in this section, reviewing key vocabulary words and practicing their meanings in context can improve your performance in the future.

- **Reading Comprehension**: This section measures your ability to read, analyze, and understand written material. A lower score in this section may suggest that you need to work on **reading speed, identifying main ideas**, and **critical thinking** in reading passages. Practicing timed reading exercises and comprehension questions will improve your skills.
- **Clarity**: A strong clarity score shows your proficiency in identifying sentence structure errors and improving the clarity of communication. If this score is lower, focus on studying sentence structure, grammar, and understanding common mistakes such as run-on sentences and fragments.

By examining your individual section scores, you can gain a more specific understanding of where you excel and where there may be areas for improvement.

How to Use Your Test Results for Future Applications

Once you have a clear knowledge of your T-score and section scores, you may utilize this information to make informed decisions regarding your future career path and application process. The PELT B Exam is widely used by law enforcement agencies to determine a candidate's readiness for entry-level positions, and your scores can play a big part in your job prospects.

1. If You Passed and Are Satisfied with Your Score

If you're content with your T-score and general performance on the PELT B Exam, it's time to start preparing for your next stages. Most law enforcement agencies need applicants to submit their PELT B Exam scores as part of the hiring process, and your scores will likely play a factor in whether or not you're invited to proceed ahead in the recruitment process.

Here's how to leverage your results:

- **Submit Your Scores**: Ensure that your exam results are shared with the relevant law enforcement agencies you are applying to. Many agencies use the **PELT B Exam** scores to evaluate candidates for entry-level law enforcement roles.
- **Highlight Your Strengths**: If you scored well in one or more sections (such as vocabulary or clarity), make sure to highlight those strengths in your **resume** and **cover letter**. You can use this as evidence of your proficiency in key areas of law enforcement communication.
- **Move on to the Interview Process**: After submitting your scores, focus on preparing for the interview process. While the **PELT B Exam** is important, it's just one component of

the hiring process. Work on improving your **interview skills** and preparing for questions related to law enforcement scenarios, your experience, and your interest in the position.

2. If You Need to Retake the Exam

If your **T-score** falls below the threshold for the positions you are applying for, you may need to retake the **PELT B Exam**. While this may feel like a setback, it is an opportunity to improve and come back stronger.

Here's what to do if you need to retake the exam:

- **Identify Weak Areas**: Use the feedback from your test results to identify which sections need the most attention. Review the material that you struggled with during your preparation and focus on improving those areas.
- **Devote Time to Focused Study**: Consider dedicating more time to studying the sections where you scored lower. For example, if you found **reading comprehension** particularly challenging, practice reading passages under time constraints, making sure to focus on identifying the main idea and answering questions related to **inferences**.
- **Retake After Sufficient Preparation**: Make sure you are thoroughly prepared before retaking the exam. Avoid the temptation to rush back into the test without addressing the areas where you struggled.

3. Using Your Results for Long-Term Career Development

Regardless of whether you passed or need to retake the exam, your results provide valuable insights into areas where you can improve. Here's how to use this information for your **long-term career development**:

- **Take Additional Training**: If you found certain sections of the **PELT B Exam** particularly challenging, consider taking additional training or classes in those areas. Many community colleges or law enforcement training centers offer courses in reading comprehension, vocabulary building, and professional writing that can help you perform better on future exams and in your career.
- **Work on Test-Taking Strategies**: Your test-taking strategies play a major role in your performance. If you struggled with time management or second-guessed yourself on multiple-choice questions, practice your **test-taking strategies** to build confidence and speed for future exams.
- **Develop Your Soft Skills**: As a future law enforcement professional, you'll need more than just technical knowledge. Develop your **soft skills**, such as communication, problem-solving, and critical thinking. The **PELT B Exam** evaluates these skills, and strengthening them will contribute to your overall career success.

Next Steps After the Test: How to Move Forward in Your Law Enforcement Career

Once the PELT B Exam is behind you, it's time to think about how to take the next steps in your law enforcement adventure. Your results will influence your path forward, but regardless of your score, there are critical activities you can take that will advance you closer to your career aspirations.

1. Analyze Your Exam Results

After you receive your exam results, it's vital to carefully study them to understand where you are and identify areas where you might need to improve.

- **Review Your T-Score**: Your **T-score** will be the primary indicator of your exam performance. A higher score indicates strong performance, while a score that's closer to or below 50 may require a deeper look at specific sections where you may have struggled.
- **Section Breakdown**: Break down the individual scores for each section: **spelling, vocabulary, reading comprehension**, and **clarity**. Understanding where you performed well and where you struggled will help you identify your strengths and weaknesses. If, for example, your **reading comprehension** score was low, you might need to focus more on understanding how to approach reading passages and answering related questions in future practice sessions.
- **Understand the Implications of Your Results**: Some law enforcement agencies may have specific **cutoff scores** that determine whether you pass the **PELLET B Exam**. Be sure to review any department-specific guidelines to understand if your score meets their requirements.

2. Decide Whether to Apply or Retake the Exam

Once you've reviewed your results, you need to decide on your next steps based on the score you received.

- **If You Passed and Are Satisfied with Your Score**: If you achieved a score you're happy with and meet the requirements of the departments you're interested in, it's time to start applying for positions with law enforcement agencies. However, be sure to research each department's specific application requirements.
- **If You Didn't Meet the Desired Score**: If your results didn't meet the desired score, you have options. You can retake the **PELT B Exam** after the required 30-day waiting period and dedicate time to reviewing and strengthening the areas where you struggled.

While it's not uncommon for candidates to retake the exam, remember that it's a learning opportunity to refine your test-taking strategies, focus on weak areas, and come back even more prepared.

3. Focus on Gaining Experience and Networking

Whether or whether you need to retake the exam, it's crucial to continue growing your law enforcement expertise and professional network. Many agencies search for people who are not just well-prepared academically but also possess a deep understanding of law enforcement practice.

- **Internships and Volunteer Work**: Consider applying for **internships** or **volunteer positions** within law enforcement agencies. This will allow you to gain practical experience, learn about the day-to-day duties of officers, and expand your network. Many agencies value hands-on experience and may prioritize applicants who have demonstrated a commitment to the profession.
- **Professional Associations**: Join law enforcement-related **professional associations** and attend conferences or workshops. These events allow you to learn from experienced professionals, stay up-to-date on industry trends, and connect with potential employers.
- **Build Strong Relationships**: Networking with professionals in the field can open doors to opportunities. Law enforcement agencies often hire candidates who come recommended by trusted professionals within the industry. By building a strong professional network, you increase your chances of securing a position.

Understanding Department-Specific Requirements for Reading and Writing Tests

Different law enforcement agencies may have distinct reading and writing requirements for new recruits, and the PELT B Exam is often just one component of the process. After finishing the PELT B Exam, it's crucial to acquaint oneself with each department's individual standards, as they can differ greatly depending on the agency and area.

1. Exam Scores and Cut-Offs

Each law enforcement agency may set its own cut-off scores for the PELT B Exam. While a score of 50 is considered typical, some departments may require a higher score to be eligible for consideration. Be sure to examine the minimum score criteria for each agency to which you plan to apply.

- **High Score Agencies**: Some agencies may prioritize candidates who achieve **above-average scores**, typically a **T-score of 60 or higher**. These departments may be

more competitive and may require candidates to demonstrate proficiency in reading, writing, and comprehension.
- **Average Score Agencies**: If you scored between 50-59, you may still be eligible for a position, but you may need to demonstrate additional skills or experience to stand out in the selection process. Some agencies may provide extra opportunities for training or remedial courses to help you improve specific areas.

2. Department-Specific Training and Requirements

Beyond your **PELT B Exam** results, many law enforcement agencies have specific **training requirements** for recruits. These training programs typically cover everything from physical fitness and law enforcement procedures to ethical conduct and community relations.

- **Physical Fitness**: Many law enforcement agencies require candidates to pass a **physical fitness test** in addition to the **PELT B Exam**. Prepare for this by maintaining an active lifestyle and working on your endurance, strength, and agility.
- **Background Checks and Psychological Evaluations**: As part of the application process, law enforcement agencies may conduct thorough **background checks** and **psychological evaluations**. Ensure that you are prepared for these by reviewing your personal history and ensuring that you meet all the criteria required by the agency.
- **Written Communication Skills**: Some agencies may require you to demonstrate strong **written communication skills** during the application process, including writing reports, essays, or taking additional tests related to grammar, spelling, and clarity.

3. Additional Testing and Assessments

Some agencies may also require additional testing or assessments beyond the **PELT B Exam**. These could include:

- **Psychological Testing**: To ensure you have the mental and emotional fortitude to work in law enforcement, some agencies may require psychological assessments as part of their application process.
- **Oral Exams**: In addition to written tests, some law enforcement agencies include **oral exams** to assess your verbal communication skills, decision-making, and ability to think on your feet. Prepare for these by practicing communication and interview techniques.
- **Polygraph Tests**: Some law enforcement agencies may conduct **polygraph tests** as part of their background investigation process. Be prepared for these by being honest and forthright during the application process.

4. Understanding Application Deadlines and Procedures

Every organization has its own set of deadlines and procedures for applying to employment. Some agencies may have open employment windows, while others may recruit year-round. Be sure to properly understand each department's application process, including when to submit your application, what materials are required, and how to follow your progress.

Tips for Applying to Different Law Enforcement Agencies

Now that you have a deeper knowledge of the department-specific requirements, it's time to focus on the application procedure. Here are some guidelines to help you effectively apply to law enforcement agencies:

1. Tailor Your Application for Each Agency

Every law enforcement agency has unique requirements, so tailor your application to reflect the specific needs and values of each agency. This might include adjusting your **resume**, **cover letter**, and **personal statement** to align with the agency's mission and goals.

- **Research the Agency**: Before applying, take the time to research each agency. Learn about its culture, values, and the specific needs of the department. This will help you tailor your application materials to demonstrate how you're a good fit for the organization.
- **Highlight Relevant Skills and Experience**: Emphasize skills that are particularly valued by law enforcement agencies, such as **communication**, **problem-solving**, **leadership**, and **physical fitness**. Make sure to include any related **internships**, **volunteer work**, or **criminal justice coursework**.

2. Prepare for the Interview Process

The **interview** is a critical part of the law enforcement application process. This is your chance to showcase your suitability for the role and demonstrate your passion for a career in law enforcement.

- **Research Common Interview Questions**: Familiarize yourself with common law enforcement interview questions, such as "Why do you want to be a police officer?" or "How would you handle a situation involving conflict?" Practice answering these questions confidently and professionally.
- **Demonstrate Your Knowledge and Commitment**: Be prepared to discuss current trends in law enforcement, local community issues, and the challenges faced by law

enforcement agencies. Your ability to show that you've done your research and are committed to the job will set you apart from other candidates.
- **Professionalism**: Always approach the interview with **professionalism**, including dressing appropriately, arriving on time, and being respectful throughout the process.

3. Be Patient and Persistent

The application process for law enforcement agencies can be lengthy, involving several rounds of interviews, testing, and background checks. It's important to remain patient and persistent throughout the process.

- **Stay Engaged**: Continue improving your skills and gaining experience in areas that will benefit your application. If you're not successful on your first attempt, don't be discouraged—many law enforcement candidates apply to multiple agencies before being hired.
- **Follow Up**: After submitting your application or completing an interview, don't hesitate to follow up with the agency to inquire about the status of your application. A polite follow-up shows initiative and interest in the position.

The PELT B Exam is a vital milestone in your law enforcement career journey, but it's just one element of the process. Whether you're preparing for a retake, moving forward with your application, or assessing your findings, it's crucial to take the following steps with confidence and clarity. By learning department-specific standards, personalizing your application materials, and preparing properly for interviews, you can put yourself up for success in the competitive area of law enforcement.

Remember, persistence and determination are crucial in law enforcement. Continue growing your knowledge, abilities, and network, and remain determined as you work toward your goal of becoming a law enforcement officer.

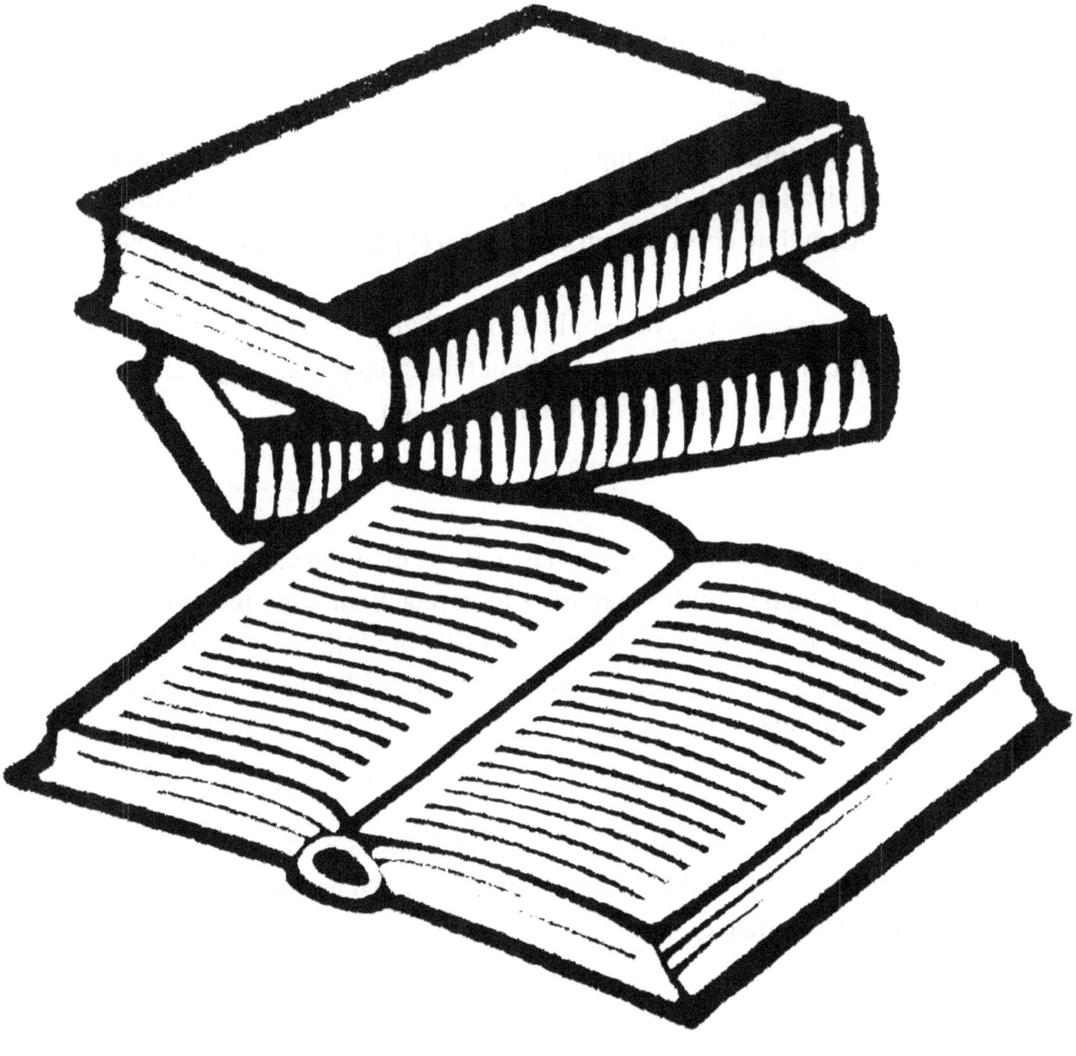

Conclusion

Congratulations! You've gone on a journey to equip yourself with the knowledge and tactics needed to succeed on the PELT B Exam and in your pursuit of a career in law enforcement. Throughout this book, we've covered everything from preparing for the exam, understanding its components, and developing successful study strategies, to analyzing your test results and charting your next actions. The knowledge and insights offered here are aimed to ensure you are not just ready to pass the exam but also equipped to succeed as you seek a career in this exciting and challenging area.

The PELT B Exam is more than simply a test; it's a vital stepping stone toward your future in law enforcement. While a passing score is necessary, what truly matters is the commitment and determination you exhibit as you pursue your goals. Whether your first attempt was successful or you're preparing for a retake, remember that each step is an opportunity to perfect your skills, strengthen your commitment, and come one step closer to your ideal career.

As you move forward, always keep in mind that law enforcement is not just about passing examinations or acing interviews—it's about the ability to serve, protect, and make a real effect in your community. Your preparation, hard effort, and dedication to personal growth will define your success, not just on test day, but in your future profession. Stay focused on your goals, welcome setbacks as chances for progress, and never lose sight of the greater cause you are working toward.

We hope this book has equipped you with the resources, techniques, and confidence you need to succeed, whether you are taking the PELT B Exam for the first time or preparing for a retake. The journey to become a law enforcement officer is packed with chances for growth, learning, and contribution to your community. You've taken the first crucial step—now, go forward with the assurance that your hard work will pay off.

Good Luck, And May Your Career In Law Enforcement Be Both Fulfilling And Meaningful.

Bonus Section

Bonus 1: Email Consultation

Dear Valued Reader,

Thank you for purchasing and reading the **"PELLET B Study Guide 2025-2026".** We hope this guide has provided you with comprehensive strategies, practice tests, and the confidence you need to excel on your journey.

Your feedback is extremely important to us, and we would greatly appreciate it if you could take a moment to leave a **FAVORABLE REVIEW.** Whether it's the in-depth explanations, test-taking strategies, or realistic practice tests that helped you the most, we'd love to hear about your experience and what made the book valuable for you.

As a special thank-you for your support, we're offering a **FREE CONSULTATION** via email! If you have any questions, need personalized guidance, or seek advice on how to tackle specific sections of this book, feel free to reach out to us at **[mintwritereview@gmail.com]**.

We Are Here To Support Your Journey!

Thank You For Being A Part Of Our Community, And Your Feedback Will Help Us Create Even More Resources For Students Like You.

Best Regards.

Bonus 2: Full-Length Online PELLET B Practice Test.

In addition to the detailed strategies and practice tests provided in this book, we're excited to offer you exclusive access to a full-length online PELLET B practice test that will help you simulate real test conditions. This online test mirrors the actual format and gives you an accurate assessment of your readiness for the PELLET B exam.

Spelling | **Vocabulary**

Reading Comprehension | **Clarity**

To Claim Access To This Bonus, Simply Scan The Qr Code Provided Above.

Thank you for choosing **"PELLET B Study Guide 2025-2026"**, and we wish you great success as you continue preparing for your Test. Stay focused and confident, and know that with the right preparation, your goals are within reach!